Comprehensive Group Work

What It Means & How To Teach It

Robert K. Conyne
F. Robert Wilson
Donald E. Ward

AMERICAN
COUNSELING
ASSOCIATION

5999 Stevenson Avenue
Alexandria, VA 22304-3300

COMPREHENSIVE GROUP WORK:
What it means and how to teach it

10 9 8 7 6 5 4 3 2 1

American Counseling Association
5999 Stevenson Avenue
Alexandria, VA 22304

Acquisitions and Development Editor
Carolyn Baker

Managing Editor
Michael Comlish

Cover design by Jennifer Sterling, Spot Color

Library of Congress Cataloging-in-Publication Data
Conyne, Robert K.
   Comprehensive group work : what it means & how to teach it /
Robert K. Conyne, F. Robert Wilson, Donald E. Ward.
        p.   cm.
   Includes bibliographical references and index.
   ISBN 1-55620-158-3 (alk. paper)
      1. Group counseling.   2. Group counseling—Study and teaching.
   3. Group psychotherapy.   4. Group psychotherapy—Study and teaching.
   I. Wilson, F. Robert.   II. Ward, Donald E.   III. Title.
   BF637.C6C5716   1997
   158'.35—dc20   96-7805
                                                                        CIP

DEDICATION

To all teachers and students
of group work in our common quest
to make groups relevant
and meaningful to all.

CONTENTS

PREFACE

The group work practice of counselors is exploding. The demand for groups to be offered by counselors is increasing in all sectors of society, from mental health agencies, to schools, to business and industry. The kinds of groups being requested are diversifying rapidly. People want group-based assistance for personal and interpersonal problems, to gain skills, to resolve organizational issues, to discuss and learn, to cope more adequately, and to prevent future dysfunction. The people with whom counselors will work in groups are becoming increasingly diverse, a fact that reflects the multicultural nature of our communities. In short, group work is in high demand for addressing diversity along many dimensions.

As counselors find themselves providing both more and more varied group work services, it is critically important that counselor education training programs prepare students (and practitioners through continuing education) with appropriate curricular experiences. Such training needs to be in group work that is comprehensive; that is, it prepares students to apply group work in a variety of ways, all of them consistent with the Association for Specialists in Group Work *Professional Standards for the Training of Group Workers* (ASGW, 1991b). These Standards (which are included in Appendix A) specify comprehensive group work competencies and supervised experiences. In addition, they explicate a broad view of group work that we think is consonant with the kinds of extensive demands for group services now occurring. In fact, the following question motivated the development of this book:

Can we identify and describe to readers outstanding examples of group work training that serve to prepare students to provide comprehensive group work and thus help to advance group work training?

Our hope was that comprehensive group work training could be advanced by making excellent examples of teaching available. If our goal is accomplished, then it will no longer be necessary to say "comprehensive group work," as we do in this book—the shorter term "group work" will be sufficient, widely understood to include a range of valid applications.

Thus, we have set out to stimulate the improvement and broadening of group work training in counseling programs. How did we identify examples of training excellence? We surveyed all counselor education programs accredited by the Council for the Accreditation of Counseling and Related Educational Programs (CACREP), and asked program personnel to nominate to us any group work training elements in their program that they considered to be exemplary. We limited our judgment of excellence to one criterion: compliance with the ASGW Professional Training Standards. Therefore, following from the Standards, we were interested in detailing for others those excellent training experiences that address what we think of as the "Group Work Rainbow," that is, group work competencies that all counselors need to possess, as well as training examples in each of the four group work specializations: task groups, psychoeducation groups, group counseling, and group psychotherapy.

The book is divided into three sections. In Section I, we define group work from a comprehensive perspective and discuss its very foundations. We also enumerate 13 difficult situations faced by all group workers and give suggestions for coping. Section II is the main part of the book. In this section we describe in detail many exemplary training approaches. Chapters are organized around core competencies, group counseling, task and psychoeducation group work, and group psychotherapy. In Section III we address application issues. We present a number of design principles for developing excellent training experiences in comprehensive group work, as well as a host of concrete action steps for faculty, students, and practitioners to take as they attempt to implement the general principles.

The five appendices contain materials that will be of particular interest. Because this book is intended to provide curricular resources to enhance teaching based on the *Professional Standards for the Training of Group Workers*, these standards are reproduced in Appendix A. The multifaceted view of group work defined by these ASGW Training

Standards is illustrated graphically by the "Group Work Rainbow," which is presented in Appendix B. The survey materials used in collecting compliance data and raw curricular materials upon which this book was based are presented in Appendix C. Then, Appendix D presents "Selected Instructional and Resource Examples"; it is a collection of interesting illustrations for group work training such as a bibliography, a journal, a laboratory group, a group plan, guidelines for critiquing articles, guidelines for portfolio development, and processing suggestions. Finally, Appendix E, "List of Contributing Programs," gives recognition to the many programs supplying the examples of excellence in group work instruction contained in this book.

Certainly, this book will be of greatest value to counselor education faculty who are directly responsible for creating, teaching, and supervising the group work curriculum. It also will be of worth to other counseling faculty who have an interest in group work, to group work practitioners, and to group work instructors from related academic disciplines such as psychology and social work. In terms of textbook adoption, this book can serve well in the introductory course in group counseling, or its equivalent, especially when faculty intend to teach a comprehensive view of group work; otherwise, the book could easily be included as a required secondary source.

We were impressed to learn about the innovative and substantive approaches being used to educate and train counselors in comprehensive group work. We are hopeful that the material contained in this book will serve to stimulate this type of broad group-work training in counselor education programs. Doing so, we believe, will not only aid programs in meeting the ASGW Training Standards but, more important, will also prepare students for the increasingly diverse demands of contemporary group work.

ACKNOWLEDGMENTS

The authors are grateful to the faculty of the CACREP-accredited institutions who completed and returned our survey on compliance with the ASGW Training Standards in their group work programs. In addition, we are also indebted to the counselor educators who contributed descriptions of their group work curricula. These contributions formed the raw data from which this book was crafted, and, obviously, without their supportive contributions the writing of this book would not have been possible. We express our appreciation to the Association for Specialists in Group Work and its leadership under President Sam Gladding, who encouraged this project.

We express our appreciation to Dr. Pete Eveland, who gave tirelessly of himself in the survey data-collection phase of the project. His contributions included facilitating bulk mailings and placing follow-up telephone calls, coding and recording of raw data, and preparing the data for statistical analysis. We also want to acknowledge that his unflagging interest in and enthusiastic involvement with our project helped to keep us going.

Finally, for the "Group Work Rainbow," we thank Zachary Conyne-Rapin, who created the design; we also thank counseling student Laura Carrol Haas, who, with her husband, Nick Haas, developed the innovative "Group Work Cafe," where we are all invited to partake of the riches embodied in group work.

ABOUT THE AUTHORS

Robert K. Conyne is a professor of counseling in the Division of Human Services at the University of Cincinnati, where he has worked since 1980. He received his BA degree from Syracuse University, his master's and PhD degrees from Purdue University, and was a post-doctoral intern at the University of California-Berkeley. For 9 years, Dr. Conyne was a professor and staff psychologist at Illinois State University. He is a fellow of the Association for Specialists in Group Work (ASGW), the American Psychological Association (APA), and the American Psychological Society (APS). He has served ASGW as journal editor, Professional Training Standards chair, CACREP representative, and president. He is the author of numerous articles and presentations and of five other books in the areas of group work, primary prevention, and consultation.

F. Robert Wilson is a professor of counseling in the Division of Human Services at the University of Cincinnati, where he has worked since 1978. He received his bachelor's, master's, and educational specialist degrees from Eastern Michigan University, and his PhD degree in counseling psychology from Michigan State University. He has 3 years of postdoctoral education and experience in Gestalt work. For 2 years, Dr. Wilson was the director of interpersonal skills training for prospective teachers at Michigan State University. He is a member of the Association for Specialists in Group Work and has served ASGW as member of the Journal Editorial Board, member of the Professional Training Standards committee, chair and member of the Research Committee, cochair of the Program Committee, and cochair of the Education and Training Committee Cluster. He has written about and presented in various aspects of group work and has developed software for the on-line collection of group process data.

Donald E. Ward is a professor, chair of the Counseling Committee, and CACREP liaison in the Department of Psychology and Counseling at Pittsburg State University, Kansas, where he has worked since 1976. He received his BA degree in psychology from DePauw University in Greencastle, Indiana, and his MS and PhD in counseling and counselor education/counseling from Purdue University. For 3 years, he was an assistant professor and counseling psychologist at Ball State University; he taught both on campus and in an overseas program on U.S. Air Force Bases in England and Spain. He is a fellow of the Association for Specialists in Group Work and has served for over 10 years in separate appointments to the *Journal for Specialists in Group Work* Editorial Board. He has also served ASGW as Convention Program chair, Research Committee chair, Professional Standards chair, and Professional Development Committee member. Currently, he serves as the ASGW representative to CACREP. He teaches and presents in the areas of group work and counseling theories and techniques, and he has published numerous articles, monographs, and book chapters in these areas.

The Foundations of Group Work— A Comprehensive Perspective

INTRODUCTION

The first section of the book is devoted to a discussion of the basic foundations of group work. In order to provide a context for our presentation of curricular exemplars, we divide this contextual material into an overview of our vision for group work which is consistent with the ASGW Training Standards and is comprehensive in scope. We then detail challenges confronting counselor educators who specialize in group work.

The first two chapters provide a conceptual introduction to teaching group work, and thus are qualitatively different from the rest of the book, which includes content closely derived from survey data. The first two chapters represent our own thinking. Here, content is much less tightly tied to data and external resources, but expresses learnings gained from our collective group work experience.

In Chapter One, we attempt to answer the question, "What is group work?" Core competencies and the specializations of task, psychoeducation, counseling, and psychotherapy groups are described. We then attempt to set the stage for much of the book by providing advance organizers, which should prove helpful to readers who choose to use our ideas and insights. Finally, we describe at length one way in which a comprehensive educational program in group work can be implemented.

In Chapter Two, we identify a set of 13 challenges that we see confronting all group workers, regardless of the type of group. This "baker's dozen" of overarching challenges is accompanied by 13 complementary strategies group workers can use to prevent the challenges from being inhibiting, if not overwhelming.

1 CHAPTER

What Is Group Work?

GETTING ORIENTED TO "GROUP WORK" THROUGH SOME EXAMPLES

Gladding (1995) detailed in his text on group work that members of all helping professions have provided services for people in groups since the early 1900s. For a variety of reasons, including efficiency of service delivery, potency of group methodologies, and personal interest, counselors are drawn to learn group work skills. Yet, as beginning group workers may discover, group work is not unidimensional. Groups differ from one another in important dimensions such as size, purpose, prerequisites for membership, outcome expectations, and expectations for leader skills.

Historically, the counseling profession has taken the view that "a group counselor is a group counselor is a group counselor" and has attempted to use one set of standards for training practitioners, regardless of the kind of group work for which they were preparing. In 1991, in a landmark action, the Association for Specialists in Group Work identified, defined, and established standards for the preparation of group workers for four distinct group work specializations: task and work groups, psychoeducational groups, group counseling, and group psychotherapy. These specialization standards serve to substantially broaden group work training and practice. In the following section, brief examples of each group work specialization are presented.

EXAMPLES OF GROUP WORK SPECIALIZATIONS

Task Group Example

Recently elected to your neighborhood association, you are attending the orientation meeting. After a short period of milling around, the group of 10 people is called to order by the president of the association. She announces that the first task is to elect officers. She calls for nominations from the floor. Looking around, you are quickly aware that you recognize several people but know the names of only three of them. To your chagrin, you realize that you are unfamiliar with the interests and expertise of everyone in the room. You wonder how you can participate in the selecting of officers, given your lack of information. You are also concerned about being able to contribute in a meaningful way to this association. You feel confused and think you are the only one in this state of mind.

Psychoeducation Group Example

You and your spouse have begun participating in a parenting education program at your child's school. This program is offered to parents of children who are 5–12 years old. Along with eight other parents, you begin learning new information, increasing skills, and experimenting with decision-making processes to enhance child-rearing practices. The leader of the program has explained her role as a facilitator, not an expert information provider, although each session is topic-oriented and emphasizes skill development. You are finding the group experience enjoyable and interesting, but you are not always sure how to use in your own family what is discussed.

Counseling Group Example

Your personal growth group is now in its eighth weekly 2-hour session, which is about halfway through its planned life. For the last two sessions, the 10 members have been working through various conflicts with each other and with you. Now the group mood seems to have calmed and the climate seems more work-like. Your leader suggests that each of you thinks about the interpersonal goal statements that you and the other members developed earlier in the group. Then your leader turns to one of the group members and says, "Sally, are you interested in learning how Bill and the other members of this group are reacting to you right now?" After Sally replies affirmatively, the leader helps Bill and each of the other group members to provide constructive interpersonal feedback and assists Sally in processing what she heard. Finally, the leader turns to you and says, "Would you be willing to share your perceptions of Sally's behavior with her?"

Psychotherapy Group Example

Susan is very fearful about today's session. She has been making small strides over the last several meetings in reaching out more to the other members and to the co-therapists. Previously, she had been unwilling to look directly at anyone in the group, and only recently had she begun establishing eye contact with some group members and maintaining the contact for longer periods. Over time, her arms had gradually come uncrossed from her chest, and she had assumed a more erect sitting posture. Yet today, for some reason, Susan looks as she did 10 months ago at the group's beginning, head and body slouched, as if protecting herself in her own kind of cocoon. Your group leader asks gently, "Susan, I am noticing you are looking away from us today.... Can you tell us something about that, about what you are experiencing today?" Because of your leader's previous explanations, you know your leader is trying to encourage Susan to reconnect with the group by first helping her connect with and express herself.

DEFINING GROUP WORK

Each of the vignettes above illustrates one of the four types of comprehensive group work. Of course, countless other examples could be given because group work is ubiquitous in Western culture. The basic definition of group work below was developed to capture the important and diverse place of groups in Western society and to provide direction for delineating group work practice:

> *Group work* is a broad professional practice that refers to the giving of help or the accomplishment of tasks in a group setting. It involves the application of group theory and process by a capable professional practitioner to assist an interdependent collection of people to reach their mutual goals, which

may be personal, interpersonal, or task-related in nature. (ASGW, 1991b, p. 14)

This basic definition is critical grounding for understanding group work from a comprehensive perspective. Therefore, the essential defining elements and components will be elaborated below.

Essential Components of a Comprehensive Group Work Definition

The ASGW definition of group work embraces several essential components (e.g., giving of help, accomplishment of tasks). To amplify the definition of group work, we will expand and elaborate upon these components.

Broad professional practice. Group work is not the province of one discipline or profession. Rather, group work is an interdisciplinary, cross-profession practice. It draws important conceptual and practical input from sociology and anthropology and from psychology and education. It is taught and applied by many professionals from these disciplines and is an important change vehicle within behavioral science professions such as counseling, psychology, social work, organization development, community organization, and others. Settings in which group work is used intentionally include, but are not limited to, mental health centers, corporate board rooms, private practice, hospitals, schools, city hall, and social agencies of nearly every kind.

Giving of help. A main purpose of all group work is to give help and support. People come together in groups to work with one another, to learn from one another, to combine forces to accomplish goals, to improve themselves in some way through the interactions inherent within the group itself. A group worker—that is, one who is trained to lead or colead groups—uses his or her skills to enhance help-giving among the group members so that the group and its members can reach their goals effectively. Some ways that help-giving can be facilitated in groups are by helping members to feel connected with one another, to demonstrate altruism, to sense hope, and to learn from each other's experiencing (Yalom, 1985).

Accomplishment of tasks. Group work helps members to achieve defined tasks and goals. These tasks may be directly related to interpersonal and intrapersonal growth or change, as in a psychoeducational, counseling, or psychotherapy group, or the tasks may be connected to producing a strategic plan, continuous quality improvement, or some other concrete product, as in a business task or work group. Therefore, in all group work, it is important for group workers to help and support groups and individual members of groups to establish clear goals and to develop the processes for accomplishing them.

Salience of group size, composition, setting, and charge. For interactive, face-to-face group work, the size, composition, setting, and charge of any group are crucial. Clearly, a group must include sufficient members with enough diversity to fuel group interaction yet not encompass so many participants as to overwhelm either the members or the leader with data generated by individual disclosures and group interactions. In face-to-face group work, the members of the group are its resource. Even in a homogeneous group, such as a group of teen-aged fathers who have gathered to learn about their parenting role, it is from their diversity of experience that the group will draw its wisdom and strength. The setting must be chosen or constructed to permit a flexible and comfortable working environment. Finally, from the charge of the group (e.g., to complete a task, to learn about parenthood, to master a developmental stage, to remediate long-standing problems of adjustment), norms evolve providing for the group members' safety and for guiding the work of the group. The trained group worker is active in the recruitment and selection of sufficient group members to provide the resource, is active in selecting and arranging a physical environment which will support the group in its work, and is active in specifying the group's charge and, from that charge, in helping the group articulate its working norms.

Application of theoretical understandings of group process. The practice of group work is based on the successful application of theory and processes that, as we have mentioned, are drawn from a variety of disciplines. Group theory includes conceptions of individual, interpersonal, and group development. *Group process* refers to events occurring within a group and their evolution over time. Group workers need to be able to effectively apply group theory and process to the particular group situation with which they are working. Competence in applying the necessary knowledge and skills in group theory and process is gained by participating in a comprehensive educational program that adequately blends theory and supervised practice in group work (Conyne, Sturm, Fishbach-Goodman, Rand, & Brown, 1995).

Leadership by a capable professional practitioner. A group worker must be a capable professional practitioner. That is, the group worker needs to possess the ability to effectively apply relevant group theory and process to the presenting group situation. Knowledge and skills are critically important to being capable. The group worker needs to know about people and groups and must be able to employ a range of group work skills in helping to promote goal accomplishment and help-giving. A large additional component of capability is found in the exercise of professional judgment. For instance, the group worker needs to develop the ability to decide, often immediately, what intervention is called for in a situation. Issues of appropriateness, adequacy, effectiveness, efficiency, and anticipated side effects are usually important to consider. A final, and perhaps most important, element in capability is the effective personal and interpersonal functioning of the group worker—that is, the group worker's level of self-awareness and interpersonal competence. Without personal and interpersonal competence, effective group work is impossible.

Recognition of interpersonal interdependence. Individuals who become part of a group enter an emergent system in which the whole becomes larger than the sum of its individual parts. As the group meets, the system becomes defined. Individuals assume a place in the group, they acquire and perform roles, relationships between and among people begin to emerge, group goals are often set, and as interaction patterns solidify, the group itself begins to develop a kind of personality. A social ecological network (Insel & Moos, 1974) becomes established in which each person stands in an interdependent relation to every other person. Members of a group form connections, similar to those formed by members of a basketball team or an improvisational acting troupe. This concept of interdependence, in which behavior is viewed as people interacting with each other and with their environment ($B = P \times E$) (Lewin, 1936), holds special implications for the group worker. The concept of interdependence suggests that although the individual level of focus and intervention is possible, it is not exclusive. It embraces the duality of being both independent (taking responsibility for oneself) and dependent (relying on the group for help and support). The interdependence perspective emphasizes that interpersonal and group foci are more salient for group workers' observation and action.

Mutuality of goals. Throughout the specializations in group work, there is a recognition that group activities are beneficial to the extent that each member is rewarded by his or her participation. This overarching understanding is coupled with a second, pragmatic, understanding that humankind works hardest at and derives most benefit from working toward goals which are individually held. Thus, group workers refrain from independently setting goals for individual members to achieve. Rather, a collaborative ethic undergirds the practice of the group worker. Although group workers may set general goals necessary for the establishment and initial functioning of the group (e.g., increasing cohesion, fostering self-exploration, heightening awareness, encouraging feedback seeking, increasing trust, autonomy, initiative, industry, identity, mutuality, helpfulness), later group goals and those for individuals are arrived at through a collaborative decision-making process. Employing a mutual goal-setting process allows group members to participate equitably in shaping the directions of the group and to determine their own involvement.

Multidimensionality of goals. All groups include various combinations of intrapersonal, interpersonal, and task-related goals. A committee, specifically established to accomplish a set of tasks, needs to accommodate intrapersonal and interpersonal goals in order to be effective. A psychotherapy group, certainly focused on personal change, needs to keep on task and to manage itself sufficiently in order to be effective. Thus, different groups emphasize different goals. Relative goal emphases lead to two large classifications of group work: task accomplishment or personal change (Conyne, 1989).

The notion of group work for task accomplishment recognizes that much of what occurs in this and other Western societies is realized through group arrangements of one kind or other. Committees, teams, task forces, skill-building sessions, planning meetings, governance boards, educational classes, learning societies, professional development activities, and other similar forms of getting work done are all group based. As such, each represents a facet of task groups, and each provides significant opportunities for group work.

On the other hand, the notion of group work for personal change recognizes that groups also are becoming increasingly prominent as a preferred mode of helping people to learn and manage change. The omnipresence of support groups, which frequently and intentionally do not include a professional group leader in order to maximize opportunities for self-help and natural support, illustrate this trend. It is estimated that some 15–20 million people in this country alone are members of support groups addressing such topics as alcoholism, child abuse, overeating, and depression. In terms of group work involving trained professional leaders, many settings, such as community agencies and elementary schools, now incorporate group work as a primary means of delivering service. Personal change groups are offered by group workers to treat or remediate existing pathology (psychotherapy), resolve problems with others (counseling), and to learn new skills (psychoeducation), in addition to those that are task oriented.

ADVANCE ORGANIZERS

To understand the ways in which knowledge and skill competencies are and can be provided for preparation in core and specialization competencies, we have adopted a set of organizing principles. These principles will be used throughout the book to facilitate communication and understanding.

Core and Specialization Preparation

As reflected in the training standards set forth by the Association for Specialists in Group work (1991b) and in the 1994 program accreditation standards of the Council for Accreditation of Counseling and Related Educational Programs (1993), all group workers need to master a set of core competencies in group work. In a sense, this is the basic tool kit of the group work trade. Mastery of these core competencies is necessary for a group worker to provide minimum conditions suitable for a group to become established and for members to get started with their work. Beyond core group work competency, individuals may choose to specialize in one or more areas of group work (e.g., task groups, psychoeducational groups, counseling groups, psychotherapy groups). As described in the ASGW Training Standards, each specialization requires mastery of additional, specialized competencies and supervised practice of the tools of the master craftsperson. For specialization work, it is assumed that the learner will have mastered the core competencies. In the following chapter, we will discuss at length a "baker's dozen" of foundational issues of group work which affect all group workers regardless of level and which are addressed directly in core group work curricula. In subsequent chapters, we will present examples of methodologies used by various CACREP-accredited institutions in preparing core and specialty-competent group workers.

Competency Content Clusters

The 93 knowledge and skills competencies listed for preparation in core and specialization competencies have five common themes that we have organized into clusters. We will emphasize these five clusters throughout the balance of the book. These clusters are as follows:

Cluster 1: Defining the nature and scope of practice. Regardless of level of preparation (core or specialization), it is critical that the group worker define the nature and the scope of practice for the level of preparation in which he or she is engaged.

Cluster 2: Pregroup preparation. Group workers need to be able to adequately match a group to prospective participants (and vice-versa) and to orient them for realistic involvement.

Cluster 3: Therapeutic dynamics and leadership skills. Once the group is formed, the major focus of the group worker's attention is to provide skillful leadership by interpreting and managing the therapeutic dynamics occurring within the group. Therefore, it is not surprising that the required key competencies for the core or for the specializations are thematically focused on leadership and process issues.

Cluster 4: Research and evaluation. Skillful blending of the art and the science of group work is necessary in order to utilize research and evaluation methodologies to achieve a practitioner-scientist orientation to group work.

Cluster 5: Group work ethics. Regardless of the group worker's level of preparation or scope of practice, all group workers need to accept the ethical standards relevant to the range of problems they are likely to encounter within their scope of practice.

In the following chapter, a baker's dozen of challenges and strategies will provide additional depth regarding the meaning of each of these clusters. In Section Two of the book, the presentation of stellar curricular examples will also be organized by thematic standards clusters.

Competency Knowledge and Skill Dimensions

A third distinction made in the ASGW Training Standards (1991b) which is preserved throughout this book is the distinction between knowledge and skill aspects of the competencies. At the risk of belaboring what may be obvious to most readers, mastery of the core of group work or a group specialization requires mastery of the body of knowledge common to the level of preparation in which the student is engaged. However necessary this information may be, it is insufficient to produce a competent group worker.

While knowledge may be learned didactically, skills cannot. Developing group work competency requires experiential involvement. The Training Standards suggest both a minimum and a desired clock-hour requirement for immersion in group life. At the core level, observation and participation in classroom and other supervised group experiences provide the best route for effectively gaining and integrating the requisite skills. At the specialization level, supervised design and implementation of a group consistent with one's specialization are required.

THE IDEAL OF A COMPREHENSIVE
CURRICULAR MODEL

Implementing a comprehensive program in group work preparation is a very complex process. Competing program emphases abound (e.g., marriage and family counseling, gerontological counseling, counseling children and adolescents, mental health counseling, career counseling, counselor education). At many campuses, there may be but a single faculty member who has an interest in promoting group work. For many campuses there are insufficient resources to permit offering specializations in group work. At these campuses, the best that can be provided is group work competence at the core level. However, a program faculty with a broad commitment to infusing group work programmatically on a campus with sufficient resources may offer comprehensive group work preparation with one or more specialization offerings.

One example of a counseling program which offers comprehensive group work preparation is the Department of Counseling and Human Development Services at the University of Georgia. The department, with 16 full-time faculty trained as counselor educators or counseling psychologists, is housed in a College of Education which has more than 200 full-time faculty members—one of the largest colleges of education in the country. The size and positioning of this department have provided the opportunity and resources for them to create an expansive program in group work. With a faculty of this size, the department sponsors four different master's programs (school counseling, community counseling, rehabilitation counseling, and college student personnel in higher education), an educational specialist program (school counseling), and two doctoral programs (counseling psychology and student affairs administration in higher education). By using specific courses in group work and by infusing group work throughout the curriculum, this faculty has been able to provide both core preparation and specialization work in task groups, psychoeducational groups, counseling groups, and, with advanced doctoral students, psychotherapy groups. A description, abstracted from material submitted by Horne and Hayes (1995), has been provided in the accompanying box to illustrate one way in which a comprehensive program in group work can be accomplished.

THE GROUP WORK RAINBOW

Group work is a comprehensive and robust helping intervention (Conyne, 1985). To illustrate, we borrow the words of Morris Goodman (1995), a past president of the Group Psychology and Group Psychotherapy Division of the American Psychological Association (a newer

(text continues on page 20)

DESCRIPTION OF GROUP WORK PREPARATION AT THE UNIVERSITY OF GEORGIA

Group work is seen by the faculty as being broad in scope and as including the four core areas of group work identified by ASGW: task/work groups, guidance/psychoeducational, counseling/interpersonal problem solving, and therapy/personality reconstruction groups. We believe that groups are essentially deliberate social arrangements among persons who share a common purpose. Further, we believe that group work, in all its forms, is intended to foster those relationships among members of the group that will encourage members' growth and development most effectively. Although our faculty members claim expertise in a particular theory, we lay no claim as a department to any particular orientation. In fact, we have attempted over the years in recruiting faculty to select persons who share different orientations in an effort to broaden the range of our own and our students' learning in group work. Presently, our faculty represent the following approaches to group work practice: Adlerian, cognitive–behavioral, constructivist developmental, family systems, Gestalt, intentionally structured/developmental, life-skills training, person-centered, psychodynamic, and social learning.

Group work is incorporated into all aspects of the department, including most courses taught, departmental administration, and the conduct of research. The faculty are committed to a democratic governance and group problem solving/decision-making model. Students are routinely involved in research groups within the department, many of which are focused on group work research. Students participate in program meetings, where appropriate, as equal members in decision making. Thereby, students learn about group work not only through academic requirements and practica offerings but also through modeling and the integration of group process into the daily activities of the department.

Curriculum and Preparation for Group Work

The sequence of course work is designed to provide a breadth of knowledge in group work and to allow students to delve in depth into a specific area of group work. Two primarily didactic group courses are available for master's degree students: group counseling and group dynamics. Master's degree students generally take one or the other, although they are encouraged to take both. The doctoral program in counseling psychology includes an advanced course on group counseling and therapy, as well as a two-quarter group practicum.

Before beginning their preparation in group work, master's students are expected to have completed most of their first year of preparation in counseling (interviewing, theories of counseling, career development, assessment, and individual practicum) and to be familiar with individual approaches to counseling. Most will also have taken a course in multicultural counseling. They take either group counseling or group dynamics in their second year as they move toward demonstrating greater knowledge of the counseling process. All students complete an individual counseling practicum and a three-quarter internship as part of their master's work. Although there is no group practicum at the master's level, students routinely engage in supervised group work practice as part of their internship experience. Depending upon their particular program, master's students, under supervision, are called upon to design, deliver, and evaluate structured group experiences in student personnel, classroom guidance, group counseling, focus group research, and personal growth groups.

Master's degree classes are structured so that faculty have the opportunity to observe students in structured class activities as they demonstrate various group leadership skills. In addition, master's students are regularly offered opportunities to earn course credit by participating in group activities led by doctoral students and professionals across campus. Students at both the master's and doctoral level are encouraged to view and critique live group interactions or review professionally prepared videotapes of nationally recognized group leaders and of program faculty conducting group experiences. All students are required to demonstrate group leadership skills commensurate with their level of preparation during their internship.

Doctoral students are expected to have completed a master's degree, which generally includes preparation in group work, before being admitted to the counseling psychology program. The few doctoral students who come to our program with little formal study in group work are required to take one or both of the master's courses early in their programs. In the second year of their program, doctoral students enroll in advanced group counseling and advanced group practicum, which continues over a two-quarter sequence.

Students in the advanced group class are required to demonstrate a comprehensive knowledge of group work at the beginning of the course; otherwise, they do remedial work before beginning the course. As part of the course requirements, students develop a written research proposal in which they identify specific questions related to group work that they would like to investigate. After having their proposal critiqued and revised as necessary, they carry out their proposals, including collecting relevant research data, under supervision as part of the advanced group practicum.

Students typically propose and carry out group practica that fit under group counseling or psychoeducational groups. Recent examples include the following: support groups for overeaters, persons who are HIV^{+}, siblings of persons hospitalized for mental illness, and persons with disabilities; personal growth groups for master's students in counseling, for high school adolescents, for secondary school teachers, for men dealing with men's issues, and for women cultivating creativity; a social skills development group for college students; encounter groups for persons with addictions; a planning group within an organization undergoing restructuring; task groups for persons wanting to improve their study, time management, or decision-making skills; and parenting groups. Only rarely will doctoral students complete a practicum with a hospitalized population largely because of the constraints of time in a quarter system. Group psychotherapy is most likely to be included in their predoctoral work as part of an internship experience.

Evaluation and Research

Students at all levels are evaluated by a variety of means. The most obvious is the assessment of their group work knowledge through written examination as a part of specific course work. Further, the comprehensive examination for master's students and written doctoral preliminary examinations include a major focus on group work knowledge.

Whether at the master's or doctoral level, students write a proposal in which they identify specific questions related to group work that they would like to investigate. At the master's level, students submit proposals for groups they might like to conduct. The focus of the doctoral proposal is on a specific research study to be carried out during the practicum. With regard to researchable questions on group work, the students' proposals range from topics such as the viability of adding moral development components to skill development groups for incarcerated adolescents to exploring the interactional components of group supervision when provided by experienced and inexperienced supervisors. They evaluate the process by using quantitative and/or qualitative methods and write the results in publishable form for submission and critique at the end of the practicum.

Ethical Practice

Ethics is a core component of all preparation in group work at the University of Georgia. Therefore, it is infused throughout the counselor preparation program. Both master's and doctoral students are required to address ethical and professional issues in all group plans and activities in which they engage.

Implementation Problems

Our experience with group worker preparation is that it is generally fun, intellectually stimulating, personally challenging, and professionally rewarding. Frankly, we often wonder why everyone doesn't enjoy leading, participating in, and generally being a part of groups as much as we do. Nonetheless, problems arise on occasion that press us to rethink our assumptions about the merits of group work and about our enthusiasm for having every counselor become a specialist in it.

At the master's level, problems generally arise among those students who do not value group work, particularly group counseling and group psychotherapy. They tend to regard it as a secondary form of treatment—a sort of holding pattern into which clients are put until they can see the "real doctor." Students who have encountered group work for the first time within a clinic or hospital setting often express this bias. Another complaint about group work comes from those students who see any group work as group "therapy," and so don't value its use in other formats. Our master's students in student personnel work often see group counseling and psychotherapy as esoteric and limited to therapeutic interventions with severely disturbed clients. They prefer task groups and have little interest in learning to address group counseling issues. Finally, our school counselors often mistakenly believe that they have come to graduate work to be trained as individual therapists who will do the bulk of their work one client at a time. They know they don't want to do paper work, but only occasionally believe that group work can be something more than classroom instruction, especially if they have come from a teaching background.

At the doctoral level, a major area of difficulty in implementation is related to "know[ing] thyself" in the process of learning to work with groups. We expect that group leaders will explore their own issues related to facilitating client growth. There is a fine line between providing growth and learning opportunities and developing dual-role relationships that provide faculty with too much knowledge of the student. At the doctoral level, however, we also expect that students will seek supervision actively and that they will see group supervision as an opportunity to solicit multiple perspectives upon their work, especially from groups. Students who do not trust the larger group or who feel uncomfortable exposing real or imagined inadequacies before their peers are especially reluctant to see group supervision as an opportunity for growth. In our experience, students feel greater vulnerability to exposure in group supervision than in individual supervision and, moreover, feel greater vulnerability in group supervision of group work practice than in group supervision of individual counseling. Despite the availability of alternative opportunities for group experiences through the University Counseling Center and through other available services both on and off campus, the issue about how experiential classes should become remains a challenge for us with some students.

Although group dynamics in organizational settings are covered to some extent in the course work, few students see such settings as viable alternatives for practicing group work. Likewise, group psychotherapy settings that are appropriate to providing field experience prior to doctoral internship are few, remote, or substandard.

Few students use available technology fully to permit an analysis of their own group work practice. Beyond the customary resistance to videotaping, students are reluctant to risk experimentation with computer simulations and distance education as appropriate group work.

Despite our encouragement, students still do not take full advantage of the opportunities available to them to be in groups. Because we are fortunate enough to have an outstanding conference facility on campus, the university plays host to several group-oriented conferences each year (e.g., the ASGW national conference, an annual family therapy conference). Nonetheless, the personal and curricular demands upon students mitigate against their full participation in such activities. Finally, our commitment as a faculty to diversity in both our faculty and our students leads inexorably to the set of issues that accompany the development of any heterogeneous group. We have often asked ourselves why we want to entertain wide faculty participation in all activities of the department or why we want to select diverse students and then encourage them to express themselves as a central part of their experience within the department. We encourage the diversity and the conflict it generates because we believe that central to our work as counselors is the stimulation of human development. We do not believe one can simply choose when and where to engage in such practices. Rather, we accept the responsibility for continued education of our students (and ourselves), and we believe that a democratic social structure is most likely to promote the kind of development we seek.

Future Directions

Greater attention is being paid to pre-screening students for an interest in group work. At the master's level, for example, our school counseling program uses a group format for interviewing candidates as a part of the interview process. Because the development of a group identity as part of a "cohort" approach to graduate education is central to the current school counseling program, efforts to evaluate candidates' interest in and propensity toward effective group functioning has become very important. We are now considering limiting doctoral study to those who have *at least an interest* in doing their work from a group perspective. A clear problem, as we become more advanced in our group focus, is that many of our doctoral students are likely to continue to come from programs that inadequately prepare them for our program. Once here, they may have several courses to make up to get to a point where the more advanced courses make sense.

Greater attention is being given to preparing students for group supervision. Too often students come to supervision with a mindset shaped by participation in individual supervision. Although we strive to take advantage of the possibilities for group interaction that arise in such a context, the added dimension of looking at one's own group's interaction within the context of a course in group work seems to create an anxiety-laden situation for some students who are ill-prepared to think of themselves in this way.

and yet more traditional group work organization than ASGW), as he advocates a wider application of group psychology than most group psychotherapists may presently employ:

> My wife, a retired social work administrator, is offering training workshops to Boards of Directors of non-profit agencies . . . she sure puts group dynamics to work. My son-in-law directs the Emergency Room at a large local hospital. He sure puts group dynamics to work. Michael Diamond . . . applied psychoanalytic theory in consulting to government, business, health service centers, medical schools and non-profit organizations. He must be putting psychoanalytic theory and group dynamics together in a very useful package. Harold Kelman . . . has been applying group dynamics to the tinder-box of the Middle East. (p. 2)

The four group work specializations developed by ASGW validate comprehensive group worker preparation, and they can be used to guide subsequent group work in the directions envisioned by Goodman and others. In a sense, the ASGW specializations can be visualized as a "rainbow of group work types," each emerging from the core competencies yet existing separately with their own unique color, texture, and hue. Please see Appendix B, "The Rainbow Cafe," for a creative presentation of the variety of group work. At the University of Cincinnati, we use these materials to introduce the differing group work types in our beginning course (and the Rainbow Cafe provided a theme at the ASGW luncheon during the 1996 American Counseling Association conference in Pittsburgh).

Allan Dye, a former president of the Association for Specialists in Group Work, observed at the Second National Group Work Conference of ASGW in St. Petersburg Beach, Florida (Dye, 1994), "When ASGW was created in 1973 no one ever imagined that we would be one day talking about the range of group work types we are today." He is right. Until recently, counselor educators and group work practitioners spoke only of group counseling. However, when pressed, they described their understanding of group counseling in very different ways. With dialogue, we have realized that for some, group counseling meant what ASGW has defined it to mean today—delivery of personal development services for essentially well-functioning individuals currently facing developmental challenges. For many others, opinions varied widely (e.g., delivery of student guidance services in a group format, offering psychoeducational or career development services in small exploratory groups or in large workshops, remedial psychotherapy for acutely or chronically disturbed individuals). Popular texts, focusing on how theories of individual therapy could be applied in a group setting, did little to resolve the divergence. If they provided no greater service, the ASGW Training Standards (1991b) clearly identified the four most common specializations (e.g., group work with task groups, psychoeducational group work, group counseling, and group psychotherapy). Each type was framed as an extension and refinement of a common set of core group work competencies, each demanded mastery of particular knowledge and skills, and each demanded supervised field practice to obtain mastery. Counselor education programs face many issues as they attempt to make their group work preparation more comprehensive. Because organizing the overall effort in group worker preparation is so important, we chose to provide early in this book an illustration of how one program at the University of Georgia has proceeded.

As we move toward the 21st century, the demand for diversified group work of the kind that we are describing in this book, and that is consistent with the ASGW *Professional Training Standards*, will increase and accelerate. According to Morganett (1993, p. 2), when referring to the specialized group types of task, psychoeducation, counseling, and psychotherapy, "ASGW made one of the major contributions to the field of group work by identifying and defining group work specialties." Educators, counselors, and other helpers will be called upon to provide these diverse types of group work to business and industry, communities, mental health centers, schools, and a variety of other settings. People will demand group work that helps them to remediate long-standing and deep-seated problems, develop and enhance skills, improve productivity, and prevent dysfunction.

Outstanding group work preparation is under way in counseling programs today. Through our national survey of group work preparation, we have been able to describe at least some of those efforts in this book. We encourage you to continue exploring the group work rainbow as you move through the next chapters.

2 CHAPTER

A "Baker's Dozen" of Challenges and Strategies

ALL GROUPS PROVIDE CHALLENGES AND REWARDS

The nature of humankind is to engage in activity in groups. The varieties are countless: sports teams, governmental bodies, car pools, educational cohorts, professional societies, religious communities, work squads. Regardless of purpose, all groups are complex, dynamic entities which provide challenges and rewards for the members and their leader.

To introduce this chapter on challenges and strategies for group leaders, we will examine a very basic task group, the book discussion group (Jacobsohn, 1994; Slezak, 1993), a national phenomenon to be found in nearly every neighborhood, community center, religious or work community. A book group is a type of task group in which members agree to read the same books and to meet regularly to discuss them. Leadership may be professionally conducted or member led.

Example of a Basic Task Group:
The Book Discussion Group

Book groups present demands and rewards that are common to all groups, and these demands require competent management by members and leaders. In terms of demands, what happens when a member comes to the discussion without having completed the agreed-upon readings? What happens if not one but, say, three of eight members are so unprepared? How does the group cope with the member who, week after week, monopolizes the discussion and tends to present her own ideas as "truth"? How does the book discussion group define what it means to stay focused on the task at hand when members often want to pursue the individual meaning of a book's passage? Is self-disclosure accepted and encouraged? If so, how much and what kind? How does the group manage task completion while also seeking to accommodate unplanned intrusions, such as sickness or weather emergencies, that delay progress? What kinds of procedures are developed to handle the departure of current members or the incorporation of new members? What factors are considered by the members in attracting new members? In fact, how are new books selected for reading and discussion?

Ostensibly formed to further intellectual needs, book discussion groups can also satisfy needs for interpersonal connection. Such groups also provide rewards for participation. Participants learn and grow, sometimes in unanticipated ways. In Slezak's (1993) book of essays on the experience of book group members, intellectual value was frequently accompanied by personal and social value: Book group members reported that their groups helped them to feel less isolated and more supported and that they facilitated friendships. In several cases, the personal–social component was at least as important as the intellectual. According to Jacobsohn (1994, p. 137), the ultimate purpose of the book discussion group is empowerment: ". . . through select reading, through trust in certain authors, story, and the group discussion process, you can teach yourself to let go, to discover more about the mysteries of life and the presence or the absence of answers."

Not all groups work well, however, and some prove to be disastrous. Book discussion groups that fail to satisfy their members' needs disband. Monopolizing can be allowed to continue, irresponsibility can become normative, the group can become permanently derailed from its purpose, intermember conflicts can become nasty and go unresolved for long periods of time, and much more. Any of these kinds of problems can lead to group failure.

No doubt you have experienced similar—and other—challenges and rewards in your groups. Your awareness of these events and situations will contribute to a broader understanding of the importance of competence in group work practice.

Group Work Practice: Challenges and Strategies

The professional practice of comprehensive group work requires practitioners to be competent in dealing with a full range of challenges and complexities germane to group work. Professional group workers, therefore, need to develop a complementary range of strategies that will enable them to anticipate and cope effectively with these challenges. What follows is a discussion of 13 major challenges (a "baker's dozen") faced by all group work practitioners, accompanied by a discussion of related group worker strategies that can help to meet each challenge. These challenges have been organized according to the major themes discussed in Chapter One: defining group work and one's scope of practice, pregroup planning, therapeutic dynamics and leader skills, research and evaluation, and group work ethics. Note that the strategies presented are drawn from the document, *Professional Standards for the Training of Group Workers* (ASGW, 1991b), which specifies both knowledge and skill competency areas.

DEFINING GROUP WORK AND SCOPE OF PRACTICE

Challenge 1: How to Know Your Limitations

In all things, one simply must know one's limitations to avoid blundering into difficulty. In their text on group work in counseling, Capuzzi and Gross (1992) devote several pages to debunking myths about group work. According to Capuzzi and Gross, it is crucial, for example, for the group worker to understand clearly that

• although many people benefit from group experience, not everyone does;
• although intentional planning for group composition is necessary, such planning does not assure positive outcomes;
• although leaders exert important influence on group life, the group does not revolve around the leader's charisma;

- although intentional structuring of group activities may facilitate certain explorations and awareness, structured exercises are not the mainstay of effective group work;
- although adopting a here-and-now focus can intensify emotional experience, outcome research suggests that greatest benefit derives from combining thought with feeling and exploring both historical and real-time phenomena;
- although self-disclosure and soliciting feedback can promote positive outcomes, such outcomes occur mainly when they serve to generate empathy among members.

Folk wisdom about what it takes to have a successful group can be wrong. Prospective group workers, armed only with conventional knowledge about groups, not only may not know their limitations but also may not know the power of the group work they have chosen to use.

Experience in groups can be a potent force for healing and for harming. The prospective group worker must understand for what people, under what conditions, what kind of group experience is likely to produce positive changes with a manageable level of risk. To answer this question, a group worker needs to understand the therapeutic power of the group, the signs which contraindicate group experience for certain people, the risk level of each of a variety of group techniques, the signs that positive changes are occurring, and the signs of impending casualties.

Strategy: Learning definitions and boundaries. For these reasons the ASGW Training Standards (1991b) require students of group work at the core level to deliver a clear, concise, and complete definition of group work in general and of each of the four group work specialties (Core Standards 13 and 14) and to state the advantages and disadvantages of group work and the circumstances for which it is indicated and contraindicated (Standard 9). Core level preparation is also required to help the student understand distinguishing characteristics of each of the specializations, the commonalities shared by all, and the instances in which each specialization is to be used (Core Standard 1). Beyond this general knowledge of definitions and boundary markers, within each of the specializations are requirements that particularize the student's knowledge of the strengths and limitations of the specialization, the populations for which that group specialization is an appropriate intervention, and the contraindicating signs. The "Group Work Rainbow," mentioned in Chapter One, can assist in helping the theoretical material come alive for students and can serve as an excellent way to introduce and compare group work specialty areas.

PREGROUP PLANNING

Challenge 2: How to Prepare for a Group— Preparation, Planning, and Screening

In our work, we have found failure to properly plan the group to be a significant contributor to poor group work. Unfortunately, it seems to be a challenge area that receives relatively scant attention in the professional literature, although this situation is beginning to improve (cf. Corey, 1990; Gladding, 1995; Jacobs, Harvill, & Masson, 1994). Too often group work is conducted without an overall plan or a session plan, so that a clear direction is absent or minimal. That is, group workers either have not put forward the effort to plan and, therefore, none has been created, or it has been only vaguely developed; or they believe that spontaneity should rule, and thus making a plan is unnecessary. However, a resulting strategy of intuitive group work, sometimes known as "winging it," is not generally desirable and, in fact, is inconsistent with ethical practice in group work (*ASGW Ethical Guidelines for Group Counselors*, 1991a). Of course, planning is too often ignored or forgotten because it takes time and effort from an already busy professional life. Moreover, if a group is to be coled, as is often preferred or necessary, planning can become even more difficult to arrange and accomplish. Ironically, this is so, even as the need for coled groups is becoming critical.

Another more subtle but equally vexing problem in pregroup preparation is the way in which many group plans are prepared. Too often plans are developed in isolation from the target population and setting. This problem is especially prevalent in preventively oriented psychoeducation groups, such as adolescent social-skills development groups. The group leader(s) design a plan that they think will work and that may even be based on a thorough literature review. However, when designed independently from the prospective group member population and divorced from the reality of the target population needs, the plan lacks the ecological validity necessary for success. An additional problem is that when the plan is produced without the direct involvement of target population members, there is the risk of foisting the plan on the unsuspecting. When this occurs, collaboration is sorely absent, and the chances for a successful group experience are severely diminished. In fact, a common circumstance is that too few prospective members may appear for the beginning session, and the group never "gets off the ground"; we have referred to this occurrence as the suppose-you-gave-a-party-and-no-one-came phenomenon.

Especially in counseling and in psychotherapy groups, screening, selection, and pregroup preparation are practical necessities (Bednar & Kaul, 1985). However, such groups are too often formed without benefit of proper screening for suitability and pregroup orientation. In such a situation, the group members may be quite unaware of the purposes for the group, of the group worker's qualifications and experience, or of methods to be used. Thus, it is not unlikely that the group might prove to be inappropriate for some of the members. All of these illustrations are inconsistent with appropriate ethical behavior for group workers and are incompatible with effective practice. The challenge is for group workers to understand that planning and preparation are critically important for effective and ethical group work practice and to convert this understanding into practice. Good group work results from what occurs within the group sessions and the planning and preparation that are expended outside (and before) those sessions.

Strategy: Planning groups and preparing members by using collaborative-ecological principles. As mentioned above, group workers must be able to deliver clear, concise definitions of group work and its specialties, be able to clarify the purposes of group work types, and know how to recruit and screen prospective group members. In addition to this general knowledge, the leader must become versed in the findings of researchers and seasoned practitioners regarding the specific application of group work to the population in which the prospective group leader is interested. With mastery of this understanding, the group worker is positioned to be able to make clear choices about the kind of group experience needed by the population of interest and to communicate to potential recruits what they can expect as participants in the group, benefits they may reasonably hope to obtain from participation, and risks they face in agreeing to become a member. Said plainly, group workers must plan their groups and prepare their members adequately in order to set the stage for an effective group experience.

A highly recommended strategy to use is based on what we term "collaborative-ecological principles." That is, the planner of group work services needs to invest his or her effort in working with members (and/or their representatives) of the target population. The plans need to be grounded ecologically in the real-world experience of prospective members, as well as in related research literature. Plans, then, emerge from the environmental context and are not imposed on that context. The leader-member works *with* setting members in plan creation rather than parachuting a plan in and *doing to* the members. This is what is meant by enacting a collaborative-ecological perspective to pregroup preparation.

Challenge 3: What Is Our Purpose?

Every group work leader will hear this question, and it is often a legitimate one. Members, busy with many of life's demands, need to understand what their group is intended to do, as well as what it will not do. In groups as in other situations, uncertainty and ambiguity are usually avoided. In contrast, knowing what is intended, if agreed to, can serve as a powerful motivator to participate in all kinds of group work.

However, group work is by definition a somewhat ambiguous endeavor. After all, much of what occurs is dependent on the unpredictable involvement and contributions of individual members and of the even less knowable subsequent interactions among these members. Because group work possesses a quality of risk and openness to experience, it thereby embraces the unforeseen and encourages creative expression. Thus, the group work leader faces a continuing and unavoidable tension between the specification of group and individual purposes as they relate to spontaneity, creativity, and the freedom of expression.

Sometimes groups never get off the ground because of perceived purposelessness or because of time spent doing things that members choose not to value. It is not unusual in some groups for members never to identify the overall group purpose and/or to be unable to clarify individual goals for participating. These groups are at high risk for dissolution or, if they continue, for very limited productivity. In such cases, the cause for this failure to define goals may be the group work leader's; in others, the continual cry for clarity may be a smoke screen hiding the unwillingness of members to move forward with the work before them.

Examples abound. A stereotypic complaint from members in counseling and psychotherapy groups is confusion over the members' reasons for being in the group. In reaction to a counselor's encouragement of members to set personal goals for their work in a personal growth group, members may complain, "We just flounder around, talk about feelings, and get stuck in silence. What are we supposed to be doing here?" Group psychotherapists also hear group members expressing confusion about "why we are here." In response to the therapist's press for members to be clear about what they want, a member might respond, "Why do you ask me what I want? I don't know what I want! I thought you were supposed to help me!" Even in such straightforward groups as task/work groups and psychoeducational groups, confusions about why we are here may occur. It is, unfortunately, not uncommon for civic committees to form, gather, and engage in weeks of discussion only to have someone in the group declare, "We talk round and round in circles but never come to a conclusion. Just what are we supposed to be doing in this committee?" In a psychoeducational group designed to teach parenting skills, some group member may complain, "Why are we playing these communication games? I've got problems with my son, and I expected this class was going to tell me what to do about him!"

Why are we here is a ubiquitous group work question, reflecting an essential existential quest common to all thinking people. As a normative issue, therefore, finding ways to appropriately respond is important. When the question hides a different feeling or dynamic, such as anger at the leader or an unwillingness to work, then it is important to find effective ways to address those issues.

Strategy: Defining purpose. The group work leader can attempt to prevent later confusion or anger about why members are in a group through early, mutual delineation of purposes. Explanation and clarification of the overall purpose of the group is essential, as indicated in the Standards. We also strongly suggest that group work leaders work closely with the members during recruitment and selection and that from the first session they mutually negotiate individual goals that directly flow from the overall group purpose. If a group is to generally address sexual abuse prevention skills, for example, Member A might be especially interested in developing assertion skills while Member B might want to enhance skills in developing supportive relationships with others. In a research and development group, in which the overall goal might be to secure external funding for a teenage pregnancy project, Member A can contribute expertise in prevention technology, and Member B skills in budget preparation.

The interrelationship of group goals and individual goals is absolutely critical to involvement and success. Maintaining this balance cannot be done by the group work leader alone, nor can it be accomplished independently by each member. This interlacing must proceed mutually. Related competency skills contained in the Standards are also involved, including encouraging participation of group members, attending to and acknowledging group member behavior, clarifying and summarizing group member statements, and keeping the group on task in accomplishing its goals.

THERAPEUTIC DYNAMICS AND LEADERSHIP SKILLS

Challenge 4: Coping with Data Overload and Fast-Paced Action

The complexity and fast pace of group work cannot be overstated! For the experienced and competent group worker, this complexity and speed, necessary for individual and group productivity, can become a source of richness to be appreciated. For the novice, complexity combined with speed frequently are experienced as data overload. This rushing stream of data can exceed the ability of the group worker to process it sufficiently and promptly. Consequently, group workers in this situation may become concerned about—or consumed with— fears of inadequacy and losing control.

Data overload begins with numbers. As counselors and therapists know, working with one client in counseling produces a considerable amount of data to be processed. These data, for example, can emerge from the client's history, intrapsychic world, present relationships with others, and experience within the therapy sessions. These data can be produced through self-report, therapist observation, observations and reports of others, testing, and diagnosis. Of course, the data are building cumulatively across the individual counseling sessions.

In a group work situation, the data set becomes multiplicative because of the number of participants and the levels of possible interaction. Depending on the type of group, any of the above individual-level data mentioned may be relevant, along with data emerging from the interactions of members with each other. In group work, as we pointed out in Chapter One, member-to-member interactions can produce a voluminous (and critically important) array of data. In addition to the individual and member-to-member levels, group work can also involve attending to the group itself, that is, seeking to monitor the group's working climate. Subsequent group-level data, therefore, supply another layer of input. Finally, the group worker's relationships with the group itself, the members, the coleader (if present), and his or her awareness of personal reactions to group activities all can contribute additional data for processing.

In addition to complex data, in groups the action usually occurs quickly. There are many words, feelings, nonverbal behaviors, open and hidden agendas, and tasks to be accomplished. A useful metaphor is table tennis, where the ping-pong ball is propelled back and forth across the net in a blur. A more accurate metaphor is the abstract notion of multidimensional table tennis, with multiple ping-pong balls being propelled back and forth across multiple nets in a blur.

Group work is even fast paced when appearing slow on the surface. That is, in those moments when it seems that little is being accomplished or when no one is talking, significant internal dialogue and meaningful nonverbal behavior may be occurring. Minds may be racing with self-talk and self-presentation rehearsals, palms may be sweating out of anxiety, legs may be crossed and uncrossed reflecting any number of meanings. Any of these events may be indicative of considerable energy flow.

In any group, it is a mistake to ever conclude that nothing is happening within or between its members. When a group worker begins to wonder whether "nothing is going on" or notices such characterizations being made by members, it is very helpful to look below the surface and beyond the obvious. Likewise, it can also be a mistake to accept apparently productive activity at face value. Without exploration beneath the surface, a group leader may be charmed by the "well-behaved group" that has learned to appear cooperative with group goals and methods. In some groups, the confluence of forced consensus may camouflage underlying conflict. Failure to delve into the meaning of the apparent successes of the group may allow the group to survive the experience of being in the group yet may result in members not challenging their fears and gaining real growth. Therefore, the group worker needs to know when to promote exploration of surface behavior to reveal hidden thoughts, attitudes, and feelings that are unexpressed verbally.

The challenge for group workers is to develop manageable and effective skills for observing, cataloging, processing, and then using these data in an efficient way. Therefore, developing effective and efficient linkages among input, processing, and output is necessary in order to both manage and to use the data available. In addition, competent group workers need to increase the real-time speed with which they can successfully perform these functions. Although reflection following a group meeting or session is necessary to help in understanding what happened and in preparing for the next session, becoming able to accomplish these activities within a session is a highly desirable goal.

Strategy: Sorting and organizing information through using a conceptual map. The ASGW Training Standards provide considerable attention to knowledge and skills that are helpful in reducing data overload and in promoting data management. All of the knowledge standards can contribute to this goal. Especially important is knowledge of group dynamics, the basic therapeutic ingredients of groups, the process components involved in typical stages of group development, and roles members can play. Thus, group workers can be aided substantially by having mastered conceptual knowledge of the role of group dynamics, such as how decisions are made or what patterns group member interaction may follow. Knowing that certain kinds of member behaviors can be generally anticipated to occur within certain points of a group's development can be inordinately helpful to the group worker. Understanding the kinds of roles that members might assume in a group can serve as a useful guide in making better sense of behaviors that are being displayed.

The most important skill available to the group worker in managing data overload is to observe and identify group process events. Critical group process events can easily occur without being noticed, and observations may be made without awareness of their meaning. In either case, it does not take long before the group and the group worker become lost. Other important skills documented in the Standards involve clarifying and summarizing group member statements, helping group members attribute meaning to their experience, and helping them to integrate and apply learnings. These skills involve doing something intentional with the data. Members can quickly become confused about all that has been said within just a few minutes or about the meaning of a long silence. Helping to clarify and summarize on a regular basis, and assisting the members to do so, can reduce this problem. What events and data mean to group members and how they might integrate and apply learnings are important for the group worker to address in an effort to make understandable and useful the data that are produced.

The fast-paced action of group work, whether it is occurring above or below the surface, requires group workers to use their skills to keep up with the action or to slow it down. That is, the group worker needs to monitor the flow of events in the group. A conceptual map is essential to enable the group worker to follow the action, to sort and organize it, and thus to prevent data overload.

We all use conceptual maps on a daily basis in our personal lives. For instance, they assist us in getting from our home to downtown or within our home from one room to another at night in the dark. While your conceptual map of a certain area and mine of that same area may differ in their details, it is generally the case that each is effective for each of us. They help us to get where we need to go and to be able to make sense of all the incoming and perhaps unexpected data that we encounter, much like road repairs and detours on a highway. Without our conceptual map we would have a far more difficult time of finding our way.

In group work, a conceptual map can function similarly. Incoming data have a place to be stored and processed. The map may give us a framework for understanding the data. It also may help us to anticipate and plan for what might happen in any particular session or meeting. In short, a conceptual map can assist the group worker in keeping up with the fast-paced flow of activities in a group.

In terms of the ASGW Training Standards, sorting and organizing strategies are directly pertinent. In fact, the challenges of fast-paced action and data overload are highly related. If the fast-paced action is not managed properly, then data overload is likely to follow.

Going beyond the Standards, it is important for group workers to develop broader conceptual maps. At the University of Cincinnati training program, for instance, students learn several different models, including the Hill Interaction Matrix (Hill, 1965), What to Look for in Groups (Hanson, 1969), and the Critical Incident Cube (Cohen & Smith, 1976a, 1976b). These materials provide overarching conceptual schema useful for keeping up with and making sense of group action. They provide, respectively, a map for following group verbal interaction, group processes, and group member and worker interventions. We encourage students to use or adapt these kinds of schema in their group work leadership experiences and thus to develop their own conceptual maps. We then draw upon this material in supervision to assist in linking the meaning of data produced through group interaction with action steps.

Challenge 5: How to View a Group

Group workers are always challenged by the need to keep up with the ongoing flow of data and to make sense of it. This challenge might suggest a stance of narrowing one's perspective. This more circumscribed vantage point would reduce the range and scope of one's attention and thereby lessen the work load. For instance, group workers might focus their attention on verbal behavior only, excluding the nonverbal, or they might attend to task issues without considering personal relations. Although this focused stance might serve to simplify the task of group work leadership, it is too restrictive. Adopting such a stance means, by definition, that other important information is ignored. In our earlier examples, both verbal and nonverbal behavior is important; both task and personal relations are critical in all groups.

Moreover, it is useful to attend to and respond to other aspects of group work, including (a) *levels of involvement*: how each individual member is feeling and behaving, how relationships between and among members are being expressed, how the group is functioning as a group; (b) *types of involvement*: how members participate, in terms of thinking, feeling, and behaving; (c) *roles of involvement*: the general styles assumed by members, such as those of helper, challenger, monopolizer, and others; (d) *communication patterns in involvement*: who speaks to whom, who is often silent, influential members, how decisions get made in the group, and others; and (e) *productivity in involvement*: Is the group engaging or avoiding its tasks? How is conflict being handled? Are the goals clear? Are members working with each other to reach goals?

These five aspects of group work illustrate the importance of the group worker's taking multiple vantage points, not a single one. Group activity naturally involves multiple and complex interactions. Therefore, it is necessary for the group worker to function in accord with that reality by employing multiple vantage points to understand what is occurring and to guide his or her actions in the group. The obvious challenge to be met is that multiple vantage points produce multiple data sets that need to be understood and acted upon but they potentially serve to increase the problems addressed earlier of fast-paced action and data overload.

Strategy: Become at ease with multiplicity and interdependence. The definition of group work contained in the ASGW Standards centrally includes the concept of interdependence: ". . . to assist an interdependent collection of people. . . ." Interdependence and multiple vantage points are synchronous. That is, interdependence suggests that everything is connected to everything else. In this view, a group is not composed of a set of separate, independent individuals. Rather, it is an interconnected network of people and interactions. Being able to understand, relate to, and assist this interdependent network requires the group worker to employ multiplicity in many ways, including the vantage points used.

All the knowledge and skill strategies contained in the ASGW Standards, then, need to be set within the twin concepts of interdependence and multiplicity. Each separate skill, for instance, represents a particular vantage point to be applied in such a way as to assist interdependence to develop within the group. The first skill in the Standards, "Encourage participation of group members" (ASGW, 1991b, p. 15), can be considered as an example. It provides one vantage point for the group worker to use in understanding the group—that is, how the members are involving themselves in the group. Also, the skill of encouraging participation provides a way for the group worker to function. The group worker can encourage greater interdependence by promoting members to participate actively and directly with each other, as opposed to encouraging them to participate as independent agents.

Challenge 6: How to Manage a Group

Keeping a group moving forward effectively and efficiently is a continuing challenge faced by all group workers. Lieberman, Yalom, and Miles (1973) termed this aspect of group leadership "executive functioning." It involves keeping time, staying on focus, allowing members to be heard, fitting methods to goals, and generally directing traffic.

For many group workers, two particularly difficult challenges, which we will use to illustrate group management, are how to begin a new group and then how to terminate when the work is done. On a smaller scale, beginning and closing issues are often experienced for each meeting or session. Both kinds of starts and finishes seem to touch sensitive areas for many of us. Along with feeling excitement, many of us are anxious about initiating something new with others. The act of meeting new people and developing new relationships is sometimes both enjoyable and stressful. Fear of the unknown can play a role for many. Performance anxiety related to how one will be able to function with these new people may be inhibiting for some. In addition, for the group worker, being responsible for the professional leadership of a task or personal change group can be daunting. Do I know enough? Am I skilled enough? Will I be perceived as competent? Do I have enough energy to last these next 2 hours? Are these people going to find the group useful? Will we be able to accomplish the goals that have been established? These are the kinds of questions that may flash through a group worker's mind before the start of a new group and before every session.

Bringing closure to an ongoing event that has been important and meaningful also can pose significant challenges. Probably the clearest and most intense instance of termination that we will know in our lives is death, either ours or that of someone whom we love. Changing residence is another life event that triggers closure issues for many. Saying good-bye to friends and family and moving on to an unfamiliar environment can be traumatic. Graduation from high school or college can be a bitterly sweet experience. These basic life events, all involving termination in some way, invite discomfort and struggle for many people.

The cycles of inclusion, control, and openness appear in metacycles and microcycles of human existence (Schutz, 1973). A lifespan involves birth (inclusion), mastery of life skills (control), bonding with a life partner (openness), aging (loss of control), and death (disinclusion). Within any of these epochs of life, microcycles intertwine: taking one job (inclusion) may entail leaving another (disinclusion). Numerous developmental theories have charted the developmental process in small groups and have noted patterns reminiscent of the inclusion–control–openness–control–disinclusion pattern noted by Schutz.

For group workers (and their members), closing an ongoing group can conjure up similar struggles. How to say good-bye to each other is sometimes painful. Approaching termination while maintaining a consistent and focused motivation to be productive within the group can cause conflict. Helping group members to integrate and apply what they have been learning or producing is a task that needs to be accomplished by the end of a group. Assessment of the group's effectiveness at a variety of levels also needs to occur before the experience is completed. In a sense, the goal of the group worker is to help group members prepare to terminate the group with a sense of completion, without an accumulation of new, "unfinished business" to carry forward beyond the group.

From session to session, these sorts of opening and closing issues also emerge. Beginning each session in such a way as to tie it with preceding work may be desirable. Warming-up members to the tasks at hand can be problematic, given the pressures and daily events they have been experiencing. Developing agreed-upon agenda for a session can be tricky. In terms of closing each meeting, ending on time in a comfortable way seems to be especially hard for new leaders. Finding ways to summarize accomplishments or learnings while anticipating the next meeting is not easily developed. Knowing when not to tie everything up in a "neat, little ball" is a learning that requires time and practice.

Opening up and closing down are two sets of skills that on the surface seem to be simple and easy to accomplish. In fact, they call for substantial group worker sensitivity and expertise.

Strategy: Beginning and ending a group and its sessions. As stipulated in the ASGW Standards, group workers must be able to explain and clarify the purpose of the particular form of group work being used. Doing this at the start of a group helps to begin the process with clarity. The skill competency of opening and closing group sessions, of course, is essential to proper management. Keeping the group on task in accomplishing its goals is another skill competency that assists group management. All of these strategies center on the group worker functioning as a process manager and guide who assists the interactions to stay targeted and timely.

Challenge 7: How to Manage Conflict

Conflict is inherent in all human interactions. Certainly, conflict is present in all group work. It can be experienced subtly or directly. Almost always, the conflict is experienced as being uncomfortable for members and leaders alike.

Conflict can take many forms in group work. Internal conflicts, those occurring within a member, are common. For instance, Seth might show nonverbal signs, such as wringing his hands or shielding his eyes, which suggest an internal struggle. Perhaps he is struggling with whether to disclose to the group his feelings of inadequacy regarding a work task to which he had been assigned.

Other forms of conflict involve members with each other or members with the leader(s). Carol finds Marguerite to be generally arrogant and insensitive to others in the group. One day Carol erupts, saying,

"Marguerite, I wish you would stop being so nasty to everyone in here!" This is a conflict-laden moment that challenges the capacity of all to respond.

Members may be much less direct in expressing feelings than was illustrated in Carol's disclosure to Marguerite. For example, Arthur may communicate his displeasure by ignoring Anna Mae, by not looking at, listening to, or approaching her in any way. In the extreme case, Arthur might stop coming to group meetings because of his disaffection with Anna Mae's behavior and his own inability to deal with it directly. These are subtle forms of conflict, sometimes thought of as "passive aggressive," in which a member withdraws and seethes inside.

Often group members conflict with the leader(s). A question about group purpose may simply be a request for information, or it may be a subtle opening for a more general attack on the competence of the leader(s). Such an apparently innocent question about why are we here may soon be followed by the more provocative demand, "Why don't you do something?" or "What we really need in here is leadership!" When Carol directly challenged Marguerite's "nasty" behavior in the group, her statement might be followed quickly with another member's saying to the leader, "This is the kind of thing I can't stand— what are *you* going to do about it?" Suddenly the opening issue, whatever it may be, is transformed into one of conflict, control, and power.

Power issues with the leader can also occur subtly. Members can become silent, seemingly unwilling to interact. Or, conversely, they might chatter about all kinds of things which are irrelevant to the purpose of the group. Members might resist the leader's suggestions. When the leader suggests that the group break into subgroups to work on a task (either work related or therapy related), members might continue to interact as they are, apparently disregarding the leader's idea. Attendance might begin to flag or a pattern of tardiness might develop. Although there might be other explanations for any of these kinds of behavior, one possibility is that the members are displaying passive aggression against the leader.

Strategy: Understand group development and confront appropriately.
Many beginning group work leaders are uninformed about the natural

occurrence of conflict at certain points in a group's evolution. Thus, even the mere appearance of conflict can be unsettling. Even with solid intellectual preparation for the inevitability of conflict in a normally developing group, inexperienced leaders are frequently disconcerted when conflict erupts. Therefore, developing a working knowledge of conflict as a necessary part of any group's development is a fundamental tool for the effective group work leader to acquire. This knowledge base is directly addressed in the ASGW Training Standards.

Over 100 theoretical models of group development exist (Forsyth, 1990). Particularly helpful examples include those proposed by Anderson (1984), Cohen and Smith (1976a, 1976b), Corey and Corey (1992), Jones (1973), Lacoursiere (1980), Schutz (1973), Trotzer (1989), and Tuckman and Jensen (1977). Each of these models represents a variant or extension of a basic four-stage model:

- *formation*, characterized by issues of trust, security, orientation, purpose, and inclusion;
- *control*, characterized by conflict, power, and regulation;
- *work*, characterized by open communication, cohesion, interdependence, and productivity;
- *termination*, characterized by application, integration, disengagement, saying good-bye, and closing.

These stages can serve as general guideposts for any group work leader, as long as it is remembered that any one group can vary in how it proceeds through the stages. Conflict appears within this general paradigm as a stage to be expected, somewhere between the early meetings of a group and before the group has become a genuinely effective operating system. In fact, many authors suggest that the successful resolution of the conflict stage is necessary before cohesion and productivity can occur.

Knowing this conceptual information, then, can be very helpful for group work leaders. Conflict should come as less of a surprise. Generally anticipating when it might occur in a group allows the group work leader the opportunity to plan for it, at least somewhat. As a product of group development, conflict should not be experienced as a personal or professional failure of the leader, but as a necessary and important part of doing group work. Conflict is a prerequisite to growth and development.

Even so, having this knowledge does not automatically make it easy to deal with conflict when it arises. A whole set of skill strategies is also important. Probably the two most directly relevant skills contained in the ASGW Training Standards are the ability to effectively "confront group members' behavior" and to "impart and clarify information in the group when necessary" (pp. 15–16). This is a potent tandem of skills in dealing with troublesome situations.

The ability to confront effectively allows the group work leader the opportunity to call conflict to the attention of group members so that constructive action can occur. As we have said, conflict can be obvious or subtle. In either case, attention often needs to be focused on the event or its underlying dynamics. The leader needs to have both the courage and the sensitivity to move into these areas, areas that are often avoided by others. Helping members to become aware of struggles, to surface hidden agenda, or to take responsibility for statements made or omitted are examples of how appropriate and effective confrontation can be useful in beginning to deal with conflict.

Moreover, helping members to understand that conflict is a natural and often growth-producing process in human interactions, such as group work, is critically important. The group work leader can accomplish this goal by using the skill of imparting information in the group, informing members about the proper role and function of conflict in their group, and helping them to learn conflict resolution skills. As members begin to understand the developmental function of conflict in their interactions, they often become better able to accept and work with it productively.

Challenge 8: How to Know and Be Yourself

Most theorists and authors in the group work field emphasize the significance of the personhood of group work leaders. In fact, regardless of the mode of help-giving—whether it be individual, group, family, or consultative—it is commonly understood that the level of functioning of the helper is fundamentally important to success. This assertion does not mean, of course, that knowledge, skills, and experience are unimportant. On the contrary, these factors also are vital to determining successful help-giving. However, without self-awareness and interpersonal competency, the effective application of knowledge, skills, and experience becomes inhibited or impossible.

The continual, often intense, interactions with a number of group members demand that the group work leader possess high levels of personal and interpersonal competency. Leaders must be self-aware. They need to know their patterns of associations, personal and interpersonal sensitivities and insensitivities, customary patterns of confusion and misperception, and personal reactivity to external trigger situations. They need to be functioning at a high level in their daily lives. They need to be able to relate well to others, to be able to appropriately self-disclose, take risks, and give feedback.

In addition to personal and interpersonal competence, group work leaders need to develop and maintain their humanity. That is, they must be good at what they do, and they must be good people. This statement may sound trite or inappropriate in a text. However, at the root of group work is the reality that it is a human endeavor, a purposeful connection of people with each other. The leader, therefore, needs to be able to relate to others, to empathize with their situations, to demonstrate caring for them as people. In fact, in the Lieberman, Yalom, and Miles (1973) classic study of group leadership, the function of caring was found to be centrally important for success across all theoretical positions.

Group work leaders need to have integrated theory and practice of group work leadership with their own personal and interpersonal style. That is, they need to have developed a functional level of comfort and effectiveness, a good fit between themselves, what they do, and how they do it in group situations. They must not be led by techniques or theory, nor by their own intuition or spontaneity. Rather, group work leaders need to have incorporated their own personhood into their professional practice in a useful and effective way.

It is important that group work leaders are cognizant of themselves during the course of group activity. Monitoring their own thoughts and feelings in relation to what is occurring provides the potential for using themselves as instruments of growth or change in the group—a vitally important source! Often, while seeking assiduously to apply techniques or to thoroughly understand the positions of each member, group work leaders unintentionally can lose sight of themselves in the process. At the surface, losing sight of self may be viewed as a technical error. Thus, leaders are exhorted to include their input appropriately in ongoing group interactions. At a deeper level, losing sight of self may be thematic for a group leader. Many individuals, when feeling responsible for the welfare of others, habitually look outward instead of inward. For them, more than exhortation is needed. Repeated examination under supervision of the process of the group may help such group leaders to flexibly shift their awareness from phenomena outside the self to their own inner-world experiencing of the group.

Strategy: Know your personal and interpersonal strengths and weaknesses. The ASGW Standards clearly set out knowledge of self and others as necessary for group work leaders. They indicate that the personal characteristics of group workers that have an impact on members must be understood. In this regard, our students have found it useful to consider becoming more aware of their "stimulus value." That is, they need to understand how they are generally perceived by others, how others picture them in their minds. Are they soft and quiet? Forceful and strong? Thoughtful and considerate? The skill competencies of the Standards call for the group work leader to be able to model effective group leader behavior, to engage in appropriate self-disclosure in the group, to give and receive feedback in the group, to confront group member behavior, and to empathize with group members. To effectively engage in these behaviors, group work leaders must integrate technical expertise with personal and interpersonal competencies and with a good working awareness of their stimulus value.

Challenge 9: How to Understand the Uniqueness of Members

In order to conduct group work effectively, the leader needs to develop a good, practical understanding of each member and of the members' interrelationships. This statement is true for all types of group work, but it is much easier said than done.

There is so much to understand in group work that the attention of any leader can be pushed and pulled in many competing directions simultaneously. What did Sarah just say? I was watching Betty and was not listening. I remember that John said his father ignored him usually, and I wonder if that is being played out here somehow. Is

Fred hiding right now or just being quiet? The group members just seem lethargic, but I am wondering if it is a lack of purpose or something else. Is Susan needing support here from me, or should I just let this discussion continue? I know we are off-task right now, but it seems that Betty and Fred are beginning to get involved.

Another increasingly important concept to aid in understanding individual members is multiculturalism and diversity. As this country becomes ever more heterogeneous in terms of ethnicity, group workers need to heighten their awareness of the effects of how cultural differences may affect group member behavior. For example, with increasing frequency, group leaders are becoming involved in working with Chinese and with Chinese-American group members. Reticence to share personal disclosures in groups composed of strangers is experienced by many (note: not necessarily all) people of Chinese and Asian descent and is perhaps even more keenly felt by them than those from other ethnic backgrounds. Recognizing and making appropriate allowance for this factor in group work with Chinese members is important.

These are just some of the kinds of ongoing questions a group work leader may raise, and they all revolve around differing levels of understanding. What to focus on? What to pursue? How important are any of them? How are they related to productive working together? How can cultural and ethnic background influence present behavior?

Strategy: Attend to and acknowledge members. There is very much to be understood about members in any group. Considerations include levels of analysis, group size, and the degree of difficulty or importance of what is being attempted. Some brief illustrations of each consideration are presented below:

- *Level of analysis—individual, interpersonal, group.* At the *individual* level of analysis, understanding can include each member's goals, concerns, strengths, weaknesses, personal-interpersonal orientation, life history, diagnoses, life stresses, physical health, expression of affect, behaviors demonstrated, cognitions, ethnic and cultural background, and so on. At the *interpersonal* level of analysis, understanding can include how each member interacts with other members, what relationships are working, which ones are undeveloped, what relationships are in conflict of some sort, and the capacity of each member to give and receive feedback. Finally, at the *group* level of analysis, understanding can include how involved each member is with the group as a whole and what roles members play in relation to various aspects of group functioning, such as decision-making, planning, goal setting, leadership, conflict resolution, and so on.

* *Group size.* The larger the group size, the more there is to understand. As would be expected, generally there is less to learn about members in a group of four than in a group of nine. On the other hand, the smaller the group size, the more scarce are the interpersonal resources needed to fuel a well-functioning group. A group of four may put undue reliance on a single member's skills or experiences, but in a group with more members, skills and experiences may be distributed more widely.

* *Degree of difficulty or importance.* Degree of difficulty refers to the extent of change or development required of the members in order to perform their task (task and work groups) or intended for the members (personal change groups). The greater the extent of change expected or needed, the more important it is to develop a good, practical understanding of group members. Degree of importance refers to the level of seriousness of a group's goals. Groups formed to accomplish goals of relatively high importance or seriousness (e.g., planning for the future of an organization, restructuring a failed life) require the leader to develop a good, practical understanding of group members.

Preceding understanding, however, is the critical competency contained in the ASGW Standards of "attending to and acknowledging members" (p. 15). Providing adequate and consistent attention to members and acknowledging their situation is fundamental to developing any good, practical understanding of them. This means that the group work leader needs to prize individuality and to look, listen, and respond individually to each member in the group. Just as important, the skilled group worker must observe and respond to the interactions of members with each other and must attend to how they (the members) are involving themselves with the group as a whole. By doing this, not only will the group members feel more understood but also the group leader will begin to acquire data necessary for developing improved understanding of each member.

A critically important facet of attending and acknowledging members that is largely missing from the ASGW Training Standards and that needs immediate attention concerns multicultural differences. Training in group work must be integrated with multicultural competencies so that future group workers can be sensitive to the differing needs of members of various cultures.

Challenge 10: How to Connect Members

In our view, group work derives much of its power from intermember connections. That is, group work of any type is much more than the dyadic interactions between a leader and each member in the group. This is a "switchboard" model of group work leadership, in which everything goes through the leader, just as in an old telephone switchboard system. By contrast, a central function of the group work leader is to promote a working environment in which members feel free to talk and work with one another directly. This is a "network" model of group work leadership, in which the group work leader intentionally seeks to foster between-member interactions, similar to how members in a computer network can directly interrelate (although face-to-face). In a very real way, the group work leader seeks to move away from being the sole repository of power and influence to empowering growth in the interrelationships of members. In this way, participation becomes broadened and leadership becomes diffused among group members.

Developing intermember connections, however, is easier written about than accomplished. Too frequently, group work can be characterized by members who are unconnected with each other and by group work leaders who are unable, or who do not see the need, to help the members form positive working relationships. When this is the situation, much value is lost. As Trotzer (1989) has pointed out, members are the most important resource in the group.

Strategy: Work to enhance cohesion among members. The ASGW Training Standards emphasize the importance of therapeutic factors and ingredients in group work. As first identified by Yalom (1970), these therapeutic factors include instillation of hope, universality, imparting information, altruism, corrective recapitulation of the primary family group, developing socializing techniques, imitative behavior, interpersonal learning, group cohesiveness, catharsis, and existential factors.

In our view, cohesion is of fundamental importance among the list of therapeutic factors. As Yalom stressed, group cohesiveness is not exclusively a therapeutic factor per se but a necessary precondition for effective therapy; it is the analog of the relationship in individual therapy (1985). That is, cohesion needs to be present in order for growth and change to occur.

By extension, we think that cohesion is a central growth factor in all group work types. When cohesion is present, members feel they belong and that others want them to belong as well. A palpable kind of "we-ness" is present. In turn, because cohesion allows members to freely share information, data, and perceptions with each other, it is easier to accomplish individual and group goals, whether they be personal or task in nature.

A group worker can build cohesion by seeking to implement the competencies contained in the ASGW Training Standards (see list), set within the overarching intent of connecting members with each other. Let us take but three examples of how group worker competencies included in the Standards can be intentionally tied to advancing inter-member connections (and cohesion):

- *Encourage participation of group members.* The group worker can continually reframe this competency as "encouraging participation of group members *with each other.*"

- *Model effective group leader behavior.* The group worker can continually reframe this competency as "demonstrating effective group leader behavior *in relation to others* in the group."

- *Help group members attribute meaning to their experience.* The group worker can continually reframe this competency as "helping group members attribute meaning to their experience *with each other.*"

In these ways, connecting members with each other and thereby increasing cohesion can become a recurrent theme permeating all that a group work leader considers doing. Behaving in a manner consistent with that theme, as appropriate to any presenting situation, will better enable connections to form, cohesion to emerge, and productivity to be realized.

Challenge 11: How to Influence Change Within the Group

Probably no goal is more important for the group work leader than that of facilitating intended change. Group work is a means to an end. The task group and the personal change group are each formed to enable group members to reach desired individual and group goals. In the personal change group, individuals may want to become less depressed or more socially skilled. In the work team, members join together to increase or enhance their collective productivity. In each case, the group work leader is committed to the group's becoming an effective means to reaching the group's desired ends.

This final challenge of influencing change is the ultimate goal for group work leaders. Its successful accomplishment depends on satisfactory and cumulative mastery of the preceding challenges and related strategies that we have discussed in this chapter.

Desired change rarely occurs easily. New questions and ideas are surprisingly hard to come by. When they appear, especially if they are imposed (Wheelan, 1994), they are often resisted with considerable force. Change is often experienced as being frightening. Working with and through others in a group can be very frustrating, confusing, and time consuming. Developing a well-functioning group work environment within which change efforts can proceed is demanding. Keeping people on task while responding to their personal and interpersonal needs is a delicate balance to achieve. Identifying learnings and gains made in the group and deciding how they might be applied outside the group are knotty problems. In fact, helping members successfully to make transitions between within-group learnings and outside-of-group applications is a fundamentally important demand for all group work leaders as they seek to influence change through the group.

Strategy: Attribute meaning, integrate, and apply learnings. The within-group/outside-of-group transition that is so endemic to influencing change through the group needs to be continuously addressed. Group work leaders can assist members in making these transitions by performing a triad of functions that are specified in the ASGW Training Standards:

- *Attribute meaning*: help members to make sense of their within-group experiences and attribute within-group events to robust explanatory concepts and frameworks (Lieberman, Yalom, & Miles, 1973);

- *Integrate*: help members to compare and synthesize and thus integrate new learnings with previous ones;

- *Apply*: help members to test out, revise, and apply within-group learnings to situations they face outside the group (Hill, 1969).

Change in group work—whether it be personal or product development—is dependent on many factors, including all the "baker's dozen" we have considered in this chapter. At the heart of it all, in our judgment, is the capacity of group members to make sense of what is happening in the group and then to do something consistent with their learnings in the real world. Understanding and learning a skill, relating it to other skills, and practicing and refining the skill outside the group are essential steps to personal growth in group work. Developing an idea, including it within a general plan, and applying and refining the plan outside the group are essential steps to task productivity in group work.

When group work leaders perform this triad of strategies, group members are better able to gain perspective of their in-group experience and then to convert their learnings to meaningful action. In our experience, change through group work is greatly enhanced whenever group work leaders are able to demonstrate these functions consistently and well.

RESEARCH AND EVALUATION

Challenge 12: How to Fit Practice with Science

Probably no one who has graduated from a counseling preparation program would seriously question if group work leadership should ideally include an effective blending of science and practice. After all, the successful integration of theory, research, and practice is thought to be one hallmark of the professional counselor. Yet, achieving this goal is a daily and unrelenting challenge.

In the real world of counseling practice, in schools, agencies, health care settings, businesses, and private associations, theory has a tendency to be driven out. The onslaught of client and work demands frequently exerts such a continual pressure on practitioners that time seems to disappear for planning, thinking, reading, reflecting, and talking with colleagues about conceptual and practical issues. As a result, with limited time available and an often burdensome caseload, group work leaders tend to become focused on practice to the exclusion of theory.

Group work practiced without the benefit of theory and data is subject to a dangerous insularity that can lead to unwittingly falling behind the state of the art. Conversely, group work leadership conducted without benefit of real-world experience, while grounded in current theory, is subject to irrelevancy and impracticality. Both stances are partial and failure-prone. Science and practice must be merged effectively and appropriately in group work leadership.

Strategy: Become a reflective practitioner. How can busy group work practitioners continue to maintain the theoretical orientation they developed in graduate school? It is unrealistic to expect that the busy group worker can adequately keep current with the comprehensive professional literature in the group work field. However, reading the quarterly *Journal for Specialists in Group Work* and the *Together* newsletter of the Association for Specialists in Group Work should be possible for most. It is even less pragmatic to expect that many group workers will formally research their group work, although they may be able to team with university and research personnel (where they are available) to produce jointly conducted studies in which the talents and experiences of both parties are merged. It is more feasible for group workers to attend local, state, and regional continuing education conferences focusing on group work issues and to at least occasionally attend the national meeting of the American Counseling Association. In fact, incorporating continuing education into their practice is an ethical responsibility which all counseling professionals must assume.

Those opportunities stated above identify important traditional avenues for remaining current in group work theory and concepts and should be pursued. In addition, we want to emphasize a less traditional conception of how to unite theory and practice, one that is meant to be rooted in the naturalistic and daily work setting: the concept of the reflective practitioner, a type of "action scientist" (Argyris, Putnam, & Smith, 1985).

A reflective practitioner, by definition, synthesizes practice with its analysis, and always strives for mutual influence to occur. That is, reflective practitioners experiment with an intervention while intentionally studying it and then use the results to guide future related interventions. A group work leader, for example, might use a new technique during a group meeting, gather data about its implementation and effects, and then consider its potential for future adaptation and application. Or, during a session when confronted with an intervention choice, a group work leader might assess in real time a range of possibilities against a number of criteria and then use professional judgment to make a choice, intervene, and carefully note intervention effects. Later, the leader might actively consider what potential effects other choice options might have had, if selected and used (Cohen & Smith, 1976a).

Data gathering, study, and analysis may be formal or informal for the reflective practitioner. For instance, data gathering can be accomplished in a variety of ways, including group leader observation and group member reactions to a questionnaire. Study and analysis also can be accomplished in different ways. For instance, they can occur through the examination of data output from a paper-and-pencil instrument or a computer, notes taken by the leader immediately following a meeting, or through observations and judgments made by the leader during the session itself. Important considerations are that the methods used for reflective practice are possible to implement and that they allow practice situations to be examined and affected through reflective analysis.

Group work leaders can become reflective practitioners and thus progress toward a functional integration of science and practice that is feasible within the context of their daily work demands. This fully embraces and gives impetus to the ASGW Standard, "Demonstrate ASGW ethical and professional standards in group practice" (p. 16), as it promotes the dynamic, ongoing synthesis of science with practice. We highly recommend this approach as providing a dynamic framework for group work leaders to use in bridging the too frequently distant worlds of theory and practice.

ETHICS

Challenge 13: How to Resolve Dilemmas and Value Choices

In individual counseling, the practitioner is often faced with difficult choices that are tied to conflicting values and moral dilemmas. Dilemmas faced by group work leaders generally are more complex than those occurring within individual counseling. Concerns emerging from working with a sole client in individual counseling are multiplied by the many members composing a group. Consider the issue of keeping material in confidence. While this condition can be more fully assured in the individual case, no comparable assurance can be made in group work because of the presence of several members, whose behavior outside the group situation cannot be monitored by the group work leader.

Group leaders in all types of group work face difficult choices. The task group leader is always balancing the degree of attention that can be given to personal relations and concerns with the dominant focus on task and productivity. For instance, in consulting with an organization on its strategic planning process, a team of eight members was formed into a strategic planning group. As the members began the various stages of the planning process, they expressed the need to process their intermember functioning on a regular basis. Two challenges faced the task group leader: (a) to hold the members to their processing commitment while continuing the progress on strategic planning and (b) to keep the personal relations focus related to task functioning and not become centered on personal issues. She was able to address these twin challenges by regularly reminding the members of their choice to process their working together and by specifically contracting with them to focus the processing on task functioning.

In personal change groups, such as psychoeducation, counseling, and psychotherapy, the ethical dilemmas often are intense. By way of illustration, even before a personal change group has met for the first time, the leader(s) may have struggled over whether to refer certain applicants to other treatment modalities because the leader perceives a marginal fit between the group goals and the applicant's needs or skills or whether to be less restrictive so that the group might have a greater number of participants.

Personal change group leaders walk a tightrope—counting on group members to encourage one another to take risks yet watchful to catch the moment when encouragement becomes group coercion. As mentioned earlier, though leaders of personal change groups are taught to respect the individual's right to set his or her own goals for change, we have goals of our own (e.g., increasing personal awareness by encouraging self-disclosure and data seeking; increasing trust, autonomy, initiative, industry, sense of identity, mutuality, and altruism; promoting reasoned discourse and discouraging avoidance or coercion). Identifying the point when the leader's goals set for the greater good infringe upon the individual's freedom of self-determination is a delicate matter.

The tools of the group worker may be encapsulated as *permission*, *potency*, and *protection*. Leaders of personal change groups try to create environments wherein participants have the freedom (permission) to experiment with their thoughts, feelings, and behavior. Leaders must have the skills and personal energy (potency) to help the participants experiment once they have decided they want to do so. It therefore falls upon the leader to insure that members can experiment safely (protection). Yet such an obvious good as providing safety can, at some degree, become an encouragement to dependency. Identifying the point of overprotection is a chronic leadership challenge. As we mentioned, even such an ethical imperative as the ethic of confidentiality becomes even more complicated in group work than it is in individual counseling. Though a leader can pledge personal confidentiality and describe the conditions under which client disclosures may or must be divulged, the leader can make no such promises for the group members. Despite exhortations to the group members, despite extracting from the members personal pledges of confidentiality, and despite the belief that personal awareness proceeds, in part, from personal self-disclosure, leaders must be watchful to help members make informed choices about how much they disclose about what. The examples given do not exhaust the kinds of ethical problems faced by leaders of personal growth groups, yet they highlight the complexities of ethical decision making in psychoeducational, counseling, and psychotherapy groups.

The distinction between task/work groups and personal change groups was drawn because the two types of groups have some important differences. The focus of task groups on product-oriented goals is often mandated or sanctioned by an authority external to the group, while the focus of personal change groups on the personal needs of its members typically is not externally mandated or sanctioned (except for the obvious case of court-remanded clients). But despite some clear differences, many of the ethical dilemmas found in either type of group are found in both. For example, task group leaders who fail to realize that their members have individual needs and goals apart from the mandated or sanctioned group goals risk task failure or task success through the use of unsanctioned or unlawful means. Work groups frequently encounter the "code of silence" problem related to protecting members from external scrutiny. In the obverse, personal change group leaders can become so focused on here-and-now goals that they lose track (and fail to notice that one or more of their members have lost track) of life outside the group—that the members are making changes in their personal orientation that may ill fit them to move back into the world from which they came.

Strategy: Become an ethical practitioner. Professional associations have developed ethical standards to assist their members in professional conduct, the discharge of duties, and the resolution of moral challenges. Recognizing the particular sensitivities involved in group work, ASGW established a set of ethical guidelines specific to group counseling (revised in 1989). These guidelines are being modified to reflect best practices in group work, and they are subsumed under the revised American Counseling Association (ACA) Code of Ethics and Standards of Practice (1995). The revised ACA document is intended to comprehensively address ethical issues relevant to the broad scope of professional counseling practice. Under the advice of ASGW, all former references in an earlier version of the ACA document to "group counseling" are replaced by references to "group work," a change consistent with the broad preparation and practice of counselors who work with groups (and with the ASGW Professional Training Standards). The exception is in the section of the ethical standards dealing with the screening of group members, which will be stated specifically with regard to counseling/therapy group work.

As was indicated in the preamble to the 1989 ASGW ethical standards, the processes of ethical responsibility are of vital importance to group workers, to the profession, and to group members. ASGW considers "ethical process" as central to group work and group workers are perceived as "ethical agents." This understanding is also central to the 1994 revised CACREP Accreditation Standards associated with group work preparation, where ethical considerations are accorded prominence. It is imperative that group workers be cognizant of the context, intent, and effects of their group work leadership because the attempts of group workers to influence member behavior and to produce change always have ethical implications.

Ethical standards provide one essential source for group workers to consult as they continuously seek to practice ethically. Because they set forth conduct judged to be appropriate for ethical behavior, ethical standards can be used to stimulate reflection, self-examination, and discussion of issues and practices (ASGW, 1989) with colleagues. Collegial support and consultation provide other critically important sources for helping group workers to clarify ethical dilemmas. It is often through discussing issues with wise and supportive others that meaning and desirable courses of appropriate action can best be achieved.

SUMMING UP THE BAKER'S DOZEN

To practice group work is to confront ambiguity and complexity. The group worker is continually confronted with challenges about which decisions need to be made and actions taken. Frequently, as Kottler (1995) pointed out, there may be no apparent explanations. Why a leader did this or did that remains a mystery, as the following honest description suggests:

> I sit alone for a few minutes, trying to make sense of what just took place. If I had to, I could offer several theories to explain what happened and why, what I did, what impact these interventions had, and what participants gained as a result of these efforts. Push me a little further, though, and I will admit to you the extent of my confusion. Do I ever really know what

I did that made a difference to any client? Do I ever really understand what it is that I am experiencing at any moment in time. . . . (p. 38)

The baker's dozen is no antidote to the human condition, of course. Nor would we want that, for access to our humanity is at the core of effective group work. However, we hope that the challenges and strategies identified will be useful for those preparing to lead groups and will help to prevent some misfortunes and to generally improve practice.

Exemplary Curricular Approaches in Comprehensive Group Work

INTRODUCTION

We now turn our attention to examining the implementation of the ASGW Training Standards within specific counseling programs (Conyne, Wilson, Kline, Morran, & Ward, 1993). Our goal is to identify exemplary curricular approaches that are being used to teach the standards. From this material, we hope readers will identify leads they can follow for improving group work preparation in their own programs.

To organize this work, we collapsed the 54 knowledge competencies and 59 skills competencies contained in the core and specializations into five broad, representative clusters:

- defining group work
- pregroup preparation
- therapeutic dynamics and leader skills
- research and evaluation
- ethics

We use these five standards clusters as organizational aids as we present exemplary methods collected from programs across the country. We believe this parsimony will aid readers in drawing from this material for their local application.

GROUP WORK SURVEY

Where did we discover these exemplary materials? During 1993, we conducted a survey to identify stellar group work preparation in group work across the United States. The specific objectives for this survey were threefold: (a) to describe group work preparation nationally and by region, (b) to identify exemplary programs for core and/or specialist level preparation in group work, and (c) to assemble a reference material library of core and specialist level preparation in group work. The survey materials are presented in Appendix C.

Survey Design

The population sampled in this study included the 86 programs across the United States which were at that time accredited by CACREP. This group was chosen as the population of interest because, as accredited programs, all could be expected to provide preparation in core competencies, which included "studies that provide an understanding of group development, dynamics, counseling theories, group counseling methods and skills, and other group work approaches" (CACREP, 1993, p. 50). A letter explaining the study and a copy of the research instrument was sent to either the individual most directly associated with group work or to the CACREP liaison at each of the 86 CACREP-accredited institutions. Follow-up telephone calls were placed to institutions not responding to the written request.

The questionnaire listed the knowledge and competency standards within each of the areas and, for each standard, provided space for the respondent to indicate whether the standard was met or not met. In addition, each responding institution was asked to indicate for which of the specialization areas they intended to provide training, regardless of whether they met specific standards within a specialization area. Finally, each institution was asked to provide examplary materials for lessons, courses, extracourse activities, or whole programs of study which illustrated how the institution was attempting to comply with the ASGW Training Standards.

Basic Survey Results

The response rate for our survey was most gratifying. Of the 86 CACREP-accredited institutions contacted, 68 institutions (79%) returned usable responses. The sample was clearly representative of CACREP-accredited counseling programs. Of the 40 states in which accredited programs are found (including Washington, DC), responses were obtained from all but one state. From 38 of the states, at least half of the accredited institutions responded to the survey, and a 100% return rate was secured from 25 of the states.

Responses to our questionnaire allowed us to profile compliance with standards within CACREP-accredited institutions. The results of this profiling were reported in Wilson, Conyne, and Ward (1994) and are outlined throughout this book. The survey data (as noted in Chapter One) revealed the following for these CACREP-accredited counseling programs:

- *Core group work preparation*: All provide core group work preparation and, though not required under CACREP Accreditation Standards, most comply with nearly all the ASGW Standards for core knowledge and skill competencies.

- *Counseling groups*: Virtually every CACREP-accredited counselor preparation program offers a group work specialization in group counseling; across the programs offering this specialization, there was generally high compliance with ASGW Training Standards.

- *Psychoeducational groups*: Eight out of 10 CACREP-accredited programs offer a specialization in psychoeducational group work; however, a small number of specific standards were consistently problematic.

- *Task groups*: Nearly two thirds of the CACREP-accredited programs offer a specialization in working with task and work groups, but, again, specific standards were difficult for many of the institutions offering this specialization.

- *Psychotherapy groups*: Four out of 10 CACREP-accredited programs offer a specialization in group psychotherapy; at this point, compliance with the full set of ASGW Training Standards, of course, is more difficult.

EXEMPLARY GROUP WORK CURRICULA

Standards can be developed for two purposes: (a) to validate what presently exists as indicative of acceptable practice and (b) to lead present practice to emergent or higher levels of excellence. Our survey research project suggests that the ASGW Professional Training Standards satisfy both of these purposes.

Part A: Validating Present Practice in Group Worker Preparation

Exemplary materials submitted clearly document that sufficient numbers of excellent curricula exist in two central areas of group work preparation within counselor education programs: (a) core competency and (b) group counseling. Therefore, these are the two areas of group worker preparation that can be described and illustrated most comprehensively in this book. On the basis of these results, we suggest that the training standards in these areas are validating existing approaches. Part A of this Section will present the exemplary curricula for preparation in core group work skills (Chapter Three) and in the group counseling specialization (Chapter Four).

Part B: The Emerging Specializations of Task, Psychoeducation, and Group Psychotherapy

By contrast, relatively few nominations for exemplary curricular elements were submitted to us in the specialty areas of task groups, psychoeducational groups, and psychotherapy groups. This outcome seems consistent with the 1994 CACREP Accreditation Standards for the core area of group work. In this accreditation section, group work standards emphasize basic core competencies, as well as those related to group counseling. A CACREP group work standard is included to accommodate what is called "other group work approaches." We have adapted this nomenclature to represent what we view as emergent group work specializations in counselor education: task, psychoeducation, and psychotherapy groups. Because of the receipt of limited descriptions of curricular materials in these emerging group work specialties, we suggest that the training standards in these areas are presently ahead of practice and thus represent targeted areas for future growth.

Accordingly, we will adopt a different approach in Part B of this Section. We will cite illustrative methods in these emergent group work approaches that were submitted for our consideration by counselor education programs. However, because few descriptions were provided in these areas, we will supplement these instructional materials from published approaches which have appeared in related literature. Published methods and curriculum elements for task and psychoeducation groups were more scarce than those available for preparation for work in psychotherapy groups. Recognizing this difference, we have organized the discussion of emergent group specializations into one chapter on "Task Groups and Psycho-education Groups" (Chapter Five) and a second chapter on "Group Psychotherapy" (Chapter Six).

We recognize that presenting this ordering of the group work core and specializations is inconsistent with the sequence contained in the Training Standards, where the core competencies are followed by the task, psychoeducation, counseling, and psychotherapy specializations in turn. In this book, the ordering was rearranged to highlight where training models presently exist (i.e., core training, group counseling specialization) and where they are emerging (i.e., task group speciali-zation, psychoeducation group specialization, and group psychotherapy specialization).

We hope that this next section of the book can serve to stimulate and guide the preparation of group workers to become increasingly comprehensive and responsive to future needs. We turn now to Chapter Three on core group work competencies.

3 CHAPTER

Core Group Work Competencies

Whatever their individual career goal might be, counselors work in groups. As was amply demonstrated in the preceding chapters, even if a counselor intends to limit his or her practice to career counseling with individuals in a private practice setting, some aspects of the counselor's professional life will involve working with groups, and skillfulness on the counselor's part will be expected. Thus, the core in group work has been defined to encompass that knowledge and those skills judged necessary for all counselors to possess.

The ASGW Training Standards for core preparation include 15 knowledge and 16 skill standards. As was mentioned in earlier chapters, these standards have been organized into five clusters: (a) defining group work, (b) pregroup preparation, (c) therapeutic dynamics and leader skills, (d) research and evaluation, and (e) ethics. Each of these subtopics will be discussed in turn, and examples of methods will be given.

STANDARDS CLUSTER 1

Teaching the Definition of Group Work

In any profession, it is critical that its members be able to identify and describe their scope of practice. A set of five core knowledge standards requires that the student be able to list and define the areas of group work practice recognized by the Association for Specialists in Group Work. These standards are as follows:

- K-13: Deliver a clear, concise, and complete definition of group work.

- K-14: Deliver a clear, concise, and complete definition of each of the four group work specialties.

- K-9: State the advantages and disadvantages of group work and the circumstances for which it is indicated or contraindicated.

- K-1: State the four major group work specializations identified in this document (task/work groups, psychoeducational groups, counseling groups, psychotherapy groups) distinguishing characteristics of each, the commonalities shared by all, and the appropriate instances in which each is to be used.

- K-15: Explain and clarify the purpose of a particular form of group work.

It is important to notice that the standards require learning different from that which is gained from study of the traditional group counseling theories (e.g., psychoanalytic theory, humanistic/person-centered approaches, Gestalt methods, and psychodrama). Though introductory courses in group work have traditionally dwelled on the study of how these classical, individual counseling theories can be utilized in a group format, the ASGW Standards encourage a shift toward the differential application of competencies.

Instructional Methods

The most common method for imparting knowledge is the assignment of readings (e.g., The ASGW Training Standards) and within-class discussion of the Training Standards for core and group work specializations. At times guest speakers may be brought in to augment the instructor's lecture. Written assignments and student presentations also are employed. The categories are

- readings and class discussion
- guest speakers

- student presentations
- letters to the instructor
- focal topic papers
- term papers
- annotated bibliographies

Readings and class discussion. Assigned readings (including the ASGW Training Standards) and in-class discussion of the four group work specializations are part of the curriculum at Rollins College, the University of Cincinnati, Indiana University–Purdue University at Fort Wayne, and other counseling programs. At the University of Maine, the four ASGW-defined specializations have become the basic organizing principle for their introductory course, Preparing Group Work Specialists. The course is divided into four modules or units so that each module focuses on one of the four group work specializations. As stated in the course syllabus, students will "comprehensively examine the four specialty areas through a variety of cognitive and experiential learning activities designed to answer such questions as: (a) What are the unique characteristics of each specialty area, (b) How is leadership viewed in each specialty area, and (c) Are there commonalities in what group leaders do across the four specialty areas?" A helpful group work reference list, developed by Diana Hulse-Killacky, to accompany this course is presented in Appendix D.

Guest speakers. Guest speakers representing each of the four group work specializations might be invited to provide a "career fair" presentation. Components of the presentation might include (a) the nature of work within the specialization area, (b) how the speaker experiences his or her work life, (c) necessary knowledge and skills for a successful professional career, and (d) excitements and difficulties encountered within that specialization. Time for questions and discussion might be planned either in a spontaneous or structured manner.

Student presentation. Student presentations also may be utilized to highlight the characteristics of each of the group work specializations. At the University of Maine, student work groups are formed and charged with the responsibility of selecting one of the four specialization areas and presenting a team report on some aspect of work within the chosen specialization area. Students are encouraged not only to include a presentation of information about the specialization area but also to involve the class in an experiential activity or demonstration which will highlight critical issues, problems, or techniques.

Letters to the instructor. Rather than having the students write journal entries each week, the students may be asked to write letters to the instructor. At the University of Maine, students write the instructor five letters, spaced 2 weeks apart. Each letter is to be used to report the student's impressions of the class, the nature of student's learning experiences, and the process by which the student is linking readings to a personal understanding of the four specialty areas.

Focal papers. Some universities may use brief focal, or focused topic, papers as a vehicle for further exploration. At the University of Maine, three short papers (four pages in length) are assigned, each focusing on a special dilemma faced by leaders in one of the specialization areas. Students are expected to utilize class readings, input from guest speakers, and other resources in preparing their paper.

Term papers. Of course, term papers also may be used either to encourage broad familiarity with the four group work specializations or to focus more intensive investigation of a particular group work specialization. At the University of Maine, students are required to focus their term paper on a single group work specialization. Students may (a) research a particular issue related to their selected area of specialty, (b) design a group proposal, or (c) develop a new idea for their chosen specialty area by incorporating current literature. In addition to submitting the term paper for grading, students are expected to make a short presentation to the class on the content of their term papers.

Annotated bibliography. Students might choose one of the four group work specializations and prepare an annotated bibliography of leadership resources focused on the uses of that group work specialization, common methods used within that specialization's groups, and leader skills necessary for successful work within that group work specialization.

STANDARDS CLUSTER 2

Teaching Pregroup Preparation

A successful group rests on solid, pregroup preparation. Accordingly, ASGW Training Standards require that core group work preparation teach the student to

- K-11: Identify principles and strategies for recruiting and screening prospective group members.

Pregroup preparation includes, but is not limited to, topics such as choosing a population of interest, developing a plan for a group, conducting recruitment, screening, and pregroup orientation for members.

Instructional Methods

In most group work programs examined, this standard is met through straightforward, didactic instruction. At some programs, students are required to demonstrate their acquired knowledge by describing an effective plan for recruiting and screening in a written proposal for conducting a group. The categories are

- class discussion
- written group plan

Readings, lecture, and class discussion. In the Group Theory and Process course, required of all University of Cincinnati counseling students, pregroup preparation is taught by lecture and discussion. Particular attention is paid to (a) needs assessment (matching the kind and structure of the group to the needs of the population being served), (b) task assessment (estimating the personal and interpersonal difficulty level of the objectives and methods to be used in the group), and (c) member screening (determining whether the proposed group will meet the needs of the individual potential member and whether the potential member has the necessary personal characteristics to have a successful experience in the group as designed). Montana State provides similar content in their Group Counseling Theory course, although students focus more on classical theories of counseling as applied in a group setting (e.g., Gestalt, Encounter, Rational Emotive Therapy).

Written group plan. Written group plans form the basis for much of the practical instruction in several beginning group work courses. The typical group application paper includes topics such as (a) background and rationale for the group, (b) relevant literature on the target population and on methods and techniques, (c) objectives for the group, (d) composition of the group, (e) procedures for running the group (including, in some cases, detailed session-by-session activity plans), (f) leadership role and functions, and (g) methods for evaluation of the effectiveness of the group. Because this activity encompasses the spectrum of learnings necessary for successful applied group work, it is noted in this section and will reappear in later sections of this chapter.

Students in the introductory group course at Rollins College and at Montana State are required to prepare a group application paper in which they develop a plan for a group they may lead in the future (see Appendix D for the Montana State example). In the Rollins College curriculum, specific attention is paid to developing a rationale for the group (why a group for this population?), literature review (what's been written about this kind of group or this particular clientele?), objectives (what I hope to accomplish, criteria to be used in evaluating the group's effectiveness), and group composition (how the group will be advertised, selected, interviewed, etc. Deselection factors. How many? Personal characteristics, etc.). In the structured group design project required of students at Southern Illinois University at Carbondale, students are expected to conduct a literature review of group research on a selected population and then use the products of the literature review in preparing their group plan. With respect to pregroup planning, the students are expected to discuss at length "all pregroup considerations on creation of [their] group." Other universities (e.g., Indiana University–Purdue University at Fort Wayne, Indiana University, University of Maine) report that they use the group plan assignment as part of their basic instruction in group work. At the University of Maine, students may choose from among three foci for their term project, one of which is to develop a group proposal. Students present their term projects orally to the class.

STANDARDS CLUSTER 3

Teaching Therapeutic Dynamics and Leader Skills

Over the course of a group's life, opportunities arise for a skilled counselor to intervene in constructive ways. For a counselor to recognize the critical incidents in task or work groups, psychoeducational groups, counseling groups, or psychotherapy groups, the counselor must possess basic knowledge about the therapeutic factors which can operate in groups and the principles of group dynamics. In addition, to separate the contribution of individual characteristics from group phenomena, skilled group leaders must understand the contribution to group dynamics made by the individual characteristics of both the group members and its leader(s). Under the ASGW Training Standards, all counselors are expected to be able to do the following:

- K-10: Detail therapeutic factors of group work.

- K-3: Discuss the basic therapeutic ingredients of groups.

- K-2: Identify the basic principles of group dynamics.

- K-7: Define the process components involved in typical stages of a group's development (i.e., characteristics of group interaction and counselor roles).

- K-8: Describe the major facilitative and debilitative roles that group members may take.

- K-4: Identify the personal characteristics of group workers that have an impact on members; knowledge of personal strengths, weaknesses, biases, values, and their effect on others.

In addition, ASGW Training Standards detail a set of skills deemed critical as core group work skills for all counselors in all counseling settings. These skills include the following:

- S-1: Encourage participation of group members.

- S-2: Observe and identify group process events.

- S-3: Attend to and acknowledge group members' behavior.

- S-4: Clarify and summarize group members' statements.

- S-5: Open and close sessions.

- S-6: Impart information in the group when necessary.

- S-7: Model effective group leader behavior.

- S-8: Engage in appropriate self-disclosure in the group.

- S-9: Give and receive feedback in the group.

- S-10: Ask open-ended questions in the group.

- S-11: Empathize with group members.

- S-12: Confront group members' behavior.

- S-13: Help group members attribute meaning to their experience.

- S-14: Help group members to integrate and apply learnings.

- S-15: Demonstrate ASGW ethical and professional standards in group practice.

- S-16: Keep the group on task in accomplishing its goals.

Instructional Methods

Of the materials submitted for review, the most common course components relevant to teaching therapeutic dynamics and leader skills include

- didactic presentation of theory and concepts
- experiential membership in a small group
- observation of group process and leadership
- writing group plans
- critiquing the literature

The counseling programs selected for illustration of Standard Cluster 3 provided the most complete descriptive materials. These Programs are from Rollins College, Montana State University, Southern Illinois University—Carbondale, and the University of Cincinnati. Other Counseling Programs we were able to review also appear to provide similar opportunities, including Indiana University—Bloomington, Indiana University–Purdue University Fort Wayne, and Wright State University.

Didactic presentation of theory and concepts. Most of the group work programs reviewed for their core offerings provide didactic presentation of theories and concepts related to therapeutic dynamics and group leader skills. Typical topics for discussion include theories of group development, leader characteristics and skills, member characteristics, group dynamics, critical incidents, and leader interventions.

At Rollins College, students enroll in the core group work course, Group Dynamics and Process, during their first semester. The course addresses knowledge, self-awareness, and competency objectives that are appropriate for various forms of group practice in mental health counseling. Topics and issues addressed include the types of group methods, techniques, leader functions and behaviors, ethical issues and professional standards, and applications of group formats to achieve specific mental health objectives. Instructional methods are varied, including lecture and discussion, demonstration, reading, and independent study. A major component is participation in a small group (to be discussed in more detail in a following section). The weekly class session format contains a lecture, discussion, and demonstration taking about 1 hour.

In similar fashion, the Group Theory and Practice course at Southern Illinois University at Carbondale features an overview of the basic theoretical components of group work and differentiation of small group formats for meeting various client needs. The course includes lecture, discussion, and laboratory experience. Content material readings, lecture, library resources (e.g., videos of group work), peer resources, and handouts are intermixed to thoroughly address core knowledge. In addition to a number of other important objectives, specifically in terms of Standards Cluster 3, this course seeks to advance student competencies in (a) demonstrating an understanding of group dynamics and theory through the analysis of a laboratory group and (b) differentiating personal leadership skills which enhance development of the group, one's personal growth, and the growth of others.

At Montana State, students enroll in a group dynamics laboratory course which focuses on the nature and effects of group dynamics by covering theory and skills related to productive group interaction, including nonverbal communication, self-disclosure, empathic listening, dialogue, feedback, confrontation, values clarification, and conflict resolution. Two major components of this laboratory course are small group participation and group observation (discussed in a following section).

Finally, in the University of Cincinnati introductory course, Group Theory and Process, students are exposed to content and processes that emerge from the core competency section of the ASGW Training

Standards, as well as from the "Group Work" core section of the 1994 CACREP Accreditation Standards. Pertaining to ASGW Core Standards Cluster 3, course objectives indicate that, after completing this course, students will be able to

- discuss principles of group dynamics, including group process components, developmental stage theories, and group member roles and functions;
- describe group leadership styles and approaches, including characteristics of various types of group leaders and leadership styles;
- display core group work competencies.

The University of Cincinnati program approaches the teaching of group dynamics and leadership by employing a course within a course. Within the overarching Group Theory and Process course, which provides the broader instructional effort relating to core knowledge and skills, students are also trained in the management of personal-learning groups in which they have the opportunity to experience both membership in and leadership of content-relevant task/work groups (to be described in detail in a following section).

Observation of group process and leadership. A second modality employed by several programs is learning through critical observation. Typically, students are provided with instruction on how to observe a group in action and are assigned a specific group to observe and critique.

As mentioned earlier, the Montana State method requires students to participate in the systematic observation of a group in action. Students conduct and turn in two specific group observations of a group that is of interest to them and that can be observed without interfering with its process. Instructions for confidentiality are stressed. The students are asked to select and use an appropriate group observational assessment method (e.g., Hill Interaction Matrix) and then to apply it while making 5-minute-interval assessments related to group members and leader(s), along with jotting down comments about the group process. An analysis is conducted from the ratings and observations, to describe group purpose, content issues addressed, concerns of members, the leader's versus the group's interaction, developmental state, and changes in interaction during and between meetings. Finally a group observation summary paper is produced, organized by the elements of communication, roles, stages, process, and the interrelationship of these four elements.

Once students at Southern Illinois University at Carbondale have completed the Group Theory and Practice course (described briefly above), they may enroll in the Career Group Practicum course. In this course, students complete 30 hours of live observation. Then they participate in a career decision-making group that is facilitated by advanced group work students. Immediately after the live observation, students process the observed group and build their conceptual base beyond that obtained in the initial course. In addition to modeling by the observation group facilitators, each core skill competency is addressed and modeled in the classroom. Objectives relevant to Standards Cluster 3 include (a) identifying group process events and developmental themes of the observation group and (b) demonstrating all core, entry-level skill competencies in group work. After observing for 10 hours, students modify the group design that was implemented to prepare for their own facilitation. Supervision is provided to overview pregroup considerations, review session plans, and to conduct any needed role-playing. This step is followed by direct group facilitation for 16 two-hour sessions, accompanied by ongoing formative evaluation and supervision. Each student in this course completes a portfolio. Its contents include (a) notes from the observation group, (b) notes from class sessions and book chapter summaries, (c) session outlines for each of the student's group sessions, (d) critiques or conceptualizations for each group session conducted, (e) personal profile of each group member, (f) supervision notes and individual session summaries, (g) personal log or journal, and (h) appendix (see Appendix D for examples of this material).

Experiential membership in a small group. A third modality used in several group work programs is providing students with involvement in an experiential group activity. In the final section of this chapter, *The Educator's Dilemma*, we discuss the ethical difficulties faced by counselor educators who specialize in group work as they attempt to provide experiential activities for their students. CACREP Accreditation Standards and ASGW Training Standards both require counseling students to participate in experiential group activities as part of their core preparation. Nowhere in the whole of counselor education has there been such extended discourse about how to satisfy professional ethics for teaching and for evaluating student performance, on the one hand, and at the same time satisfy professional ethics regarding the avoidance of dual relationships. Several of the institutions submitting materials for inclusion in this chapter have developed novel methodologies to solve the educator's dilemma.

A major component (75 minutes per class) of the introductory group work course at Rollins College is participation in a small group (to be discussed in more detail in a following section), each session being coled by recent graduates of the Rollins program. This provision seems to adequately address competency issues while at the same time reducing any problems that might be associated with dual relationships. A unique feature of this approach is that the coleaders receive supervision and practice credit toward their licensure requirements. Exemplary features of this program include a laboratory experience handout, a purpose and agreement handout, and the use of weekly journaling (see Appendix D for examples).

(a) "The Laboratory Experience in a Small Group" handout. The small group sessions are introduced in this handout. Its contents generally emphasize the role of confidentiality in relation to important aspects of the small group experience, such as interactions, observations, and the weekly journal; also, the supervisory process used is discussed.

(b) "Group Dynamics and Process Purpose and Agreement" handout. In addition to the description of the small group laboratory experience, an informed consent form is read and signed by each participating student. This form includes a brief description of the small group meetings, their rationale, who leads them, and their potential benefits and risks. A tear-off signature form is provided for students to indicate their understanding of the experience, as well as conditions surrounding their participation.

(c) Weekly journal. This independent activity is intended to provide a thoughtful, carefully written summary of the following topics: (a) what happened in the small group this week, thoughts about it, plans to participate differently, self-learnings or those about others, etc.; (b) reactions, observations, questions about what I've read or heard this week regarding group methods or applications, my future performance as a group practitioner, etc.; and (c) submission of a "Self-Evaluation of Group Behaviors and Skills" form that is provided. The journal length is between two and three double-spaced pages, with a journal summary of between three and five pages due near the end of the semester.

The Montana State "Group Dynamics Lab" focuses on the nature and effects of group dynamics by covering theory and skills related to productive group interaction, including nonverbal communication, self-disclosure, empathic listening, dialogue, feedback, confrontation, values clarification, and conflict resolution. Two major components of this laboratory course are small group participation and group observation (discussed above). Participation in a small group discussion lab offers the opportunity for practicing interaction skills and for experiencing group dynamics. The description of the lab makes it clear that the opportunity for personal growth is not intended to serve as a therapy experience and that participation in the group is ungraded.

At Southern Illinois University at Carbondale, their laboratory group experience is a training group, or T group. Its purpose is to help students experience participation in a small group while studying communication and process. The skill of using feedback and immediacy in the here and now of the group describes much of the T group's focus. Student members also have the opportunity to learn about themselves within the small group process. Explicit attention is given to strategies to reduce dual relationship ethical issues, including the provisions that participation in the training group is not evaluated and that self-disclosure is not required. The training group experience provides 24 hours of member participation. Students prepare a written analysis of their group as part of their experience in the laboratory groups.

Analysis of the training group. The integration and application of knowledge about group dynamics and leader skills is the focus of this requirement. This written analysis of the T group requests that student participants maintain objectivity about their group, just as the group leader must. Midsemester and final analyses are produced, each one centered on mass group processes and their illustration through specific group incidents. Students are asked to avoid personalization and to consider issues such as changes in relationships, conduct of sessions, interaction of members with the facilitator, and the general flow of the group across sessions.

Finally, the University of Cincinnati program approaches the teaching of group dynamics and leadership by employing a course within a course. Within the overarching Group Theory and Process course, which provides the broader instructional effort relating to core knowledge and skills, students are also trained in the management of personal-learning groups in which they have the opportunity to experience both membership in and leadership of content-relevant task/work groups.

One of the key course components in the Group Theory and Process course at the University of Cincinnati is participation in a structured, small group, member-leader experience called the "Personal-Learning [P-L] Group." Total or partial portions of eight class sessions are devoted to building skill in and implementing the P-L group design. The overall goals for the P-L are to provide an educational method for core group work skills that can

- fit within the introductory group work course in counselor education programs,
- develop group work leadership skills and provide group member experience,
- increase group work competencies *and* learning of assigned academic content, and
- accomplish the above goals and conform to ethical guidelines related to dual relationship issues.

Personal learning groups. The first four class sessions are devoted exclusively to learning the P-L method. The P-L method is adapted from the learning-through-discussion (LTD) method of William Fawcett Hill (1969). His time-tested group discussion method has recently been published in its third edition (Rabow, Charness, Kipperman, & Radcliffe-Vasile, 1994). This method trains group members in a "group cognitive map" that designated facilitators use to guide the group discussion of selected material which has been previously experienced (e.g., read or viewed). In addition to addressing content, the method explicitly incorporates group dynamics, group participation, and group leadership considerations. The P-L adaptation retains much of the original, yet heightens attention to group process issues and slightly truncates steps included in the group cognitive map.

- The first session occurs during the course orientation itself through a 60-minute microlab. Students become acquainted, and small groups are formed through a series of meetings beginning with dyads, through quartets, and ending with octets. Guided discussion occurs at each successive step.

- In the second session, 60 minutes are devoted to core skill discussion, and a demonstration group is led by the instructor. The "ASGW Core Group Work Skills List" is distributed and emphasized. After completing the demonstration group, for 30 minutes the instructor discusses group development and distributes a handout, the "Group Development Graph" (from Jones, 1973), which suggests a relationship occurring over time between task and personal relations functions.

- During the third session, the entire class period is devoted to group observation and feedback. Hanson's (1969) "What to Look for in Groups" material is discussed at length and is used by assigned student observers in a fishbowl design to provide feedback to the inner group of students who are charged with completing a structured task. The intent is to identify important group processes (e.g., participation, norms) that characterize group functioning and to sharpen the skills of the students so that the observation–feedback function may effectively occur during the P-L groups to follow.

- The fourth and final session preparatory to conducting the P-L groups is dedicated to learning the P-L method. The entire class period is devoted to this task (140 minutes). Students are taught the steps of the P-L group discussion method, and the instructor facilitates a demonstration group in a fishbowl design, with an outer ring composed of students in the role of observer–feedback giver. Students are reconvened into their small groups to discuss the P-L method, to select cofacilitators, and to establish a schedule for cofacilitation for the next four sessions; as a team building exercise, they also have been asked to choose a tentative group name by which their P-L group will be known during the next four weeks. If there are more than two P-L groups in the course, the instructor prepares a rotational discussion–observation schedule to assure that the groups will mix and match over the weeks and thus promote diversity.

The P-L groups are assigned to read each week one journal article drawn from the *Journal for Specialists in Group Work (JSGW)*. A particularly useful source has been DeLucia, Coleman, and Jensen-Scott's (1992) edited special issue on "Group Counseling with Multicultural Populations," as it addresses an important topic through articles that are both informative and stimulating for group discussion. A fishbowl design is continued for the P-L groups. During the next four classes, a P-L group functions for 35 minutes to discuss the assigned article by using the P-L method; that is followed by 10 minutes of feedback from the group members who have been observing group process from the outer ring. The instructor observes, occasionally coaches, and in general facilitates this process. Thus, over the course of four class sessions each P-L group will both discuss and observe in every class, and all students will have at least one opportunity for cofacilitation.

Activity with "Group Skills Workshop: Developing Core and Task Group Work Skills." A creative approach to teaching selected core group work skills (e.g., encouraging participation of members, clarifying and summarizing members' statements, observing and identifying group process events) in a workshop format was developed by Conyne and Rapin (1994, in press). The method involves teaching the core skills within the context of a task or work group. The goals for the group, therefore, are

- to illustrate selected core group work skill competencies, as identified in the ASGW Training Standards (encourage participation of group members, clarify and summarize group members' statements, observe and identify group process events); and
- to illustrate selected task group work skill competencies, as identified in the ASGW Training Standards (obtain goal clarity, implement group decision-making methods, manage conflict in task/work groups).

After introducing the purpose of the workshop and a summary of core and task group skills needed for successful leadership of a school-based committee, the workshop leader forms a double-ring fishbowl with a work group of six members in the center. The work group is given instructions on the purpose, context, and role of the committee, and individual members of the six-person work group are assigned specific roles (e.g., teacher, assistant principal, counselor, parent, community representative). After group members have had opportunity to familiarize themselves with the group instructions and individual roles, they are given a specific topic (e.g., improving the interracial and intercultural understanding at the school) and a charge to discuss the topic and identify major events and tasks to achieve success. Members of the outer ring are given a "Group Observer Feedback Sheet" and asked to provide feedback at the conclusion of the work group's discussion. During its discussion, the work group is interrupted to receive feedback from the observers. The workshop leader leads discussion of the feedback and acts as an external consultant, making suggestions based on the feedback to improve the work group's task accomplishment and group maintenance. When time is called to end the work group's deliberations, feedback is again solicited. Naturally, this exercise could be taken through multiple cycles to provide opportunities for all workshop participants to participate in an experiential work group. Further instruction and summarizing may also be provided by the workshop leader. Obviously, this exercise could also be used in preparing group workers involved with task/work groups; the core skill objectives would serve as a reminder to the participants that generic group maintenance skills are necessary to the success of task/work groups.

Personal counseling. While many counseling programs may suggest to their students that enrolling for their own personal counseling could be both personally and professionally useful, of the institutions submitting materials for our review, only one institution reported requiring personal counseling. Rollins College requires each student to pay for and complete at least 10 hours of personal counseling at an off-campus facility selected by the student. Students acquire an understanding of the client experience and a deeper understanding of self, both of which are highly valuable in becoming a competent practitioner of group counseling.

Writing group plans. As noted earlier, several of the programs reviewed require students to develop a plan for a group experience, presumably to be led by the student at some future time. To facilitate understanding of therapeutic dynamics and leader skills, some programs require students to provide detailed, session-by-session planning guided by a theory of group development. For example, at Rollins College, in addition to addressing pregroup issues (discussed above), students are required to discuss leadership role and functions, the focus of which is upon their anticipated behavior as the leader of this group. Students at Southern Illinois University at Carbondale must include structured sessions with appropriate objectives and behavioral expectations, appropriate sequencing and pacing of activities, activity- and session-closing processing questions, and a rationale for decisions made for each session. In addition to citing and synthesizing information from relevant literature in preparation for their group, students at Indiana University–Purdue University at Fort Wayne are expected to specify the form and content of each group session, and to state session objectives.

STANDARDS CLUSTER 4

Teaching Research and Evaluation in Group Work

Though most students with an interest in group work seek training in the standard techniques of the field, the fully informed counselor is grounded in the research literature which undergirds the practice of group work. To insure that group workers have read and understand the research literature in their chosen area of group work interest, ASGW Training Standards require that the student

- K-6: Discuss the body of research on group work and how it relates to one's academic preparation in school counseling, student personnel education, community counseling, or mental health counseling.

Further, the Training Standards emphasize the necessity of conducting personal evaluation of the outcomes of group work activities in which the student engages by requiring the student to

- K-12: Detail the importance of group and member evaluation.

Instructional Methods

The most frequently cited method for teaching research and evaluation is within the context of preparing a group plan. Several contributing institutions require a group plan in their beginning course on group work. Within these group plans, students are required to ground their proposed group offering in relevant theoretical and research literature and to propose a method for evaluating the effectiveness of the group they have designed. At one institution, students do systematic reviews of outcome literature in group work. The methods used, therefore, are

- grounding a planned group in research literature
- evaluating the effectiveness of a group
- reviewing and evaluating outcome literature
- direct instruction in research methods

Grounding a planned group in research literature. Several institutions, including Rollins College, Montana State University, and Southern Illinois University at Carbondale, require students to devise a group plan in preparation for a future group leadership activity. As mentioned earlier, students are typically required to include sections on (a) the background and rationale for the proposed group, (b) grounding of the proposed group in relevant research literature, (c) goals and objectives for the proposed group, and (d) targeted membership for the proposed group. The intended instructional objective is to have students set goals and pick methods for their target clientele after attaining an understanding of documented best practice.

For example, at Rollins College, the required group application paper for students in the course Group Dynamics and Process includes sections on (a) background and rationale, (b) relevant literature, (c) objectives for the group, (d) composition of the group, (e) logistics for the group, (e) leadership role and functions, and (f) evaluation. Students are required to detail how the effectiveness of the proposed group will be measured and reported. Similar requirements are found in the group plan assignments at Montana State University and Southern Illinois University at Carbondale.

Evaluating the effectiveness of a group. The group plan is also used as a vehicle for teaching program evaluation skills. A required component in most group plans is an evaluation component in which the student is required to describe how the effectiveness of the proposed group may/will be evaluated.

For the evaluation section of the group plan required in the course Group Counseling Theory offered at Montana State, students are provided with detailed suggestions for the content of the evaluation effort:

• How will termination and follow-up appraisals be performed to evaluate the effectiveness of the group?
• What provisions will be made for persons who do not progress or who are harmed as a result of the group experience?
• What kinds of research questions might be asked about the process and outcome of the group? Describe potential research designs for answering questions about the group.
• How will members' involvement in research be managed?
• What measurement techniques will be used in evaluating and doing research on the group? Address the following characteristics of measures used to evaluate and/or do research on the group: relevance, appropriateness, unobtrusiveness, reliability, validity, and availability of norms.
• What statistical analysis will be used to process data? How does the analysis manage multiple independent and dependent variables and the interdependence among group members' scores?

Detailed instruction on evaluation is also provided for students in the Group Theory and Practice course at Southern Illinois University at Carbondale as part of their structured group-manual assignment. This manual is intended to be functional and appropriate for 12 two-hour sessions. Its contents include three sections—introduction, session outlines, and evaluation—in which all material is practical and explained in detail. The evaluation component of the group plan is described in the syllabus as follows:

> The purpose of evaluation is to determine group effectiveness. In order to determine effectiveness, pretests and posttests are necessary. . . . It is important that more than one instrument (preferably 2–3) be used so that assessment is not too narrow. For this task, at least one standardized instrument should be used to provide a base-line for comparison. Discussion should include rationale for instrument selection. Why is this instrument suitable for use with your population? How is it relevant to group goals? Consider the functioning level of group members. Samples of test items

should be used in the discussion to verify face/content validity or instrument appropriateness. Further, issues of validity and reliability should also be included. In addition, other non-standardized indices such as rating scales, check lists, etc. . . . should be used to provide a quantifiable measure of behavior.

Article critiques. A third method for acquainting beginning group workers with research literature involves reading and critiquing extant research. Two different approaches have been taken.

Members of the course Theory and Practice of Group Counseling at Southern Illinois University at Carbondale are required to prepare article critiques. Students select and critique articles which will help them to make decisions about the structured group they have selected to design. For critiques of research articles, students are asked to examine method, subjects, purpose, research questions, hypotheses, results, and the implications of the study's results for their group design. If the article to be critiqued is not research based, the author's key points are examined, accuracy of the message is assessed, and implications for the student's group design are sought. Each student submits 10 two-page critiques applying these criteria.

To familiarize students with the degree to which group treatment of personal and interpersonal problems is supported by outcome literature, students enrolled for the initial course in group work at the University of Cincinnati are required to select a mental health issue (e.g., anxiety, depression, substance dependence, recovery from emotional or physical abuse) and thoroughly review the research literature to determine the extent to which the use of group work is supported by outcome studies. Students are alerted to the difference between primary and secondary source articles and are given a brief review of research designs (e.g., controlled experimental studies, comparison studies, case studies, surveys). Students' papers are organized into four sections: (a) an introduction to the general problem area being researched; (b) a thoroughly annotated bibliography of outcome studies, comparison studies, and case studies; and (c) an integrative summary of the research reported in the annotated bibliography, ending with a conclusion about the degree to which group approaches to treatment were supported or not supported in the research literature.

Direct instruction in research. A final method for acquainting students with group work research methods is direct instruction. For example, the Group Counseling Theory course at Montana State includes obtaining research skills as one of the specific course objectives. Students in this beginning class are expected to learn about research on groups, process and outcome studies, and group-specific methods of research.

STANDARDS CLUSTER 5

Teaching the Ethical Practice of Group Work

Ethics are omnipresent in counseling programs. In various courses, students are taught the American Counseling Association *Code of Ethics and Standards of Practice* (1995), and ethical problems are often discussed in practica and internship supervision meetings. Because of special problems arising in the conduct of group work, ASGW has developed additional ethical standards for group workers; these are being revised to form a set of "best practices" in group work. To insure that all students understand the additional ethical considerations which accompany work with groups, the ASGW Training Standards require students to

- K-5: Describe the specific ethical issues that are peculiar to group work.

Instructional Methods

Again, the most typical method for teaching group work ethics is the lecture–discussion approach. *Ethical Guidelines for Group Counselors* (Association for Specialists in Group Work, 1991a) may be assigned as required reading. Gumaer and Scott (1985) presented an approach for preparing group leaders in ethical decision making organized around Carkhuff's goals for helping (e.g., facilitating student self-exploration and self-awareness, increasing student self-understanding, and initiating action). Case examples of ethical dilemmas in group work are presented in several sources including Gumaer (1982), 12; Gumaer and Scott (1985), 18 cases; Miller and Rubenstein (1992), 3 cases; Corey, Corey, and Callanan (1982), 8 discussion situations; and Kottler (1982), 9 examples. In addition, students may be introduced to Kitchener's (1984) moral principles which underpin ethical decision making and Miller and Rubenstein's (1992) seven-step plan for applying ethical decision making. Discussions of group worker values may be supported by referring to Corey, Corey, and Callanan's (1990) examples of ways in which group leaders may subtly impose personal values on group members. Forester-Miller and Davis (1996) have produced a helpful practitioner's guide to ethical decision making that is sensitive to the revised ACA code.

Though group worker ethics may be taught within a single class instructional unit, ethical learnings may be reinforced by infusing discussion of ethical issues into the discussion of all aspects of group work (e.g., pregroup preparation, recruitment and screening, conducting the group, dealing with difficult situations within the group, termination, evaluation, and follow-up). A common dilemma for group workers is the ethical application of structured group activities. Corey, Corey, Callanan, and Russell's (1982) work on ethical considerations in using group techniques may be a helpful adjunct to within-class technical discussions and skill practice.

THE CORE EXPERIENTIAL COMPONENT

Within the core preparation of group workers, student learnings gained from readings, lectures, and discussions are to be augmented through observation and participation in group experiences. Though the minimum amount of supervised practice is listed as 10 clock hours, 20 clock hours of supervised practice is recommended. This experiential work may occur in a classroom group or elsewhere.

A variety of methods have been discussed earlier in this chapter (see Instructional Methods for Teaching Therapeutic Dynamics and Leader Skills). In addition to these methods, arrangements could be made for students to observe a group in process (e.g., a committee meeting, a workshop on substance abuse prevention, or a counseling or psychotherapy group session), either live or by videotape.

THE EDUCATOR'S DILEMMA

Providing the Experiential Component without Violating Ethical Standards Regarding Dual Relationships

One of the most vexing problems faced by counselor educators teaching group work skills is the provision of a high-quality, experiential component without violating professional ethics regarding the avoidance of dual relationships. The ASGW Training Standards require 10 clock hours (and recommend 20 clock hours) of observation of and participation in a group experience. Though the Standards permit wide flexibility in just how this experiential requirement is to be satisfied, for many counselor educators it proves problematic.

As most texts in group work explain, counselor educators are to avoid requiring or allowing students to participate in group experiences led by a faculty member in their counseling program because of the potential conflicts of interest which may arise. Kitchener (1988) outlines the potential sources of difficulty as including (a) problems arising when the expectations of one's faculty role are in conflict with the expectations befitting the leader of an experiential group, (b) problems arising when the obligations of one's faculty role are in conflict with the obligations befalling the leader of an experiential group, and (c) problems arising because of the power and prestige which derive from the experiential group leader's faculty role.

Lloyd (1990) asked the following question and provided insight into ambiguities embedded in it: "Can we resolve the dilemma of requiring counselor educators to offer a group activity to promote self-understanding, self-analysis skills, and interpersonal skills but not in the same process providing their students with counseling, and thus creating a dual relationship?" As noted by Lloyd, the misuse of trust has always been held to be unethical; what is new in the ethical standards is the structure to avoid situations where increased opportunity for misuse of trust might exist. Lloyd argues that the term *group activity* is ambiguous in its operational definition and that resolution of the ambiguity rests with the profession, not the individual counselor educator. Lloyd also raises the possibility that the counseling profession could choose to accept as necessary the use of faculty in the provision of experiential group activities and thus eliminate the dilemma by decision.

Forester-Miller and Duncan's (1990) suggestions focus on providing for informed consent and avoiding the conflict-of-interest situation in which the group leader grades his or her group members on their group participation. To insure informed consent, Forester-Miller and Duncan suggest the following:

• Whenever possible, inform the students they have the right, without prejudice, to refuse to participate in the experiential activity;

- When an experience is required, as a condition for program completion, the student must be informed in writing before entering the program and again before the experience is offered;
- All evaluations must be restricted to the student's level of group-skill acquisition;
- No aspect of the student's personal life, value system, or personal group behavior may be considered in evaluating the student's academic performance in the group experience;
- The personal growth experience is not tied to entrance into or continuance in the academic program.

To implement these guidelines, Forester-Miller and Duncan suggest using post–master's degree students or nonfaculty group work professionals as group leaders and using a blind grading system in which students turn in work under coded numbers for grading.

Since the early 1980s, several approaches have been proposed for preparing prospective group workers in the requisite group work skills. The first three address the ethical dilemma of how faculty can remain involved in the process of preparing group workers yet protect the student from becoming overly disclosing in the presence of the faculty member; these approaches borrow microcounseling methods from Carkhuff (Carkhuff & Berenson, 1967) and from Ivey (see Ivey & Authier, 1978). The fourth method approaches the dilemma by strengthening the group participant's ability to make an informed choice about his or her level of disclosure.

Pearson's (1985) method utilizes a group-based format focused on basic small group leadership skills. This method features a four-step approach:

- Verbal presentation of the skill (e.g., definition of the skill, identification of the skill's function, description of typical situations in which the skill might be used, description of leader statements that represent the skill's implementation);
- Modeling the skill (e.g., visual presentation through role playing or videotaped examples);
- Structured practice (e.g., identifying group situations in which the skill under consideration could be used, developing a role-played scene within which to work, implementing the skill within the role-played scene, participating in group critique of the scene and the skill implementation);

• Unstructured practice (e.g., group members interact in an unstructured, shared leadership format; observers give periodic feedback on interventions made and gaps in leadership).

Clearly, the first three steps in the Pearson method circumvent many of the dual-relationship concerns by structuring the learning in a manner in which the depth of self-disclosure risked by a group member is minimal. Safety for participants in the unstructured practice can be protected by a pregroup briefing which emphasizes that the purpose of the group is to provide sufficient personal material that members may have the opportunity to practice their leadership skills and that the leadership of the group is to be considered a shared function— members are responsible for contributing to the group those resources they believe will increase the group's effectiveness. Group observations focus on leadership skill usage.

Smaby and Tamminen (1983) developed an approach based on Carkhuff and Berenson's (1967) philosophy of helper preparation which provides a systematic framework and corresponding skills that can be used to guide the group. In the first stage of the group, members explore their here-and-now world to develop general awareness. Associated modules include microcounseling (e.g., attending, questioning, paraphrasing, summarizing) and primary empathy (e.g., reflecting content, reflecting surface feelings). During the second stage of the group, awareness is expanded to consideration of one's here-and-now world in relationship to where one wants to be. Associated modules include additive empathy (e.g., reflecting deeper feelings, reflecting behavioral reactions, reflecting self-expectations and self-beliefs), personalizing (e.g., concreteness, specificity, immediacy), and confrontation (e.g., incongruities, ineffective behavior, negative consequences of behavior, getting commitment to change). The third and final phase of the group involves taking action to achieve one's behavior change goals. Associated modules include decision helping (e.g., decision processing, relating values to process, relating actions to beliefs) and contracting (e.g., establishing a working relationship, identifying change methods, concluding agreements, evaluating the process being followed). At the outset, the instructor makes it clear that participants will practice by helping to teach each other. Students are instructed to share relatively minor concerns (especially at first) because their helping skills are not well developed. As the level of skill increases, members, who are presumably now more competent to modulate their level of disclosure, may choose to share at deeper levels.

The Jacobs, Harvill, and Masson (1994) method, grounded in the Carkhuff tradition, relies heavily on the Cormier and Cormier (1991), and Ivey methods for preparing counselors in individual counseling skills. In addition to traditional basic relationship skills (e.g., clarifying, questioning, confronting, summarizing, restating), Jacobs, Harvill, and Masson (1994) identify six specific group skills to be taught. These skills, based on Ivey's microcounseling method, are cutting off, drawing out, holding the focus, shifting the focus, use of eyes, and tying things together. Students are engaged in reading about and discussing each skill to be learned, observing by live demonstrations or videotaped segments of group life, and practicing each skill in situations which successively approximate real group phenomena. Harvill, Masson, and Jacobs (1983) have outlined the process as follows:

- Each student is assigned a discussion topic (e.g., love relationships, religion, family of origin, dealing with anger).
- Each student leads his or her group in discussion of the target topic. The discussion is videotaped.
- Students are given written descriptions of the skill(s) to be learned.
- Each skill to be taught is demonstrated live or through videotaped example.
- Students review their videotaped discussion groups; students are encouraged to identify their own effective and ineffective behaviors; feedback is given by the course instructors.
- Each student leads his or her group in another discussion while attempting to implement the feedback received from review of the previous videotape.
- Students review their videotaped discussion groups; feedback is focused on the students' increased ability to utilize the targeted skill(s).

This cycle is repeated each time new skills are to be introduced to the students. A quasi-experimental study by Harvill, West, Jacobs, and Masson (1985) demonstrates that the systematic approach is an effective method for teaching behaviorally defined skills. Both between-group (trained leaders vs. untrained controls) and within-group analyses reveal that gains were made by those leaders who participated as learners. As with the previously cited methods, this method provides some degree of protection from overdisclosure by placing the emphasis on individual skill acquisition. Though topics used in the discussion groups have a personal quality, students can be instructed to control the level of disclosure in which they engage. Moreover, focusing instructor feedback on specific leadership skills provides boundaries for instructor interventions and instructor grading practices.

The three approaches presented above all attempt to solve the educator's dilemma by being grounded in microskills training. Although this affords some measure of safety, it may not be wholly satisfactory. As Pierce and Baldwin (1990) point out in their article "Participation versus Privacy in the Training of Group Counselors," several of the logical solutions to the educator's dilemma eliminate or cripple the group process and abdicate the institutional responsibility to evaluate the competence of the counseling student (e.g., eliminating the experiential requirement, arranging for the experiential component to be led by nonfaculty persons who do not submit evaluations of student performance, utilizing role-playing—as opposed to real self-presentation—within the group, limiting participation to only here-and-now interactions).

Pierce and Baldwin (1990) offer a nine-step plan for "responsible training" in group work. The authors focus on the risks which follow from self-disclosure and provide students with specific skill-building in risk assessment and appropriateness of self-disclosure. Further, they emphasize the necessity for congruity between leader expectations for self-disclosure and leader willingness to self-disclose. By emphasizing the value of personal choice in self-disclosure, this plan is thought to protect student privacy while allowing faculty to participate in and evaluate student performance in experiential groups.

SUMMING UP CORE COMPETENCY PREPARATION

Our survey results revealed that most responding CACREP-accredited programs comply with nearly all the ASGW Training Standards for teaching core knowledge and skills. From the submitted curricular materials, we were pleased to find multiple techniques and approaches for teaching the knowledge and practicing the skills required within each of the five group-work competency clusters.

Although this is wonderful news, we must also remember the expectation contained in the standards that every counseling graduate should be competent in all the group work core competencies and that every counseling training program should provide adequate core competency preparation. In addition, because we surveyed only CACREP-accredited programs, the data cannot be used to draw inferences applying to the wider population of counseling programs. Of the 540 institutions with counseling programs listed in the Hollis and Wantz (1994) survey of counselor preparation programs, only about 100 programs have achieved CACREP accreditation. Therefore, although many promising training approaches have been identified, considerable work remains to be done to insure that all counseling graduates develop minimal core competency preparation in group work.

4 CHAPTER

Group Counseling

I t is perhaps redundant to note that counselor education programs prepare counselors. Therefore, we expected group counseling to be a main focus in most programs that are providing group work preparation. Our survey data gathering validated this expectation. In fact, submissions describing self-assessed exemplary group counseling training outnumbered those for any other type of group work, including those for core group work preparation. We will draw selectively from 13 of these programs as we discuss group counseling preparation.

The ASGW Training Standards (ASGW, 1991b) for group counseling identify group counseling as one of four possible group work specializations. The group worker who specializes in group counseling is defined in the Standards as seeking to

> help group participants to resolve the usual, yet often difficult, problems of living through interpersonal support and problem solving. An additional goal is to help participants to develop their existing interpersonal problem-solving competencies that they may be better able to handle future problems of a similar nature. Non-severe career, education, personal, social, and developmental concerns are frequently addressed. (p. 14)

The ASGW group counseling standards include 8 knowledge competencies and 12 skill competencies. In addition, course work and

95

skills through supervised practice are indicated. As for any of the four group work specialties (the others being task group work, psycho-education group work, and group psychotherapy), these competencies, course work, and supervised practice skills are in addition to the core group work competencies previously discussed.

We have organized the 20 group counseling knowledge and skill competencies into the same five clusters used for the core and specialization competencies: (a) Cluster 1: defining group counseling; (b) Cluster 2: pregroup preparation; (c) Cluster 3: therapeutic dynamics and leader skills; (d) Cluster 4: research and evaluation; and (e) Cluster 5: ethical practice. Each of these standards clusters will be discussed, and examples of exemplary group worker preparation methods will be provided.

STANDARDS CLUSTER 1

Teaching the Definition of Group Counseling

This cluster is operationalized by two standards. The individual standards included in this cluster are these:

- K-1: State for at least three major theoretical approaches to group counseling the distinguishing characteristics of each and the commonalities shared by all.

- K-3: List advantages and disadvantages of group counseling and the circumstances for which it is indicated or contraindicated.

Instructional Methods

Highly interesting instructional approaches are used by a number of counselor education programs in seeking to help students define group counseling. Major categories of approaches include

- field interviews
- presentations
- reading, lecturette, and discussion

Field interviews. The counselor education program at the University of Nebraska at Kearney requires students in its Group Counseling course to conduct interviews with counselors in the field about group work and group counseling. Core questions for the interviews are designed to distinguish among the four group work types. Interviewees are asked to specify which types of group work they employ most often. They are then asked several follow-up questions, including what are some benefits and limitations, to what extent respondents are involved in forming groups, and what recommendations do the respondents have for counselors who are beginning to lead groups for the first time.

Presentations. In the Group Counseling Theory course at Montana State University, students must develop and orally deliver, with handouts, a presentation of a counseling group. The assignment states, in part:

> Clients are being hurt because they are not in the right group for them. Putting together a compelling presentation and handout will prepare you to help them make the right decision about joining a group. . . . By observing other group presentations and actually presenting their own, group counselors will learn optimal methods for conveying information about their group.

This project emphasizes the importance of describing the purpose of the group. Particularly stressed is the need to specify the relationship between group goals and the theoretical model that is selected to guide the group.

Reading, lecturette, and discussion. Most group counseling courses appear to include lecturette and discussion when instructors seek to inform students about group counseling and its relationship to other forms of group work. In the Theory and Practice of Group Counseling course at Rollins College, for example, course objectives include developing an understanding of the many types of group experiences and applications of group methods, knowledge of several styles of group counseling and therapy, and the ability to develop a rationale for engaging in a variety of counselor–leader–therapist behaviors.

A chronic difficulty in the training of group counselors has been the lack of a comprehensive theory of group counseling which is grounded in the special environment of the group. Because of this lack, group counseling has relied on attempts by various authors to apply the theories of individual counseling and psychotherapy to the group context. Typically, texts are selected which present counseling theories, and students are assigned weekly readings that are keyed to particular topics related to group leadership.

At the University of Cincinnati, focus is placed more on differences in leader and member role than on the specific content of the classical theories of counseling. The classical theories are grouped as examples of differences in goals—gaining insight versus taking action (London, 1964). Theories are also grouped according to differences in process or strategies—rational techniques versus affective techniques (Patterson, 1966). Frey (1972) conceptualized the London and Patterson continuae as forming two orthogonal dimensions upon which counseling theories could be arrayed. Discussion focuses on how these differences in goals and overarching strategies yield differences in group style (leader centered vs. member centered) and orientation (group process vs. individual outcome) (Hansen, Warner, & Smith, 1980). During the discussion of the four cells in the goal-by-strategy matrix, specific counseling theories (e.g., behavioral, Adlerian, Gestalt, existential) are briefly discussed, and general similarities and differences are noted.

We eagerly await the development of a theory of group counseling that is interpersonally based and articulates the systemic dynamics of persons in groups who have gathered to improve themselves and their connectedness with others. Until such a new theory emerges, reading, lecturette, and discussion, within a seminar environment, provide central ways that these objectives are met. In addition, supervised laboratory skill practice, viewing video training tapes, and class presentations account for other important instructional strategies that are geared more directly to practice applications.

STANDARDS CLUSTER 2

Teaching Pregroup Preparation in Group Counseling

Pregroup preparation is especially important in group counseling, where prospective members may present inclusionary challenges. Decisions need to be made by both the prospective member and the group leader(s) about whether this group counseling experience will be a good fit. In that regard, it is necessary for group leaders to realistically inform possible members about important elements of the group counseling being planned, as well as about their own experience and expertise. Possible members need to provide descriptive information about their goals and level of functioning in order for appropriate decisions to be reached regarding the member–group match.

Three knowledge and skills competencies from the ASGW Professional Training Standards for group counseling coalesce to compose this cluster:

- K-6: Discuss interpersonal assessment in group counseling.

- K-8: Describe group formation principles in group counseling.

- S-1: Recruit and screen prospective counseling group members.

Instructional Methods

Major categories of instructional approaches employed within counselor education programs to teach about pregroup preparation include

- developing detailed group counseling proposals or plans
- cognitive input

Developing detailed group counseling proposals or plans. A consistent approach for instructing students in pregroup preparation is to ask them to write a group proposal or plan (e.g., Rollins College, East Tennessee State, University of Cincinnati, Indiana University, and Indiana University–Purdue University at Fort Wayne). In most cases, after receiving feedback and evaluation from the instructor, students use their revised plans as a leadership guide, as they work under faculty supervision.

During the Group Counseling Theory course at Montana State University, for instance, students must submit a 5- to 10-page proposal for a counseling group, featuring references and following publication guidelines of the American Psychological Association. Four elements of the assignment are especially pertinent to pregroup preparation. The first element is titled "population and concerns." Here, students are asked to address the following issues:

> What population will be helped by this group? What kinds of problems will it help with? Describe the populations in some depth, addressing relevant culture, gender, and developmental issues. Use a theory (or theories) to explain the population's concerns and to identify goals for improvement.

A second element of the proposal assignment that is focused on pregroup preparation is called "leadership." Here, students are asked to address these questions:

> What personal characteristics will be important for leaders working with the population. . . . What training and/or supervision should the leaders have? What functions will the leaders fulfill and what leadership techniques will they employ to fulfill them. . . . How will the leaders fulfill their responsibilities to protect the rights and promote the welfare of members?

A third element of the assignment is termed "membership." Here, students are asked to address these considerations:

> How will group members be recruited and what effects might this recruitment process have? What is the optimal and acceptable number of group members? What criteria and methods will be used for screening out and selecting in group members? What information will be gathered on members prior to entering the group? How will this information be used? . . . In what ways will the group be homogeneous and/or heterogeneous? What would be the ideal group composition? How will group members be prepared for the group experience? What are members' rights and responsibilities? What roles and behaviors will be expected of members in the group? What risks are there in participating in the group?

A last assignment element that is directly aligned with pregroup preparation is termed "ethics." Here, students are asked to review the "Ethical Guidelines for Group Counselors" (ASGW, 1991a) and to evaluate the extent to which their proposal addresses the ethical guidelines (see Appendix D for more detail).

Cognitive input. In addition to readings, counselor education courses in group counseling sometimes include specific cognitive inputs that address pregroup preparation. Again, taking the Montana State University program as an example, one portion of the Group Counseling Theory course is devoted to preparation and screening. A "Group Counseling Intake and Referral" handout is used to orient students to important considerations related to client preparation and selection. In terms of client preparation, pregroup meetings are discussed as being an important strategy in order to prepare the client for optimum participation in the group and to allow the group counselor to assess the client for appropriate placement. In terms of selection, identification and exclusion of clients having serious problems in a range of areas is discussed in order to ensure the optimal functioning of both the client and the group. Conversely, in order to develop effective groups and services to members, selection also is discussed from the perspective of identifying and including clients who will benefit from group counseling.

Teaching Therapeutic Dynamics and Leader Skills in Group Counseling

The materials submitted by counselor education programs to describe exemplary preparation in group counseling focus on this cluster. Indeed, this situation reflects accurately the emphasis of the ASGW Training Standards on competencies necessary for directly leading groups. Therefore, we were pleased to have received an impressive array of curricular descriptions for teaching about therapeutic dynamics and leader skills in group counseling.

The competencies involved in direct counseling group leadership are enumerated through 3 knowledge and 10 skill competency standards. These 13 standards are organized below.

- K-4: Describe interpersonal dynamics in group counseling.

- K-5: Describe group problem-solving approaches.

- K-7: Identify referral sources and procedures.

- S-2: Recognize self-defeating behaviors of counseling group members.

- S-3: Conduct a personally selected group counseling model appropriate to the age and clientele of the group leader's specialty area(s) (e.g., community counseling).

- S-4: Develop reasonable hypotheses about nonverbal behavior among counseling group members.

- S-5: Exhibit appropriate pacing skills involved in stages of a counseling group's development.

- S-6: Intervene effectively at critical incidents in the counseling group process.

- S-7: Work appropriately with disruptive counseling group members.

- S-8: Make use of the major strategies, techniques, and procedures of group counseling.

- S-9: Use procedures to assist transfer and support changes by group counseling members in the natural environment.

- S-10: Use adjunct group counseling structures such as homework (e.g., goal setting).

- S-11: Work cooperatively and effectively with a counseling group coleader.

Instructional Methods

Of the variety of curricular experiences provided to us by counselor education programs, most fit into one of six general categories of instruction:

- class exercises/laboratory experiences
- observation and critiquing of a group
- participation as a group member
- participation as a group leader or coleader
- actual supervised group leadership or coleadership experiences
- laboratory manual

Class exercises/laboratory experiences. Stand-alone training exercises and laboratory experiences within a course are important and often-used means of teaching about therapeutic dynamics and leader skills. Two examples of this approach follow.

MULTIPLE T

In the Theory and Practice of Group Counseling course at Rollins College a training exercise called the "Multiple T" is used. This is described as a minimum-structure procedure that has been developed to train group leaders in the use of human relations and small group counseling techniques. Steps of the procedure include the following:

(a) Students identify and discuss dilemmas they have encountered or expect to encounter in their group work.

(b) One or more dilemmas are selected for simulation and practice; students describe as many alternative strategies as possible. Each of these strategies is analyzed for feasibility and anticipated results.

(c) Small groups (of 6–10 members) are formed randomly or on the basis of similarity, such as professional specialty, level of training/ experience, age, gender, etc.

(d) Simulated experiences are designed either by a student who wishes to practice one or more strategies or by a student chosen to administer the training experience for another student. Roles are assigned to as many students as appropriate.

(e) Time schedules for each training session ("round") are developed, allowing for practice, process feedback and evaluation, retrial, and total group evaluation. The round is conducted.

(f) Steps (c) and (d) are repeated with different students volunteering for a new situation. The group engages in as many rounds as time, energy, and interest allow.

Here is one example of a Multiple-T situation that occurred during the early stage of a counseling group:

> This is the third meeting of a personal growth group being conducted by a university counseling center. Each member has had a screening interview and has joined the group to develop some aspect of social behavior— loneliness, dating, speaking in class, etc. Having met twice, the group has gone over typical ground rules and each member has made a brief statement about reasons for being in the group. In this simulation, several characteristics are to be included.
>
> Member A has never dated, having been too busy earning money to attend school and working for good grades. "A" would now like to date but is ill at ease with the opposite sex and fearful of behaving foolishly or of being a bore.
>
> Member B has recently been dropped by a boy/girl friend after a period of six months of steady dating. This has happened four times previously with relationships lasting from two months to a year. "B" feels used but realizes s/he contributes to the pattern—but how?
>
> Member C has explained, "I just feel empty inside. I get interested in someone, we date for a while and everything is great. Then I gradually lose interest and just don't care anymore." This has happened several times and "C" worries that s/he is actually incapable of caring deeply about anyone, ever.

The Multiple T was developed to emphasize training and practice. It is claimed that the method typically generates a multitude of observations, ideas, feelings, new strategies, and, occasionally, some interpersonal conflict. Reminders are given to students that most conversations started will not be completed, not all reactions will be surfaced, resolution of personal and interpersonal conflicts may need to be deferred, and the value of the Multiple-T method will evolve from repeated practice.

"HERE & NOW RESPONSE PRACTICE SHEET"

Activation and illumination of the here and now is an important training theme for group counseling at the University of Louisville. An exercise that is used to focus on the here and now is called the "Here & Now Response Practice Sheet." The format of the exercise is that statements by example group counseling members are presented individually, followed by examples of here-and-now leader responses. Fill-in blanks are then provided to contain the original response of the student.

> Member statement: "I find myself cutting off my friend Joan. I get so impatient with her when she talks. It really bothers her and me."
>
> Here & Now leader responses:
> A. "When have you found yourself being impatient as members talk in this group?"
> B. "Who are the people in this group with whom you would be most/ least patient with when they talk?"
>
> Your response: "_____
> _____
> _____."

In this way, students practice generating leader responses and then are able to check them against those leader examples that are provided.

Group observation and critiquing. The projects considered in this section refer to observation and critiquing conducted on groups other than one's own—that is, the assignments serve to ready students for their own group leadership. Many programs include this form of group observation and critiquing in their group counseling curriculum. Groups being observed may range from those presented through a videotape production (e.g., "Leading in the Here and Now," by Peg Carroll [1987]; "Developmental Aspects of Groups," by Rex Stockton

[1992]), to the live observation of a group which has given its permission to be observed, or through viewing videotapes of actual or role-played group sessions or excerpts of sessions that are provided by the instructor or obtained from some outside source. One illustration is provided below.

In the Advanced Group Counseling Theory and Practice course at the University of Louisville, one of the requirements is for students to observe and critique 10 videotaped group counseling sessions provided by the instructor. A "Group Observation Critique Form" is used as a guide. Contents of the form are excerpted below:

1. Stage of the group
2. Therapeutic factors
   a. Instillation of hope
   b. Universality
   c. Imparting of information
   d. Altruism
      (Others cited by Yalom, 1975)
3. Group norm development
   a. Speaking in the first person
   b. Questions to statements
   c. Speaking directly to each other
   d. Approval seeking
   e. Premature advice giving
4. Rescuing behavior
5. Resistance
6. Trust issues
7. Leaders challenged/confronted
8. Group flight
9. Avoiding addressing one's feelings
10. Here-and-now implementation

Participation as a group member. Some programs provide a course which, among other requirements, features ongoing group membership for students. It appears that many such programs link group membership with opportunities for leadership or coleadership of the group. This member-leader format will be described later. For this present section on group membership, we will illustrate the group membership format only.

The course Introduction to Group Leadership at the University of Cincinnati is an elective open to those students who have opted to take the complete three-course group leadership sequence. In this second course in the sequence, students are aware that a main activity is for them to participate in a small-group personal learning experience as a member, with coleadership typically coming from outside experts or, if unavailable, from advanced students in the program who have previously completed the group work sequence successfully. The premise that guides this course is that students can learn substantially about how groups work, what the membership experience can be, how coleaders can function, and how their own group leadership style and functioning can develop through (a) actively participating as a group member; (b) integrating the actual group experience with cognitive learning developed through readings and instructor inputs, both of which occur separately from the group experience itself; (c) critiquing the group experience and their involvement in it through weekly logs that are turned in to the instructors, who return them with feedback; and (d) evaluating the total group experience through a final paper.

The group of 8–12 members meets with experienced cofacilitators for 10 weekly 1½-hour sessions. No academic matters are discussed. This time is devoted to group activities. If advanced students are serving as coleaders, then weekly supervision is provided by the instructor. If the coleaders are drawn from outside the program, they function independently. Student participation in the group is ungraded, except for attendance. Other graded aspects of the course include the final paper, in which a comprehensive evaluation of the participant's group experience is provided, and an extensive group plan each student creates for later application.

Participation as a group leader or coleader. Providing group leadership opportunities as part of group counseling preparation is very much a part of good programs. Three general approaches seem to be taken, and these are not mutually exclusive within any one program: (a) structured learning opportunities for group membership and group leadership with peers within a course, (b) separate workshops in group leadership for students with peers, and (c) leadership or coleadership of an actual group under supervision. We will provide an example of each approach.

MEMBERSHIP–LEADERSHIP WITH PEERS

Advanced Techniques in Group Counseling is an elective course at Idaho State University. It is intended to introduce students to advanced concepts, skills, and theoretical principles of leading groups. Course enrollment assumes that students are willing to be participants in a group that will be led by their classmates under instructor supervision and, possibly, by a doctoral student supervisor. The syllabus states that students who are unwilling to participate as group members should drop the course, and it includes several cautionary statements regarding ethical conduct.

Main methods of instruction include participation as a group member, supervised experiences as a coleader with a classmate, and completion of directed readings and learning logs. The syllabus states: "By choosing to participate in this course, you have offered yourself an opportunity to develop a clearer understanding of what you need to do to become an effective group leader" (p. 1).

The class functions as a group for 1½ hours of each class meeting. The group is led by student coleaders on a rotational schedule so that each set of coleaders obtains two leadership opportunities. Students, then, are able to participate both as members and as leaders. The faculty supervisor provides observations and supervision at two points each week. The first occurs at session's "half-time." The supervisor enters the group room after 45–50 minutes of the session to process and consult with the coleaders about how the group is progressing and to help plan for the balance of the session. This intervention is accomplished in front of the entire group. The second supervision occurs immediately after the completion of a session and involves the coleaders and other group members processing with the supervisor the events that transpired in the session.

The faculty member reports two interesting outcomes. The learning and dynamics generated through the half-time intervention and post-session processing are valuable and highly interesting. Second, awareness resulting from the boundaries between member and leader roles, stemming from a covert design purpose, leads to students' reporting greater clarity about their ethical involvement as group leaders.

SEPARATE TRAINING WORKSHOPS WITH PEERS

The California State University–Fullerton includes a course called Practicum in Group Leadership. As a part of this course, students participate in a 3-day training and supervision workshop in group process. As above, this workshop utilizes a member–leader format. Students are provided with several opportunities during the 3-day period to colead a small group of their peers, to give and receive feedback, and to process any dual-role issues that emerge. They also receive ongoing feedback from faculty supervisors. Learning about self, others, group process, and group leadership proceeds from an experiential base to cognitive understandings in this workshop.

In a typical workshop day there are approximately four small group sessions held, each one lasting about 2 hours. In the first hour of a session, group interaction time is led by participant coleaders. The second hour of a session, which is led by the supervisors, emphasizes feedback, critique, process commentary, and teaching. Some time during each day is spent combining the small groups into a large group meeting. These workshops suggest that participants learn best when the material emerges from actual group experience.

Actual supervised group leadership or coleadership. A number of programs describe how they provide opportunities for students to lead or colead actual counseling groups under supervision. We will draw from aspects of these programs in showing how this can be accomplished. Generally, these leadership opportunities occur in a supervised clinical experience, such as a practicum or internship, or in a course which simulates such activities.

For instance, in the course Practicum in Group Counseling: Child & Adolescent at Governors State University, Illinois, students are expected to organize and conduct two counseling groups during the trimester, with each group meeting for eight sessions. One of these groups needs to be conducted with five or more students from grades K–6, and the other with five or more students from grades 7–12. These groups can be coled with a classmate or with a trained professional. Observation, critiquing, supervision, and reading also are integral parts of this group counseling practicum.

In the Advanced Counseling Practicum at Indiana University–Purdue University at Fort Wayne, one set of course objectives addresses development of group leadership skills. These skills include conducting screening and/or orientation interviews with prospective members, beginning and ending a counseling group, and demonstrating group leader interventions such as active listening, facilitating, modeling, giving feedback, cutting off, linking, drawing out, using exercises, and others. Students are asked to develop a group plan with a coleader that details the sessions of an assigned group. This plan includes a statement about group purpose, number of members, group format, length of the group and its sessions, structuring to be used, materials required, and how evaluation will occur. All group sessions are audiotaped (videotaped, if possible). A detailed group summary paper is required at the group's conclusion. The Group Leadership course at the University of Cincinnati, although not a practicum course, is very much in accord with this orientation.

At Montana State University, students in the Group Counseling Practicum usually lead two counseling groups for a minimum of 40 hours of client contact time. Each group includes a minimum of six consecutive sessions. The groups can be developmental or remedial, structured or unstructured, time limited or ongoing. Adherence to ASGW ethical guidelines is expected, and leadership functions used are to include executive functioning, emotional stimulation, caring, and meaning attribution. All sessions are tape-recorded and reviewed. A process transcript is made while the tapes are reviewed; the transcript includes direct quotes, process comments, "should've said" afterthoughts, questions, and a summary analyzing leadership strengths during the session and suggesting areas for future improvement. Transcripts are intended to focus on relationships between group members and how members' development can be enhanced. Summary notes for all counseling sessions are written. Students participate in a weekly seminar on group counseling, where they give two case presentations, and they participate in a weekly support group for group leaders and a weekly supervision session.

During the Advanced Group Counseling-Leadership course at Indiana University students lead or colead an ongoing counseling group.

In addition to showing selected excerpts of videotaped sessions during weekly supervision meetings and developing weekly written summaries of their group sessions, other specific skill-building activities are used. For instance, after the fifth group counseling session, students are asked to compare their first taped group meeting with the most recent tape in terms of number of leader interventions, variety of interventions, leader confidence, and other variables.

As a part of the Advanced Group Counseling Theory and Practice course at the University of Louisville, students colead a counseling group with another classmate. This group meets outside of class for twice a week over 6 weeks. Each session lasts 60–75 minutes. Leaders alternate submitting "Group Counseling Leader Intentions Critiques" of videotaped sessions.

Therefore, the teaching of therapeutic dynamics and leadership skills in group counseling is being addressed in a number of interesting ways by counselor education programs. Appropriate combinations of class exercises/laboratory experiences, observation and critiquing of a group, participation as a group member, participation as a group leader or coleader with peers, and actual supervised group leadership or coleadership experiences afford programs with a set of valuable choices.

Laboratory manual. The University of North Texas counselor education department uses an unusual text, *Group Counseling: Laboratory Manual*, as a required reading resource in the course Group Counseling Theories and Procedures. Although its contents also address other group counseling standards, the focus is on assisting the practice of group counseling. The table of contents from this 44-page manual includes group counseling reference listings, guided reading assignments, specifications for the journal ("daybook") students keep to help process their in-class group experiences, summary forms to be used in their outside-class group leading experiences, a sample consent form, group ground rules, models of group developmental stages, a description of the Hill Interaction Matrix, and a wide variety of other resources (e.g., self-assessment forms, leader performance scales, group leader evaluation forms) that a student could choose to use in group leadership. Organized into a manual, this highly pragmatic material seems to be highly useful to students.

STANDARDS CLUSTER 4

Teaching Research and Evaluation in Group Counseling

This cluster consists of one large standard. This standard encompasses assessment, research design, and program evaluation:

- K-12: Use assessment procedures in evaluating effects and contributions of group counseling.

Instructional Methods

Relatively little explicit attention appears to be devoted in group counseling curricula to the research literature on group counseling. Rather, research and evaluation in group counseling preparation appears to be grounded in ongoing and qualitative assessment approaches that are used to document, describe, analyze, and make judgments about actual group counseling activities. Presented below is one example of how training in group counseling has been structured to focus on the group counseling research literature in order to promote learning about the contributions and effects of group counseling.

Research literature review. In the Montana State University Group Counseling Theory course, an assignment is to write a critique of a group counseling research study. The following questions are considered by the student:

- What were the questions or hypotheses being examined?
- What theories were used to explain and guide the procedures and questions?
- What previous studies does this study build upon and expand?
- What are the characteristics of the group participants' population, and how were they selected?
- What are the characteristics of the group which affect group process (composition, leadership, format, location, schedule, length, potency, etc.)?
- What measurement techniques are employed, and how do they meet criteria in the following areas: reliability, validity, norms, prior use, population appropriate, closely related to the purpose of the group, conceptually meaningful, cognitive, affective, behavioral, unobtrusive/nonreactive, outcome *and* process?

- Was the study experimental (research initiated) or correlational (research studied an event that would occur without the researcher)?
- Was the study carried out in a laboratory (setting established for research purposes) or in the field (the natural place where this group would occur)?
- How many experimental, control, and placebo groups were there, and how were subjects assigned to groups?
- Was a time series design employed (pretesting, posttesting, and follow-up testing) which allows subjects to serve as their own controls?
- What statistics were employed? Did they account for the relationships between multiple dependent and independent variables? Were individual members or whole groups (usually small n nonparametric statistics) used as units of analysis?
- What indications are there that this study contributes to programmatic research by building on previous studies and serving as a base for future studies? To what extent is the information reported above offered in a clear and standardized format to allow for comparison and replication?
- How are the ethical issues such as informed consent, confidentiality, right of exit, and follow-up dealt with?

Ongoing assessment of group counseling. As we mentioned, the emphasis in teaching research and evaluation in group counseling is on involving students in assessment and evaluation procedures to determine the effectiveness of group counseling, either their own or that of others. In fact, learning and applying ongoing assessment procedures seems to be a central element of preparation in group counseling. These assessment procedures can be organized into the following categories: intervention critique, session-by-session process analysis, self-assessment paper, and summary group evaluation.

Intervention critique. Group counseling leader interventions are critiqued frequently and in different ways. Three examples will be presented in text; refer to Appendix D for a more detailed example of a log contributed by the University of North Texas.

At Indiana University in the Advanced Group Counseling—Leadership course, one objective is for students "to develop a repertoire of leader interventions and techniques and a sense of when their use is appropriate" (p. 5). One activity used to accomplish the objective clearly illustrates the linkage between doing and evaluation. Students are asked to write three instances from the group they are coleading in which they have intervened. They are asked to make the narrative as specific as possible and to identify the consequences of their interventions. Moreover, they are asked to write three instances where they did not intervene and, in retrospect, wish that they had. Finally, they are instructed to discuss these observations.

In the Advanced Group Counseling Theory and Practice course at the University of Louisville, students are required to critique several videotapes of others leading counseling groups and to critique their own coleadership of a counseling group. The focus of these critiques is on group counseling leader intentions. When critiquing their own counseling group, students use the "Group Counseling Leader Intentions Critique" form to review a session within 24 hours of its completion. In doing so, the students follow five steps: (a) Indicate in column 1 of the form what the member(s) said/did just prior to your intervention. (b) To judge your leader's intentions in column 2, stop the tape before each intervention is made. Try to remember exactly what you were thinking at the time of the intervention. There are no right or wrong answers. The purpose is to identify what you planned to do at the moment. Choose the intention that best applies from the Group Counseling Leader Intention form (Note: An accompanying handout defines for students 18 group counseling leader's intentions, such as norming, connecting, process illuminating, and socializing). (c) In column 3, indicate what you actually said to facilitate your leader intention. (d) In column 4, indicate how the member or others responded. (e) In column 5, indicate what you would say differently if you did not accomplish your intention, or indicate if the intention was improper.

In the Practicum in Group Counseling: Child and Adolescent course at Governors State University, students engage in different types of critiquing procedures. They observe two group sessions conducted by other classmates or professionals and then analyze them by using the "Observation Form: Group Counseling." They submit one minitranscript and critique of a 20-minute tape segment which they think best reflects their group counseling skills; the critique follows a structured format. They submit a best tape, along with group history and detailed analysis of group process, a critique of their interventions, and a suggested evaluation method for their group. Also, they complete and submit a "Group Analysis Form," on request. The contents of this form are described in the next section.

Session-by-session process analysis. Describing and analyzing processes occurring within group counseling sessions are important instructional methods. These session-by-session process analyses frequently take the form of a log, diary, journal, or some otherwise structured format. Three examples follow.

As we mentioned, students in the Practicum in Group Counseling: Child and Adolescent course are asked to submit a "Group Analysis Form" on request. Its contents are as follows:

- Your name
- Coleader's name
- Date of session
- Number of group members present at this session
- Age or grade level of group members
- This group session focused on the following issues
- During this session I was feeling
- During this session I was thinking
- If I could do this session again, I would
- If I could do this session again, I wouldn't
- Describe *your* coleader role in this session
- Specifically identify and justify your best intervention in this session
- State your goal(s) for the next session

In the Human Relations and Group Processes course at East Tennessee State University, students submit a weekly diary/journal addressing the experiences of students as members of a growth group. The journal is personal and is read by the instructor only. Each group member keeps a one- to two-page journal of each week's group experiences. Entries focus on the member's feelings, reactions, thoughts, and insights regarding the group work, not on summarizing the group activities. Some examples of relevant material include the following: (a) How do I feel about being in the group? (b) How do I see people in the group in general? (c) How do I see myself? (d) How do others react to me? (e) What do I fear most about the group?

At the University of Cincinnati, the elective course Leading Groups is the third course in the group work sequence. It involves students in group coleadership, under supervision. Students usually implement the group plan they developed and received feedback about during the preceding course, Introduction to Group Leadership. One of the course assignments is to submit a weekly log detailing activities and observations related to the counseling group being implemented. The weekly assignment is described as follows:

> The purposes of the personal log are fourfold: (a) to provide a structure for systematically reviewing one's own group leadership plans, actions, thoughts, and feelings; (b) to facilitate examination of member behavior and member experience in the group; (c) to facilitate examination of co-leadership issues; and (d) to provide a mechanism for ongoing supervision.
>
> In preparing your log, here are some topics which you ought to consider: (a) group member behavior; (b) group member problems in working within the group; (c) what group members are likely to be feeling or perceiving; (d) level of group development; (e) who talks to whom about what; (f) who is doing the work in the group; (g) your own feelings as a leader and as a person; (h) coleadership issues and problems; (i) your own role in the group; (j) the goodness-of-fit between your plan for the group and the group members' needs and abilities. This is not an exhaustive list—just some suggestions to get you thinking.
>
> The following is suggested as an outline for each of your weekly entries in the log. We are suggesting this outline to help you organize the log in a way which will be easiest to read quickly (ordinarily, each of the five topics should take no more than one page to discuss): (a) What went on in the group this week? (b) Group member behaviors and feelings. (c) Leadership/coleadership issues. (d) My own thoughts, feelings, and self-assessment. (e) Plans for the next session.

These logs are turned in to the instructor before the next supervision group meeting and the next group session. The instructor quickly returns the session log with feedback. This timing allows the student to consider instructor feedback in preparation for the next session.

In the Advanced Techniques in Group Counseling course at Idaho State University, logs are structured around assigned reading content and then tied to anticipated events occurring in the developmental life of the group of which the students are a part. An example (p. 4) is taken from Log 3, question 3 (of three questions):

> In chapter 6 Yalom discusses two critical concepts, here-and-now and process. Briefly describe the meaning of these concepts (be sure to include

discussion that differentiates process from content!). Give two examples of group interactions in which you were involved as a member and offer your process interpretation of what occurred. For each of these examples give also a process observation you could have offered if you had observed these interactions as the group leader.

Self-assessment paper. In the Idaho State University course, a self-assessment paper is required. This paper is intended to stimulate student reflections on their learning and experience as a group member and leader. It is suggested that a diary of the group experience be kept to assist in producing this paper. The paper outline contains the following excerpts:

1. Discuss your perception/assessment of your skills as a member and as a group leader. Compare how you see your abilities at the beginning with your perceptions at the end of the semester.
2. Discuss what happened to you in terms of your development over the course of the semester. Describe any critical incidents, work done in the group, etc., that had a notable influence on you.
3. Discuss how you saw your role and perceptions of yourself as a leader evolving over the passage of the semester. Discuss fully how you have worked to differentiate your roles as group member and group leader. Include commentary on how you have defined leader versus member boundaries and the conflicts you have experienced in each role.

Summary group evaluation. Students are sometimes required to submit a summary group evaluation report at the conclusion of the leadership experience. Two examples of this instructional method follow.

In the Advanced Counseling Practicum at Indiana University–Purdue University Fort Wayne, students use their practicum group coleading experience to write a summative paper that addresses various group leadership concepts. Coleaders write their own papers, although they are encouraged to share their perceptions of their group and of its members. The paper is a 7–10 page product, written in response to these questions:

- What is your idea of a healthy person, and how is your group guiding its members in that direction?
- What are the counseling theories to which you subscribe, and how are they incorporated in your leadership style?

- What is an effective group? How are you going to determine if your group has been effective?
- What are the strengths and weaknesses of each of your group members?
- What is currently blocking their strengths, and how can you as a leader help them to become aware of and eliminate these blocks?

Finally, *evaluate* the group experience:

- Do you believe the group has been (or will be in the few remaining weeks) effective for group members? In what ways? What are you considering in making this assessment?
- What unexpected problems occurred during the planning for and/ or implementation of the group? How did you address these problems?
- What would you do differently if you were to lead such a group again?
- What did you like best—and least—about this group and your group leadership experience? Identify at least five things you learned about groups and/or about yourself as a group leader (or coleader) as a result of this experience.

In the Leading Groups elective course at the University of Cincinnati, students colead groups under supervision. We have previously described the process analysis assignment of weekly logs. The Group Experience Evaluation is a summative report of the group experience. Its purpose is to assist students to consider the outcomes of their group plans, developed during the preceding course and implemented during the present course. It is also important for any counselor to learn ways to evaluate the effects of plans and methods on clients being served. Skillful evaluation of group effects can be helpful in preparing presentations one might give to consumer and professional groups, and thoughtful evaluation of one's efforts may be the best way to learn new and more effective group leadership skills. The following outline for the evaluation report is proposed:

1. Summary of the group experience: Briefly summarize (a) the purpose of the group, (b) the methods employed within the group, (c) the population your group was designed to serve, (d) how participants were recruited and selected, and (e) the theoretical basis for

selecting the purposes and methods chosen for use with this population.

2. Evaluation data: Present data collected to facilitate evaluation of this experience. Include (a) personal observations of group members, (b) personal observations about leadership (or coleadership) issues, (c) personal observations of the group process, and (d) participant evaluation data. For the first three topics, your log books will be an important source of data. Formal participant evaluation data might be collected using some form of participant evaluation questionnaire. Note both problems and successes—it is as important to be aware of what went right as it is to attend to what went wrong. Try to report the data objectively—leave the inferences for the next section.

3. Discussion: Integrate the data into a coherent discussion evaluating this group experience. Tie your evaluation to relevant course readings from this and previous terms. Make inferences about why things happened as they did.

4. Recommendations: What recommendations would you make to other group leaders who would like to run this sort of group or who would like to serve this sort of population?

STANDARDS CLUSTER 5

Teaching the Ethical Practice of Group Counseling

This cluster also consists of one large standard. This standard focuses on the specific ethical issues arising in group work:

- K-2: Identify specific ethical problems and considerations unique to group counseling.

As we discussed in reference to the material on core knowledge and skills, ethical concerns exist about requiring students to participate in group experiences as a part of their own training or to report on personal aspects of their group leadership experiences. For instance, in reference to an assignment of turning in a weekly journal of one's group leadership, including components of personal sharing, the East Tennessee State course syllabus states:

> One of the primary objectives of the group class is self-exploration. Therefore, grading for the journal will come mainly from doing it and not content.

However, journal entries which fail to process what you are experiencing will be graded down. In other words, you will not be graded on your issues, but on the exploration and handling of your issues.

Instructional Methods

Most counselor educators who teach group counseling courses agree that an experiential participation is necessary for developing the competencies needed to function as an effective group counselor. They have found instructional methods to accommodate ethical concerns surrounding student's personal participation, including not grading the experiential portion of a course and employing external experts to lead a training group. These are strategies we use at the University of Cincinnati, for instance, in an effort to include the experiential involvement we think is vital to learning group counseling competencies while we also seek to exclude grading and the professor from that particular phase of training. See the discussion of ethics presented earlier in the section on core competencies for applicable detail.

Course syllabi contain some emphasis on ethics in group counseling as a separate area of study. Often, as in the Rollins College course Theory and Practice of Group Counseling, the syllabus contains a separate week's emphasis on group counseling ethics, and usually the ASGW Ethical Guidelines material is used as a primary source. Also, ethics as a topic appears. to be folded into the ongoing review and supervision of group counseling practice.

For instance, the group proposal assignment in the Group Counseling Theory at Montana State University specifically requires students to include ethical considerations in their plans with regard to the population to be worked with, relevant theories to be used, appropriate training of leaders, how members' welfare will be protected and promoted, how members will be recruited and screened, and what provisions will be made for persons who do not progress or who are harmed as a result of the group experience.

Another example of how ethics as a topic is examined within the ongoing context of group counseling preparation is found in the Advanced Group Counseling—Leadership course at Indiana University. An objective of the course is "to develop a personal understanding of ethics involved in group leadership" (p. 6).

At some point in the semester you will undoubtedly face a situation in which ethical considerations are involved and you must make a decision. Write up the incident, the ethical issues involved, and your handling of it in a one- to two-page paper.

SUMMING UP GROUP COUNSELING TRAINING

Our review shows that training in group counseling is the most advanced of any group work specialty. To find otherwise in counseling programs would be a surprise, indeed. When this specialized training is added to the impressive training approaches in the core competencies of group work (see Chapter Three), group counseling training seems especially vigorous.

Especially attractive are the instances where cognitive, experiential, and reflective judgment components are well integrated. When that is done, students are introduced to the multiple connections among knowledge, skills, and meaning, and thus they are better able to provide quality service delivery. More of this linkage is still needed.

Specifically, what remains to be accomplished more widely in group counseling preparation is the complete installation of knowledge, skills, and reflective judgment with consistent and appropriate supervised group counseling applications. The creation of field-based practica and internships, along with adequate off-site supervision, awaits development in many programs.

5 CHAPTER

Task Groups and Psychoeducational Groups

The task group and psychoeducational group specializations are truly emergent specializations in counseling group work. Although study of the development and leadership of task and work groups has a long history in the organizational consultation literature and although the use of psychoeducational methods is documented in the organizational training and development literature, little of this material is directly applicable to group work training in counselor education, and precious little can be found in the counseling literature.

This chapter on task and psychoeducation groups, as well as Chapter Six on psychotherapy groups, will contain few curricular examples because instructional designs for these specializations are just emerging. To offset the scarcity of curricular exemplars, we will provide considerable conceptual material to support and guide the development of future curricula in these areas. The specializations of work with task groups and work with psychoeducation groups are distinct specializations; thus, to provide clear differentiation between them, this chapter will be divided into two parts. First, we will discuss curricular designs and related conceptual support for the specialization in task and work groups. This will be followed by similar material related to the specialization of psychoeducational groups.

TASK GROUPS

> The U.S. is in a time of transition, moving from an industrial society to a post-industrial society. This means that social values are in transition as well. The changes . . . will affect group leadership and should be considered in the training of group workers. (Schindler-Rainman, 1981, p. 171)

As is referenced above, this introductory paragraph from Eva Schindler-Rainman's article "Training Task-Group Leaders" appeared in 1981 in the *Journal for Specialists in Group Work*. What was true in 1981 is only accentuated and intensified some 15 years hence. Let us review just a few examples.

Vast and continuous technological changes are causing unprecedented effects of substantial proportion in social values, as predicted, and in work, productivity, social interaction, and community life. Advances realized through computing and information processing have led to quantum leaps forward in the productivity of worker and work site alike, to global communication, and to personal entertainment options bordering on the fantastic.

Organizational life is changing significantly. Multilayered, hierarchical structures are quickly being reengineered and replaced with flatter, more streamlined designs. Likewise, organizational leadership is in transition as it changes from more authoritarian, top-down models to collaborative, team-based approaches wherein employees assume shared participation and leadership roles.

Multicultural diversity represents a societal value-wave change. With it, comes a developing appreciation for the richness of cultural differences that reflect the variety of cultures evident in contemporary American society. Aspects of this evolving diversity are the feminization of the work place, the validity of cooperation as well as competition, of the group and family as well as the individual, and of differing world views within a global marketplace.

These and other transitions have not come easily, however. Economic shifts into the information age have meant that legions of workers have been displaced at enormous financial and personal cost. Organizational reengineering has accounted for considerable job stress and related illness, as well as substantial unemployment. Multicultural diversity, a critically important goal for contemporary society, is a difficult value change for many to accept, and it has contributed to hostility and conflict within many communities and work sites. Among other appellations for it, the 1990's have been dubbed the "decade of dysfunction," marked by appalling and unacceptable levels of abuse, violence, and illness (Conyne, 1994b).

The Need for Effective Task Group Leadership

As the ASGW Training Standards state, "Much work in contemporary Western society is accomplished through group endeavor" (p. 14). Many of the sweeping and accelerated changes we quickly reviewed above are associated with task groups. The emphasis on teamwork within organizations is dependent on effective group functioning. Interactions of culturally diverse individuals and groups within communities and on the job can be enhanced through effectively organized and delivered task group activities. Organizations charged with downsizing and/or moving to install group-based innovations, such as Total Quality Management, can benefit substantially from skilled task group leaders and from members who are able to interact well in group settings. Employees displaced through job redesign can be helped through effective outplacement group services to reconfigure their employment readiness.

Task groups are usually developed to achieve either of two broad purposes: (a) to serve organizational needs, through vehicles such as committees, task forces, delegate assemblies, and administrative groups of various kinds; or (b) to serve client or member needs, through means such as teams, treatment conferences, and social action groups (Toseland & Rivas, 1994). In general, counselors will find themselves working most frequently in task groups that are formed to address client needs, but not exclusively so. For instance, counselors with task group expertise are increasingly being called upon to help improve program planning and evaluation within organizations. In either case, whether the task group is centered on organizational or client issues, the central processes of task groups deal with decision making and problem solving (Fatout & Rose, 1995). Learning groups formed within community centers and spiritual groups that are created within churches illustrate how task groups can be used to serve client needs by informing, developing strengths, countering anomie, and addressing critical social and political issues. Let us briefly describe study circles, which are one positive way that task groups are being operationalized in communities across the country.

Study circles (e.g., Christensen, 1983; Oliver, 1987; Study Circles Resource Center, 1990), which are intentionally democratic small group meetings of citizens, have a long history in this nation and abroad. Members voluntarily come together to discuss a critical issue facing their community or organization. Study circle discussions are facilitated by a trained person. The discussions informally follow a series of group discussion steps which generally include introductions, ground rules, discussion of personal connection to the selected issue, exchanging a range of views, discussion and deliberation, summary and common ground, and evaluation and next steps. Focal issues and related content discussed in study circles address anything of particular interest to a community. The Study Circles Resource Center, for example, has prepared content materials appropriate for stimulating discussion on pressing social and political topics such as racism and race relations, violence, homelessness, sexual harassment, welfare reform, the environment, and others.

Significantly, and consistent with good group work practice, the Study Circles Resource Center advocates that one vital function of the study circle leader is to stay aware of and assist the group process. Their handbook for training study circle discussion organizers, leaders, and participants (Study Circles Resource Center, 1993) provides a valuable and pragmatic basic primer in discussion group leadership, how to form these groups in a community or organization, and how group participants can best involve themselves in order to promote both an effective discussion and to deepen their own understanding of the issue under consideration. Study circles represent a valuable way that task group leadership is being employed at the grass roots level of American society to improve understanding and to generate positive change. They illustrate one approach for implementing effective task group leadership and membership to achieve both personal and societal change.

In general, however, to what extent are task groups being led effectively? As one way to answer this question, consider for a moment the various task groups with which you have been, and are, personally involved. Thinking of the major spheres of your life may assist you in identifying these groups: work, school, neighborhood and community, religious worship, politics, professional associations, recreation, general leisure, volunteer involvements, and so on. Our guess is that you will be surprised, if not amazed, at the extent of your connection with a number of task groups.

Now take your thinking one step forward. Consider the effectiveness of each of these task groups. How well are goals being met? What is the quality of task group functioning? How competent are the leaders? Are resources being used well? How satisfied are you with your participation and with that of others in the group?

Next, we invite you to imagine how the functioning and overall effectiveness of these task groups might be improved. Can you identify some specific strategies for change? What could a trained task group leader do differently? How could trained task group leaders be connected with these groups, for example, through consultation and training? Is your counselor education program training students to lead task groups effectively?

Finally, if these groups were improved, what could they then do better? Pull out your crystal ball and envision what more fully functioning task groups could accomplish.

This brief, informal personal survey of your task group experience may serve to connect you with the ubiquitous role of task groups in our society, how inconsistently they often function, and how they can be improved through more competent leadership. An urgent need for competent task group leadership exists throughout all levels of organized social functioning. This need provides significant work opportunities for well-prepared counselors.

All task groups would benefit from skilled leadership and membership. Unfortunately, leaders frequently associated with such groups are glaringly deficient in the awareness, knowledge, skills, and experience needed to function effectively. As a consequence, much of the group endeavor so evident in contemporary Western society fails to positively address the significant societal needs being faced. Well-trained, effectively functioning task group leaders are sorely needed. Also in demand are consultants who can help task groups to correct or to enhance their present functioning.

The ASGW Task/Work Group Training Standards

As with the other specializations, we have organized the task group training standards into the same five clusters. A discussion of each cluster follows, and we have cited curricular examples where possible. We have drawn from curricular experiences at the University of Cincinnati for a large percentage of these illustrations, a fact which reflects the existing dearth of materials submitted in this area by respondents to our survey.

STANDARDS CLUSTER 1

Teaching the Definition of Task Groups

The individual standards included in this cluster consist of three knowledge standards. They are the following:

- K-1: Identify organizational dynamics pertinent to task/work groups.

- K-4: Describe standard discussion methodologies appropriate to task/work groups.

- K-7: List consultation principles and approaches appropriate to task/work groups.

Our survey results suggest that counselor education programs are providing relatively little formalized training in task group leadership. This area, then, appears to need development. Occasionally, we found a component of a group course focusing on task groups; for example, at the University of Maine at Orono one such course includes a very clear discussion of task groups and other types of groups as identified in the ASGW Training Standards.

The ASGW Training Standards for task group leadership describe the specialist as being

> . . . able to assist groups such as task forces, committees, planning groups, community organizations, discussion groups, study circles, learning groups, and other similar groups to correct or develop their functioning. The focus is on the application of group dynamics principles and processes to improve practice and the accomplishment of identified work goals. (p. 14)

Defining Training Issues

Thinking interdependently and systemically. Task groups seldom stand alone but are almost always connected to a larger system, such as a school, mental health center, or company. For instance, members of a task group within a mental health agency that has been formed to create a strategic plan for agency review must be concerned about the group itself and with how it fits within the total agency. Therefore, it is necessary for leaders to help group members to view the group as being connected to, influenced by, and influencing that larger system. At the same time, the leader must help the group to develop independently within the larger context. Balancing these sets of demands requires an adroitness uncommon to other forms of group leadership.

Recognizing the important role of performance. Individual and interpersonal growth or change are not the central missions of task groups. While holding member participation and satisfaction as important, the student needs to learn how to elevate the attainment of performance outcomes, in relation to performance expectations, to a heightened position. This is so because any task group exists to produce a product, achieve a specific set of goals, or in some other way to positively affect the "bottom line." This shift, so necessary in task group leadership, is of lesser significance in other forms of group work.

Including problem-solving interventions. Task group leadership in many ways involves the solving of problems being faced by both the group and the larger system to which it belongs. Salient questions include the following: What is the problem? What can be done about it? Of all the possible strategies, which shall be tried? How will this strategy be implemented? How will we know if it worked? It is essential to include these problem-solving steps in task group leadership, along with an appropriate blend of more familiar group process interventions. With the exception of psychoeducation, other group work types typically do not involve such attention to problem-solving interventions.

Developing a facility in weighing intervention choices. Task group leaders need to develop a facility in weighing intervention choices and then making the proper best fit with the group situation being faced. These intervention choices result from an intentional intersection of the type, level, and function intervention domains. Each of these domains can best be understood as whirring in space like a computer disk, under the control of the group leader, and affording multiple options for intervention selection. The intersection of the three whirring disks represents the application chosen for the current situation. This facility for weighing and selecting intervention choices, although very important for the task group leader, is not unique to these types of groups but, we believe, is germane to all group work.

Articulating core values. As Schwartz (1994) has emphasized, the task group leader (or "facilitator," in his lexicon) bases interventions on three core values. These are the core values: (a) to be sure to work with group members to produce and understand alll relevant information, (b) to assist members in arriving at free and informed choices, and (c) to help members to become internally committed to choices that are selected. The task group leader, like other group work leaders in the counseling profession, do not coerce members or make decisions for them. Task group leadership is completely consistent with the overarching professional ethics of the counseling profession.

Instructional Considerations

Given the changes in society that we illustrated at the beginning of this discussion of task groups, Schindler-Rainman (1981) presented several areas that task group work preparation needs to address. In total, they account for seven significant functions that task group leaders need to be able to perform skillfully.

To help the task group to make decisions. Making decisions is a vital part of task group functioning. Responsibility for decision making may reside with the chairperson of a board of directors, a staff group, or any other collection of people who are charged with policy-making responsibilities. Effective decision making in task groups involves brainstorming about alternatives, using subgroups, setting goals, using techniques for determining priorities, and helping members to recognize the consequences of decisions that are made.

To deal with and use differences. As heterogeneity and diversity become increasingly a part of task groups, leaders must learn effective ways to help groups cope with and utilize these differences. Task group leaders must be able to work with others to harness the variety of resources present and to find strategies for managing conflict and impasses. Employing structured experiences such as the fishbowl technique and other dialogue aids can be very facilitative.

To use feedback and guidance to improve the work of the group. Participants of task groups and their leaders need to know how they are doing. Keeping a group on task and relevant to the purposes being addressed is very important. Being aware of how well the differing resources of each member are being incorporated is empowering information. Therefore, finding methods for generating feedback in order to help the group be productive is essential to success. Stopping the group action along the way to invite such feedback can be of help, as can routinely using postmeeting reaction periods. Once information is obtained, it is critically important that the task group develop the capacity to consider and act on it.

To mobilize and use resources needed for the task. How to get the job done well is an important practical question. Task group leaders need to develop ways to identify what resources are needed to accomplish the task, which group members possess what resources, and what is missing and how to acquire it. Once resources are known, then matching task assignments to individuals becomes an essential skill.

To develop, clarify, and act on goals. Goalless task groups are tantamount to failure. Of all group work types, the task group must produce long-term and short-term goals that are specific, realistic, feasible, and measurable. The leader must be able to assist this goal-setting process through helping members to envision the future, to use such techniques as force-field analysis, to help translate goals into achievable action steps, and to enlist member input and generate member support along the way. Clarity in goal setting is a motivating process.

To individualize member abilities, needs, and skills in relation to the group. Task group leaders must be keenly aware of individual, interpersonal, and group process in order to promote appropriate relationships and contributions to the group. Each member varies from the other in terms of interests, skills, energy, work commitment, time available, and life demands. These legitimate individual differences need to be recognized and interwoven into a pattern of connectedness with others and with the group itself.

To share leadership. Task group leaders work best when they share leadership appropriately with members. This can occur formally through designated roles, such as coleader or committee chair, or it also can occur more informally through distributed leadership, where members begin to assume selected leadership functions naturally.

To balance process and content. Even though the task group is focused on goal accomplishment, the leader must be vigilant about balancing process with content. Inattention to human relations and problem solving processes is sure to reduce the task group to a spiritless and, most likely, ineffective exercise.

Characteristics of Task Group Leadership

Performance emphasis. Of course, task groups and personal growth groups share much in common (Conyne, 1989). This is perhaps an obvious statement since group leadership across all these groups is predicated on mastery of the core competencies. In addition, task groups, as well as other groups, tend to develop generally in similar directions over time as group processes and member roles are consistent. However, in other ways, task groups are unique in their orientation and emphases.

The chief goal of task groups is to meet organizational or community performance goals (Katzenbach & Smith, 1993). Task groups are established in order to get something done to explicitly benefit a larger system, such as a neighborhood council, or an organization, such as a counseling center or corporation, of which the task group is a part. Thus, task groups are very purposive in their creation and direction, operated to effect tangible performance goals that are important to a connected and larger system (Hackman, 1987; Schwartz, 1994).

To emphasize external performance in task groups is not to suggest that the personal and interpersonal goals and experiences of members are unimportant. However, the realization and satisfaction of members' personal growth agenda are always in the service of accomplishing group-level goals. Group accomplishment, in turn, is directly associated with meeting designated external needs and performance expectations.

Task group performance outcomes can be attained in any of four general areas: (a) practice—improving the service delivery to customers or clients through technical support, resources, and improved working conditions for staff; (b) procedures and policy—developing better conceptions and ways to organize and conduct business; (c) product—producing new or improved goods and services consistent with the organization's mission and customer needs; and (d) people— enhancing the awareness, knowledge, and skills of staff. Task groups, then, function in relation to goal accomplishment in one or more of these areas.

The *team* is a unique form of task group that is the center of much attention in the contemporary work place (Muriel, 1993; Reddy, 1994). In addition to emphasizing performance goals, the team also is dedicated to developing a common vision, building mutual commitment and responsibility, and taking interdependent action (Carr, 1992; Robbins, 1993).

STANDARDS CLUSTER 2

Teaching Pregroup Preparation in Task Groups

Two knowledge standards operationalize teaching pregroup preparation in task groups:

- K-2: Describe community dynamics pertinent to task/work groups.

- K-3: Identify political dynamics pertinent to task/work groups.

Instructional Methods

Developing competency in understanding and using community and political dynamics can be achieved through taking appropriate courses in sociology, community psychology, management, and organization development. The Task Group Performance Model (Conyne, Rapin, & Rand, 1995; in press), which we discuss in this chapter, illustrates the important relationship of task group leadership to outside-the-group dynamics.

All Counseling students at the University of Cincinnati take the course Program Development and Evaluation. In addition to learning and applying in a group a coherent program development and evaluation model (Craig, 1978), which will be discussed further under Standards Cluster 4, students also learn how to consider the problem situation within the context of a larger organization. Specific attention is given to analyzing the organization's capacity to change, understanding processes of organizational change, anticipating problems in introducing the plan within the organization, and preparing a strategy for getting the plan accepted. Techniques learned include force field analysis, analyzing characteristics of management systems, and the change process of unfreezing, changing, and refreezing (Lewin, 1951; Lippitt, Watson & Westley, 1958). This kind of study helps students to understand and find ways to apply important organizational, community, and political dynamics in relation to task group work.

STANDARDS CLUSTER 3

Teaching Therapeutic Dynamics and Leader Skills in Task Groups

For the standards cluster on teaching therapeutic dynamics and leader skills, there are eight skill standards:

- S-1: Focus and maintain attention on task and work issues.

- S-2: Obtain goal clarity in a task/work group.

- S-3: Conduct a personally selected task/work group model appropriate to the age and clientele of the group leader's specialty area(s) (e.g., school counseling).

- S-4: Mobilize energies toward a common goal in task/work groups.

- S-5: Implement group decision-making methods in task/work groups.

- S-6: Manage conflict in task/work groups.

- S-7: Blend the predominant task focus with appropriate attention to human relations factors in task/work groups.

- S-8: Sense and use larger organizational and political dynamics in task/work groups.

Task Group Leader Intervention Choices

Task group leaders need to keep performance expectations and related goals firmly in mind, and they need to help members to do the same. Their within-group functioning can be thought of as an interrelated series of intervention choices. This conception is analogous to that of Cohen and Smith (1976a, 1976b), who proposed a critical incident model of intervention choices for leaders of personal growth groups. Conyne, Rapin, and Rand (1995, in press) adapted the critical incident approach to task group leadership through their Task Group Performance Model. This conceptual and skill-building model in task group leadership is generally compatible with leadership models appearing in the management, human relations, and organization literature (e.g., the Group-Effectiveness Model of Schwartz, 1994), but it is thought to be the first one developed specifically for counseling students.

Task group intervention choices, depicted within the large circle contained in Figure 1, emerge from three domains: (a) intervention type—a combination of problem-solving or of group process; (b) intervention level—either individual, interpersonal, group, or organizational; (c) and intervention function—a combination of caring, meaning, motivating, or managing. A task group leader considers making a leader intervention within an ongoing group situation by intentionally weighing the dynamic possibilities existing between the presenting group situation and the three domains of intervention type–

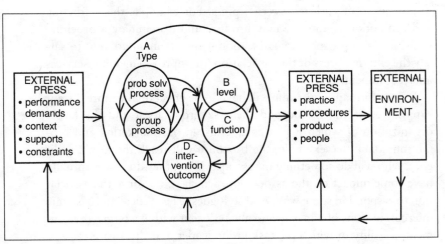

Figure 1.   Flow of Events in an Intervention Choice

level–function. The leader intervention choice results from a perceived best fit, which is represented in the Figure by the term "intervention outcome" (at letter *D*). In turn, this intervention outcome will affect subsequent group interaction and productivity, a result signifying the importance of systemic influence in task group interventions. This systemic factor also can be seen in the other ingredients of the Task Group Performance Model: (a) external press, (b) performance outcomes, and (c) external environment. We have already mentioned the importance of performance outcomes to task groups. Further, because task groups are usually created to solve existing problems or to plan for future actions, these groups cannot be viewed as existing independently. Rather, task groups are part of a relevant larger environment whose press is significant.

For instance, in considering the factor "external press," a marketing and promotion committee may be formed by an association to reach certain goals. The committee (the task group), then, is at the service of the larger association. The press of the association is illustrated through demands and expectations it places on the committee, by the resources and supports it provides, by the constraints imposed (such as deadlines), and by its overall cultural and political context.

As the task group works, its performance outcomes are of vital importance. These performance outcomes, as we mentioned above, can be in several forms, including practices, procedures, products, and people (e.g., training regimens). What the task group produces needs to be consistent with its external press. For example, the marketing and promotion committee may produce and disseminate a brochure to present and prospective association members in an attempt to satisfy the external press of the association for improved member services and recruitment.

Any performance outcome will have some effect on the more distant external environment, beyond the task group itself and the larger organization of which it is a part. Thus, in our marketing and promotion committee example, the brochure will reach the target audience, who will do something in response. What they do will eventually have some impact on the association, which could cause the association to respond in some way. And so it goes: The cyclical and systemic interconnections of a task group always occur within a larger environment, a reality of which the task group leader must be aware.

Instructional Methods

At the University of Cincinnati, the beginning course in Group Theory and Process includes reading in task groups and a complete course meeting (2½ hours) is devoted to the topic. In terms of readings, students are assigned Conyne's (1989) *How Personal Growth and Task Groups Work*, and Bradford's (1976) *Making Meetings Work*. Much of the entire course is built around an adaptation of Hill's (1969) *Learning Through Discussion*, which has been recently revised and extended by Rabow, Charness, Kipperman, and Radcliffe-Vasile (1994). The "Core Group Work Training Method: Personal-Learning Group" (Conyne, 1994a) incorporates a hybrid form of personal growth-task groups, called the "Personal-Learning Group," to train students in the core leadership skills of group work. This Personal-Learning Group approach, described briefly in Chapter Three on core competencies, will be detailed more completely below.

1. *GOALS*
   a. To provide a method for training in core group work skills that can be used within the introductory group work course in counselor education programs.
   b. To provide a training method that can develop group work leadership skills and provide group member experience.
   c. To provide a training method that can increase group work competencies *and* learning of assigned academic content.
   d. To provide a training method that can accomplish the above goals and that responds positively to ASGW ethical guidelines related to dual issues.

2. *GROUP SIZE:* Each Personal-Learning group has five to eight participants.

3. *TIME REQUIRED:* Approximately 13 hours.

4. *MATERIALS*
   a. Individual handouts:
       i. "ASGW Core Group Work Skills List"
      ii. "Group Development Graph" (Pfeiffer & Jones, 1980a)
     iii. "What to Look for in Groups" (Hanson, 1969)

      iv. "Group Leader Characteristics Worksheet"

      v. "P-L Group Steps" (adapted from Hill, 1969)

      vi. Any relevant, short practice article (e.g., from "The Cutting Edge," *Together*).

      vii. "Reactions to Group Discussion Sheet" (Hill, 1969)

      viii. Assigned, stimulating group work readings (e.g., DeLucia, Coleman, & Jensen-Scott, 1992, "Multicultural group work," *JSGW, 17*).

5. *PHYSICAL SETTING*: Classroom large enough to accommodate formation and comfortable operation of as many groups as needed, with eight in each group.

6. *PROCESS: (60 MIN) MICROLAB ORIENTATION*

   a. At the first meeting of the course, include a microlab of forming groups in order to become acquainted and to show how group processes can be used to accomplish goals:

      i. (5 min) Students write in large letters on a piece of paper their names and a one-word description of themselves; they tape the paper to their chest and move about the room, nonverbally looking at each other's signs.

      ii. (5 min) Students are asked after 5 minutes to form dyads by choosing someone whom they do not know and who appears different from them in some way. The dyads discuss for 5 minutes "Why I am in graduate school" or some other fairly safe topic.

      iii. (10 min) Students are asked to form quads in any way they want while seeking to maximize diversity, and then to discuss for 10 minutes "Why you are in the Counseling Program" or some other fairly safe topic.

      iv. (15 min) Students are asked to form octets in any way they want while seeking to maximize diversity, and then to discuss for 15 minutes "What are your goals for this course" or some such slightly more personal question.

      v. (15 min) Small groups are asked to spend 15 minutes discussing their reactions to the microlab experience.

      vi. (10 min) Instructor facilitates a total class discussion of the experience and emphasizes group process.

7. *PROCESS: (60 MIN) CORE GROUP WORK SKILLS DEMONSTRATION*
   a. (5 min) Instructor asks for eight student volunteers to form a circle for a group demonstration.
   b. (30 min) Instructor leads a group discussion for 30 minutes and attempts to illustrate as many of the core group work skills as possible. A topic is suggested for the discussion, such as "Select a person in your life who served a valuable mentor role and then describe to group members the mentor's finest characteristic."
   c. (10 min) Instructor concludes by spending 10 minutes helping the members to process the experience.
   d. (15 min) Instructor distributes the handout "ASGW Core Group Work Skills List" and engages all students in a discussion of the skills they saw demonstrated.

8. *PROCESS: (30 MIN) GROUP DEVELOPMENT*
   a. (30 min) Instructor distributes the "Group Development Graph," and conducts a minilecture on how groups generally develop. Emphasis is placed on the relationships between task and personal relations functions over time.

9. *PROCESS: (140 MIN) OBSERVATION OF GROUP PROCESSES*
   a. (30 min) Instructor distributes "What to Look for in Groups" and conducts a minilecture on the nine processes presented. Application examples are both sought and provided.
   b. (5 min) Instructor asks for eight student volunteers to participate in a group fishbowl demonstration. The others sit in an outer circle to function as group process observers and feedback givers.
   c. (10 min) Instructor distributes to the group members the "Group Leader Characteristics Worksheet" (or some similar exercise). Members are asked to read the instructions and to begin the individual rankings. While the members are working, the instructor assigns group processes from the "What to Look for in Groups" handout to observers. They are asked to watch for that particular process and to be prepared to give feedback, when asked, by following the guidelines of describing (not judging) and giving immediate (not delayed) feedback.

   d. (25 min) Members are instructed to spend 25 minutes com-
      pleting the task while observers make notes.
   e. (60 min) Instructor calls time at the end of 30 minutes. Mem-
      bers are asked to give any comments about experience or learn-
      ings (10 min). Observers are then asked, one at a time, to
      provide feedback based on their assignment and its application
      to the group (30 min). Members respond, as appropriate
      (20 min).
   f. (10 min) Instructor highlights and summarizes group pro-
      cesses.

10. *PROCESS: (140 MIN) PERSONAL-LEARNING (P-L) GROUP
    STEPS*
    a. First Session
       i. (30 min) Instructor distributes the "P-L Group Steps"
          sheet and the "Reactions to Group Discussion Sheet"
          and describes each step for a group discussion:
          (1) PREPARATION: Students are asked to thoroughly
              read and prepare the assigned reading material. Us-
              ing the headings of theme/subthemes, analysis, in-
              tegration, and application is useful.
          (2) STEP 1 (5 min): Members identify the main theme
              of an author's message and, within it, what sub-
              topic to discuss.
          (3) STEP 2 (15 min): Members discuss the subtheme
              and analyze the author's message (not their reac-
              tions).
          (4) STEP 3 (5 min): Members are asked how the ma-
              terial relates to their own experience or to other
              readings and how they might be able to apply learn-
              ings.
          (5) STEP 4 (5 min): Members are asked to evaluate
              group discussion by using the "Reactions to Group
              Discussion Sheet."
      ii. (5 min) Students are informed that none of their par-
          ticipation in the P-L group is evaluated by the instruc-
          tor; only their attendance is noted. Materials that are
          read can be tested for mastery, if desired.

    iii. (10 min) Instructor emphasizes the role of group process in successfully conducting a P-L group. A P-L group facilitator needs to use core group work skills, be aware of group development, and use observation of group processes in moving through the P-L group steps.

    iv. (10 min) Instructor emphasizes that the P-L group method is intended to integrate the process of group membership and leadership with the group work content that was read and prepared for discussion.

    v. (15 min) Instructor asks for eight student volunteers, drawn from across the separate groups formed during the microlab, to form a demonstration group. These members are asked to read a one-page article relevant to group work (e.g., "The Cutting Edge," from *Together*).

    vi. (35 min) Instructor demonstrates the role of P-L group facilitator by conducting a 35-minute meeting that follows the P-L steps and incorporates core group work skills; instructor calls attention to group development (early, in this case) and appropriate group processes.

    vii. (20 min) Instructor leads a total group discussion of the demonstration by emphasizing group process and the P-L group steps.

    viii. (15 min) Instructor asks students within their groups of eight to pair, in anticipation of the pairs functioning as cofacilitators of a P-L group discussion. Instructor then asks the pairs to schedule themselves over the next four class sessions to conduct a 35-minute P-L group meeting. They are encouraged to meet before and after their assigned meeting for preparation and review, respectively.

b. Within the next four classes, the following 90-minute schedule applies: In each of the next four class sessions, the P-L group implementation schedule (based on a two-group model) is as follows:

    i. Group A: Meets for 35 minutes and follows the P-L steps.

  ii. Group B: Observes and gives 10 minutes of feedback.
  iii. - - - (Break) - - -
  iv. Group B: Meets for 35 minutes and follows the P-L
   steps.
  v. Group A: Observes and gives 10 minutes of feedback.
Content to be read should be manageable within the time period for the discussion (which is fairly brief), related centrally to group work (and testable), and stimulating. Other material can be addressed through other instructional methods for the balance of each class session.

Group work in college teaching. The "Using Group Work in College Teaching" workshop (Langer, 1994) at Eastern Michigan University presents strategies for how professors can employ cooperative learning through group work. Langer draws comparisons between typical classroom groups and cooperative classroom groups.

  The typical group is homogeneous, composed of students who are similar in style, gender, interest, ethnicity, age, and so on. It emphasizes independent functioning and goal attainment. One leader is appointed to direct the action. If cooperation is desired, students are asked simply to cooperate. The teacher's role is to observe, interrupt to solve problems, or answer questions. The clear top priority is to accomplish a task.

  By contrast, Langer describes the cooperative group. It is designed to be heterogeneous, formed to maximize variety and diversity. Positive interdependence is stressed, with the group itself being responsible for mutual goal setting, developing interconnected roles, production, accountability, and rewards. Shared leadership is promoted, group size is maintained at two to five students, with eye-to-eye and knee-to-knee interaction arranged within a circular configuration. Because cooperation is an important goal, students are actually trained in social skills necessary to perform cooperatively through a structured process involving definition, teaching, practicing, observing, and processing. Note that these training steps are highly similar to those used in psychoeducation group preparation. The teacher's role is to train and to encourage group problem-solving. Finally, the top priority in cooperative groups is the combination of task and social skill accomplishment.

Johnson and Johnson (1994) have further specified the teacher's role in cooperative group learning as involving four main set of responsibilities: (a) make decisions, (b) set the lesson, (c) monitor and intervene, and (d) evaluate and process.

Each of these responsibilities will be detailed below, because they are very relevant for counselor educators seeking either to teach task group skills or to use task group training formats in their teaching of group work. These are the responsibilities:

Make decisions:

- Specify academic and collaborative objectives.
- Determine group size, of from two to five.
- Assign students heterogeneously to groups.
- Arrange the room so that groups can meet in circles.
- Plan learning activities carefully to fit goals.
- Assign roles such as recorder or observer.

Set the lesson:

- Explain the academic task and teach anything in advance that students may need to know.
- Build norm of positive interdependence by using concept of "sink or swim together."
- Structure individual accountability, to instill personal responsibility for learning and helping the group.
- Structure intergroup cooperation across separate groups.
- Explain success criteria to be used.
- Specify expected behaviors, including listening, caring, contributing, helping, and asking for help.
- Train collaborative skills one at a time by using defining, teaching, practicing, observing, and processing: consider skills such as encouraging, summarizing, and praising.

Monitor and intervene:

- Arrange face-to-face interaction.
- Monitor students' behavior by circulating to check their understanding, giving immediate feedback, and positively reinforcing good use of group skills.

- Provide task assistance by clarifying, elaborating, or backing-up to instruct again.
- Intervene to improve collaborative skills by making suggestions, asking students to problem-solve around group problems, retraining.

Evaluate and process:

- Evaluate student learning and give feedback.
- Process group work functioning by individuals, small groups, and/or whole class.
- Provide closure, for learning, integration, application.

A task group component that has been used to acquaint students with task groups follows.

Group Skills Workshop: Developing Core and Task Group Work Skills (Conyne & Rapin, 1994, in press). This workshop was briefly described in the core competencies section of this book. It was developed by Conyne and Rapin and presented both to students in class and at the Second National ASGW Group Work Conference, held in St. Petersburg Beach, Florida (1994a); it is revised and published in its entirety in Conyne and Rapin (in press). A portion of the workshop contents is presented below.

1. *GOALS*
   a. To illustrate selected *core* group work skill competencies, as identified in the ASGW Training Standards:
      i. Encourage participation of group members.
      ii. Clarify and summarize group member statements.
      iii. Observe and identify group process events.
   b. To illustrate selected *task* group work skill competencies, as identified in the ASGW Training Standards:
      i. Obtain goal clarity.
      ii. Implement group decision-making methods.
      iii. Manage conflict.

2. *GROUP SIZE:* One group of six to eight participants. Additional participants can be assigned as observers, asked to give feedback at designated portions of the workshop.

3. *TIME REQUIRED:* Approximately 3 hours.

4. *MATERIALS*
   a. Individual handouts developed for this exercise:
      i. "About the Decisions Committee: Definition and Context Sheet"
      ii. "Meeting Directions Sheet"
      iii. "Individual Member Role Descriptions"
      iv. "Group Observer and Feedback Sheet: Parts 1 and 2"
      v. "Training Standards Excerpts Sheet"
   b. Newsprint and felt-tip markers for each group
   c. Masking tape
   d. Paper and pencils
   e. Name tags for role designation

5. *PHYSICAL SETTING:* Table and chairs for the working group. Room large enough to accommodate the number of observers, who may sit in an outer circle to facilitate ease of observation.

6. *PROCESS: (180 MIN) GROUP SKILLS ACTIVITY*
   a. (15 min) The facilitator provides a workshop overview and summary of the ASGW Training Standards in relation to core- and task-group work skills.
   b. (5 min) The facilitator forms a group of six to eight and asks members to assemble around the table; observers are asked to assemble in an outer circle.
   c. (5 min) The facilitator hands out the "About the Decisions Committee: Definition and Context Sheet" and briefly discusses its contents.
   d. (5 min) The facilitator hands out the "Meeting Directions Sheet" and asks members to read its contents.
   e. (5 min) The facilitator hands out roles to each member, asks members to become acquainted with their assigned role, and then asks them to write their role designation on a name tag, which members then wear.
   f. (10 min) The facilitator hands out pencils and the "Group Observer and Feedback Sheet, Part 1" and discusses how the observers can use the sheet during the exercise; observers are assigned to either core- or task-group work skill competencies.

g. (30 min) Once all the materials are read, the facilitator instructs the task group members to follow the directions contained in Step iv above and conducts a brief meeting. Members
may use newsprint, marker, and tape to post their work.

h. (30 min) The facilitator asks the group observers to give feedback and then facilitates a discussion, highlighting core- and
task-group work issues they noted on the "Group Observation
and Feedback Sheet, Part 1"; observers then perform the role
of "external consultant" to offer recommendations for improving group effectiveness.

i. (30 min) The facilitator instructs the group to "pick up where
it was" and continue its work as it seeks to implement the
core- and task-group work competencies selected for this exercise (see "Goals" above).

j. (30 min) Group observers provide feedback, drawing from
their notes on the "Group Observation and Feedback Sheet,
Part 2" and guided by the facilitator; any final recommendations to the external consultant are provided.

k. (15 min) The facilitator passes out the "Training Standards
Excerpts Sheet" and conducts both an instructional and summary session.

Examples of observation and feedback forms used with this training
workshop are provided on 145 and 146.

STANDARDS CLUSTER 4

Teaching Research and Evaluation in Task Groups

A single standard encompasses the necessary knowledge for group
workers in the area of research and evaluation:

• K-6: Identify program development and evaluation models appropriate for task/work groups.

Instructional Methods

As mentioned above, Program Development and Evaluation is a required course for Counseling students at the University of Cincinnati.
Although not a part of the three-course group work sequence, this
course focuses on learning how to apply a program development and

GROUP OBSERVATION AND FEEDBACK SHEET

Use this sheet to assist your observation and feedback for the Group Skills Workshop. Jot down any specific observations in the appropriate spaces. At the meeting's end, write a brief summary statement suitable for feedback and include any recommendations for meeting improvement.

Core group work skills	Skills demonstrated by:	
	Leader	Members
• Encourage participation of group members		
• Clarify and summarize		
• Group processes (e.g., influence, atmosphere, norms, membership)		

evaluation model (Craig, 1978) to both individual and to group situations. Students are placed in classroom task groups. Attention is given to their team development first. Then, as they read the program development and evaluation model, they are led to apply its six steps to an organizational case situation as a group. They learn how to

- define the problem
- set the objective
- choose among alternative strategies
- prepare for implementation
- design the evaluation
- use the evaluation

GROUP OBSERVATION AND FEEDBACK SHEET

Use this sheet to assist your observation and feedback for the Group Skills Workshop. Jot down any specific observations in the appropriate spaces. At the meeting's end, write a brief summary statement suitable for feedback and include any recommendations for meeting improvement.

Task group work skills	Skills demonstrated by:	
	Leader	Members
• Goal clarity		
• Group decision-making (problem-solving)		
• Conflict management		

GENERAL SUMMARY OF THE MEETING, WITH ANY RECOMMENDATIONS:

These steps are applied by each small task group against the same case situation (e.g., interracial difficulties in a school). In addition, specific attention is given to the group dynamics emerging from their work. Typical is a press which stresses task accomplishment to the minimization of maintenance or process issues. Corrective feedback and selective consultation from the instructor allow the groups to recreate a desired balance between task and process (Donigian &

Hulse-Killacky, 1995). This improvement facilitates task group functioning and reinforces important group work principles.

As students learn the program development and evaluation model and begin to apply it within a task group, they realize a significant advancement in their overall task group membership and leadership competencies. In effect, they are learning how to apply problem solving in a group as they also attend to group process. Effective task group leadership demands that practitioners be able to blend problem-solving skills with process skills, as was pointed out in the Task Group Performance Model. As we learned through our survey research, attention to problem solving in group work preparation is an area that seems largely neglected in counselor education programs.

STANDARDS CLUSTER 5

Teaching the Ethical Practice of Task Groups

Likewise, a single standard defines the requirements for knowledge of ethical practice in task group work:

• K-5: Identify specific ethical considerations in working with task/work groups.

Instructional Methods

The nature of task groups introduces special ethical considerations for group leaders. These considerations flow from the unique purpose of the task group, which is to attain work goals rather than individual or interpersonal growth. This purpose stands out from that found in any other group work specialization. In psychoeducation, counseling, and psychotherapy groups, the purpose centers on helping members to reach personal or interpersonal goals, not work goals.

Yet, task groups obviously accomplish work goals through members interacting together. Leaders of task groups mobilize group dynamics and member transactions in the service of production. In the process, members are asked to become involved with each other, to share ideas and concerns, to give and get feedback, and to take risks. All of these behaviors are essential to the effective functioning of task groups.

One particular ethical dilemma that leaders of task groups face is how to combine an emphasis on task and work goals with the desired personal involvement of members. Keeping clear that member sharing and feedback, for example, are encouraged for their enhancement of work production is both a challenge and a necessity. Helping members to understand that task groups are human endeavors without being counseling or therapy is sometimes a delicate art. Allowing members to express feelings in the task group without fear of reprisal is another form of ethical challenge unique to task groups.

This fear of reprisal links to a second major form of ethical consideration in task groups. This one stems from the relationship of the task group to its larger environment, usually a parent organization of some sort which has caused the group to be created or sponsors it in some way. As we described earlier, task groups generally do not stand alone but exist in order to meet performance demands set, at least initially, by others; for example, a department is required by the corporation to produce a 5-year strategic plan which is nestled within the overall mission of the corporation. This systemic relationship pressures the task group members to function in ways that are ethical not only within the group's own boundaries but also in relating to the parent group. Norms of the group must allow task group members to feel confident that their disclosures within the group will be treated responsibly by all members and not brought outside the group to other colleagues or to superiors. While this kind of concern relates directly to confidentiality in all group work, here it takes on a special edge because of the work nature of the group itself and because it immediately raises issues of employment, worker security, and advancement.

PSYCHOEDUCATION GROUPS

Efficiency has become a critically important criterion for survival and success in contemporary society. Complementing effectiveness and quality concerns, efficiency of service delivery is now a central motivating force. Like all systems, the mental health and educational delivery systems are experiencing external pressures to become more cost efficient. In mental health, health care reform and managed care represent twin sources of such pressure. In education, reduced public funding coupled with continued expectations for optimal services combine to exert a potent force for educational reform in schools at all levels.

Certainly, the four types of group work discussed in this book represent one important response strategy. It is, after all, more cost efficient to work with 10 people in a 2-hour group session than to work with the same 10 people in 10 separate 50-minute sessions.

Kaplan's (1989) observation that there is no possible cost effectiveness when treatment efficacy is reduced is pertinent to the psychoeducation group, which is a form of group work designed to maximize cost efficiency, but not at the expense of effectiveness. When used appropriately, that is, for the right purposes and with the right populations, psychoeducation groups also can be highly effective and of high quality. Indeed, they have become a mainstay in the fields of mental health and education today, just as they occupy an important place within the managed care environment (Hoyt, 1995).

Psychoeducation groups in counseling practice are not new. Rather, they have evolved from group guidance (Gazda, 1984). Group guidance has a long history in the counseling profession. Guidance groups were used and are still appearing in instructional settings, such as classrooms, to reach a large number of participants. Group guidance is known generally as the process of providing to an audience personally relevant information and skills, accompanied by the encouragement of interpersonal discussion and sharing, in order to enhance group members' understanding, development, and decision making (Trotzer, 1980). Group guidance tends to focus on four basic life skills (Trotzer, 1989): (a) interpersonal communication and relationships, (b) fitness and health, (c) problem solving and decision making, and (d) personal identity and life purpose. Regardless of focus, a guidance group emphasizes skill building that members can take away with them from the group setting to apply in their daily lives.

The psychoeducation group is consistent with group guidance. In fact, the ASGW Professional Training Standards for psychoeducation groups links them with group guidance through the title used: "guidance/psychoeducation groups." In addition, psychoeducation groups even more clearly emphasize cognitive, affective, and behavioral skill development through the incorporation of a structured and sequenced set of procedures or exercises within and across group sessions. Careful planning and structuring are integral to these groups, as is harvesting group dynamics skillfully.

Psychoeducation groups are intentionally structured to teach knowledge and skills (Winston, Bonney, Miller, & Dagley, 1988). These groups may be applied in a number ways, such as in social skills and social problem solving (Knoff, 1988); life skills (Botvin & Tortu, 1988; Gazda & Pistole, 1986); focused, short-term groups (Klein, 1985); human relations skills training (Authier & Gustafson, 1976; Clack, 1985); in addressing life themes, life transitions, or life skills (Drum & Knott, 1977; Shaffer & Galinsky, 1974); and values clarification and decision making (Moyse-Steinberg, 1990).

The organization of psychoeducation groups is consistent with six overlapping elements of effective short-term group therapy (Hoyt, 1995):

(a) Brief time limits. As emphasized by Budman and Gurman (1988), these groups are time sensitive, that is, effective and efficient. The length of the group is relative to the problem or need being addressed, but time limits, often expressed as a certain number of sessions, are a central feature.

(b) Member homogeneity. A common, unifying theme characterizes psychoeducation groups, such as a presenting issue, lifestyle, or situation. For example, a group may be formed to develop social skills or to help preteens get ready for teen-age years. Individuals that are likely to present substantial management issues—such as those who show suicide risk or those with active psychosis, significant personality disorders, or characterological impairments—might be excluded from participation.

(c) Focus. Vague, general goals are rejected in favor of specific, delimited, focused goals that are accomplishable within the group. For instance, improved communication between couples or increased understanding of retirement options might provide such a focus.

(d) Quicker cohesion. Member homogeneity in terms of common issues assists the goal of fast-paced cohesion, as does the emphasis of the leader on identifying and linking intermember similarities and interdependent functioning within the group. Cohesion development is given high priority, as is consistent with the principle that it is a precursor to member growth and change in groups (Yalom, 1985).

(e) Here-and-now orientation. Past history is given relatively little time. Attention is accorded to present interactions within the group and to current life situations that fall within the identified theme for the psychoeducation group.

(f) Leader activity. Transference and unstructured interaction within the group are minimized. Instead, the active and direct psychoeducation group leader may often use elements of structuring to stimulate and guide member participation.

For any psychoeducation group following the above general principles to succeed, its purpose, process, and design must be quickly integrated, after the careful planning, shaping, monitoring, and managing provided by the group leader(s) (Ettin, Heiman, & Kopel, 1988). Contrary to much typical understanding and belief, perhaps the most critical success variable in psychoeducation group leadership—as in all other group leadership—is the knowledge and effective application of group development, group process, and group dynamics. In our experience, we have noticed a tendency of those leading psychoeducation groups to elevate content and structure over everything else, almost as if the psychoeducation group were a lecturette or a series of unlinked training episodes. Doing so is a critical mistake, in our estimation, because the very power of the interpersonal situation is vitiated and thus saps the extent of learning that potentially occurs.

At the same time, however, as Ettin et al. (1988) rightfully observe, group dynamics must be meshed appropriately with the choice, order, and method of content and structure presented, and the entire "package" must be linked to the developmental readiness of participants. The discussion below demonstrates how the ASGW Psychoeducation Group Training Standards address the needs of the group leader as a content expert, task organizer, and monitor of group processes.

Psychoeducation Group Training Standards

As defined in the ASGW Professional Training Standards, psychoeducation groups are set within educational and prevention goals. The psychoeducation group work specialist

> seeks to use the group medium to educate group participants who are presently unaffected about a potential threat (such as AIDS), a develop-

mental life event (such as a transition point), or how to cope with an immediate life crisis (such as a suicide of a loved one), with the goal of preventing an array of educational and psychological disturbance from occurring. (p. 14)

The training standards include 11 knowledge competencies and 7 skill competencies. In addition, course work and skills through supervised practice are indicated. As with the other three group work specialties (task group work, group counseling, and group psychotherapy), these competencies, course work, and supervised practice skills are in addition to the core group work competencies previously discussed.

The 18 psychoeducation group knowledge and skill competencies have been organized into the same five clusters used previously: (a) Cluster 1: defining psychoeducation groups; (b) Cluster 2: pregroup preparation; (c) Cluster 3: therapeutic dynamics and leader skills; (d) Cluster 4: research and evaluation; and (e) Cluster 5: ethical practice. Each of the standards clusters will be discussed and illustrated. In addition, to supplement this material, we will provide instructional material drawn from sources other than counselor education programs.

STANDARDS CLUSTER 1

Teaching the Definition of Psychoeducation Groups

The individual standards included in these clusters are the following:

- K-1: Identify the concepts of primary prevention and secondary prevention in psychoeducation groups.

- K-2: Articulate the concept of "at risk" in psychoeducation groups.

- K-4: Develop a knowledge base relevant to the focus of a psychoeducation group intervention.

- K-6: Describe human development theory pertinent to psychoeducation groups.

- K-11: List advantages of guidance/psychoeducation groups and be able to articulate where they are indicated or contraindicated.

Learning Concepts of Prevention and "At Risk"

Psychoeducation refers to the education and training of persons in psychological competencies. Psychoeducation can be delivered individually or in groups, and its goals can be remedial or preventive (Watkins, 1985). Competencies taught in psychoeducation are thought to be pertinent to the psychological health of those receiving training. Gazda and Pistole (1986, p. 2), in discussing the "Life Skills Training" model, indicate that it is "a comprehensive delivery system designed to facilitate functioning throughout the life span." When the life skills training program, or any other psychoeducation group, is introduced to persons who are generally healthy and free from dysfunction, it is a preventive program offered to persons at risk for future dysfunction (Conyne, 1987, 1994b). The intent is to equip group members with the knowledge and skills now that they might need to better cope with future life events and thus to bolster their resources and reduce risk. Psychoeducation groups with a prevention orientation are the main focus of the psychoeducation group specialization contained in the ASGW Professional Training Standards.

Applying Knowledge of Group Developmental Theory

Over 100 group developmental theories have been created (Forsyth, 1990). They all are highly congruent, whether they contain three, five, or even nine stages or phases. All of the training curricula we have examined from counselor education programs teach students about group development. Knowledge and use of group developmental theory is obviously an essential component for good practice.

A particularly useful conception of group development for psychoeducation groups is Trotzer's model in "Group Process: Stages and Developmental Tasks" (1979, 1989). This model first appeared in the 1979 special issue he edited for the *Journal for Specialists in Group Work* dealing with group counseling and the dynamic of structure. The model is conceptually sound. Its explicit association of group developmental stages with concrete developmental tasks provides a highly pragmatic template for planning and monitoring psychoeducation groups. Trotzer's group development–task planning schema is summarized below. Keep in mind that, as with any conceptual model of this kind, both stages and tasks within them overlap in practice to some degree.

Trotzer's Group Development—Task Planning and Monitoring Model

Trotzer developed a five-stage model which is generally useful in understanding the progression of events in groups, including psychoeducation groups. These are the individual stages in his model:

- *Security* stage of group development: developmental tasks of getting acquainted, interpersonal warm-up, setting boundaries, and building trust.

- *Acceptance* stage of group development: developmental tasks of personal sharing, giving feedback, surfacing and resolving conflict, building group cohesiveness, accepting self, and accepting others.

- *Responsibility* stage of group development: developmental tasks of self-assessment, recognizing ownership, building responsibility, giving respect, and doing a fair share.

- *Work* stage of group development: developmental tasks of problem solving, mobilizing group resources, and reality testing.

- *Closing* stage of group development: developmental tasks of giving support, confirming and affirming growth, saying goodbye, and follow-up.

Why is this schema so useful? It provides a blueprint that psychoeducation group leaders can follow in planning the overall focus and direction of their group. Moreover, it lends guidance for the creation of instructional and skill-building strategies that might be used during the course of the group. We will extend and apply this discussion later as we focus on pregroup preparation.

Developing a Relevant Knowledge Base

Psychoeducation groups are organized around a particular knowledge or subject matter base which is then delivered to group members. Watkins (1985) provides a few examples: training college students in assertiveness, training medical students in interpersonal skills, training elementary students in problem-solving competencies, and training nurses in stress inoculation. Students at the University of Cincinnati have designed and coled psychoeducation groups that are preventively focused in such areas as pregnancy prevention, academic survival skills, decision making, parenting, couples communication, substance abuse prevention, child abuse prevention, and many others. In each of these psychoeducation groups, it is necessary for the leaders to possess content expertise in the topic, because specific information is transmitted within the group to members. This information base needs to be practically relevant to the prospective target population, and it must be consistent with current research.

Therefore, in a substance abuse prevention group the leaders might need to develop and deliver an information base on topics such as common attitudes and beliefs about substances, current prevalence rates, differential effects of substances, social acceptability of substance use, and the difficulty of breaking habits. In addition to knowledge about the topic itself, the leaders also might need to understand principles underlying decision making, behavior change, coping with anxiety, and social skill development (Botvin & Tortu, 1988).

In addition to developing content expertise in designated areas, students also need to refine their training and presentation abilities. Practice in creating instructional plans and then in delivering brief minilectures is useful for building competency as a psychoeducational group leader. Abilities as an instructional developer and deliverer also are consistent with the educational/developmental role long advocated by the counseling and counseling psychology professions.

STANDARDS CLUSTER 2

Teaching Pregroup Preparation in Psychoeducation Groups

Four standards encompass the knowledge and skills necessary for competent pregroup preparation training. These standards are the following:

- K-5: List principles involved in obtaining healthy and/or at risk members for psychoeducation groups.

- S-1: Plan a psychoeducation group in collaboration with target population members or representatives.

- S-2: Match a relevant psychoeducation topic with relevant (and currently unaffected) target group.

- S-4: Design a psychoeducation group plan that is developmentally and practically sound.

Developing Ability to Determine Need

How does a leader for a prospective preventively oriented psychoeducation group identify likely group members? These members need to be presently at risk but not suffering from the problem, dysfunction, or disorder to be addressed in the group experience.

One of the best methods for member identification results from collaborative planning with members of the target population or with those from that setting. That is, the group should emerge from the context and not be independently developed. Students need to learn how to connect with staff from important settings—such as schools, human service organizations, and churches—and then to collaborate with them in assessing need and identifying focal areas for interventions, such as psychoeducation groups. If topics for the groups and selection procedures are mutually selected, they provide greater ecological validity and improved chances for success.

Training in consultation skills and in program development processes is strongly suggested to provide students with the skills for establishing entry and collaboration with personnel in the target setting. Students need to learn how to make contact, develop working relationships, discover what setting personnel are concerned about in their work, find ways to blend mutual expertise, and produce psychoeducation group plans that are developmentally and practically sound.

Developing Ability to Create a Sound Group Plan

The psychoeducation group plan emerges from the above collaboration. The plan generally is consistent with those plans described in connection with other group work training in core competencies and other specializations. However, it specifically emphasizes content and particular instructional processes.

Ettin et al. (1988) have provided useful guidance for developing sound group plans, which they refer to as psychoeducational group "protocols." Their protocol building process includes four steps:

- Developing a group blueprint (e.g., group theme, target population, major concepts, skills).
- Sequencing major areas within expected group development [relating major content and skills to a group development model, such as Trotzer's (1979, 1989) developmental tasks model that we discussed earlier].
- Using phase-specific group dynamics to build exercises and structures.
- Developing within-session lesson plans.

Students in the University of Cincinnati's second group work class, Introduction to Group Leadership, are required to design a focused, structured plan for a group that they might lead under supervision in the third group work class. Many of these students submit psychoeducational group plans with a preventive orientation. What follows is an example of one such plan that was submitted by MacNeil (1993). This psychoeducation group plan is derived from the work of Popkin (1993) on active parenting. Note its general correspondence with the suggestions of Ettin et al. (1988).

1. *General Scope*: Parenting education program for parents of 2- to 12-year-old children.

2. *Philosophy*: By teaching key parenting skills, parents will be better able to prevent their children from using tobacco, alcohol, and other drugs (TAOD).

3. *Nature of Group:* Primary and secondary prevention program.

4. *Content of Group*: Focused on skills that will assist parents in child-rearing practice.

5. *Goal*: To teach parents the skills and processes that will expand their role and/or alleviate distressing situations.

6. *Format of Group*: A videotape-based group program. Information is presented in six 2-hour sessions. Group is centered on discussions, structured activities, practice, and feedback.

7. *Group Development*: Follows anticipated stages consistent with the Trotzer development-task model.

8. *Process of Group*: Primarily cognitive-behavioral in emphasis, the group process is devoted to problem-solving processes and effective decision making, as follows:
   a. Leader introduces new material through discussion and/or video.
   b. Skills are modeled on video by "the players."
   c. Material is experienced through group activity or video practice.
   d. Participant reads material at home and completes home activities in parent's guide.
   e. Skills are applied at home with parent's guide support.
   f. Feedback and encouragement are given during group "share and tell."
   g. Participant applies skills regularly, improving with practice.

9. *Leader Role*: Leader is a facilitator, not an expert, who helps group members to attribute meaning and to understand how they can apply learnings to their families.

10. *Session Format*: Each topic-oriented session emphasizes skill development. Sessions are devoted to various sequenced topics and skill development, each one building successively on those previously introduced. Activities and discussions are established so that members are able to move through individual session phases in a planned, developmental progression.

11. *Session 1 Objectives*: The Active Parent
    a. Introduce leader and group members to each other
    b. Introduce videotape format
    c. Clarify leader and participant roles
    d. Develop understanding of active style of parenting
    e. Understand use of choices in parenting
    f. Begin to develop group cohesiveness

12. *Session 2 Objectives*: Instilling Courage and Self-Esteem
    a. Understand relationship among thinking, feeling, and doing

  b. Understand relationship among self-esteem, courage, and positive and negative behavior
  c. Identify ways parents discourage their children
  d. Identify ways parents encourage their children
  e. Practice building encouragement skills

13. *Session 3 Objectives*: Understanding Your Child
  a. Recognize goals of behavior
  b. Recognize how parents and children influence each other
  c. Practice analyzing misbehavior of one of their children

14. *Session 4 Objectives*: Developing Responsibility
  a. Define responsibility and role of choice and consequences in developing responsibility
  b. Present model for handling problems in a family
  c. Construct "I" messages
  d. Understand and apply natural and logical consequences
  e. Understand importance of mutual respect

15. *Session 5 Objectives:* Winning Cooperation
  a. Define cooperation
  b. Understand how to handle child-owned problems
  c. Sensitize group to avoid communication blocks
  d. Begin to develop active communication skills

16. *Session 6 Objectives*: Active Parenting in a Democratic Society
  a. Build on positive changes
  b. Learn how to hold a family talk
  c. Learn how to hold a problem-solving discussion
  d. Understand procedure for holding a family council meeting
  e. Determine how parents can continue to build upon their group experience

This plan, with appropriate and necessary alterations, is then used to guide the psychoeducation group.

  Another example of how a psychoeducation group has been used for preventive purposes is provided by Rice and Meyer (1995), who targeted adolescent depression. Their school-based psychoeducation group model indicates that the manner in which adolescents adjust to situational and developmental challenges, so-called "stressful life events," can be influenced positively by a prevention-oriented psychoeducation group which intentionally seeks to modify relevant internal and external variables. The group program is geared to bolster intrapersonal and interpersonal buffers to challenge. Each group session is focused on a particular social skill, coping method, or challenge and is administered in such a way as to promote member interaction and group process.

A brief summary of the 16 topical sessions constituting the psychoeducation group for the prevention of depression among adolescent members is presented below to provide another example of how psychoeducation groups are constructed:

Session 1: Introduction to challenges of adolescence
Session 2: "Wheel of Life" (awareness of differing areas of life)
Session 3: Problem-solving method
Session 4: Generating alternative solutions
Session 5: Assertiveness
Session 6: Emotion-focused coping
Session 7: Relaxation training
Session 8: Anticipating consequences
Session 9: Review and practice
Session 10: Wheel of Life game
Session 11: Self-esteem
Session 12: Shyness
Session 13: Friendship
Session 14: Peer pressure
Session 15: Problem solving in the family
Session 16: Summary and wrap-up

Detailed and carefully crafted group plans, therefore, are a central component of psychoeducation groups. Training programs need to provide students with instruction and opportunities for mastering the needed set of knowledge and skills in this area.

In designing structured exercises or experiences for psychoeducational group work, several conditions should be considered (Pfeiffer & Jones, 1980b), such as the following: understanding group purposes and context, assessing the developmental stage of the group, determining if leader intervention is appropriate or needed at the moment, sensing the willingness of the members to experiment and take risks, ascertaining how the possible structured exercise fits within the ongoing culture of the group, and weighing the opportunities for processing and evaluating the effects of the intervention. Once such considerations are worked through, a structured exercise can be planned. Important planning steps include giving concrete attention to (a) goals, (b) group size, (c) time required for the entire exercise, as well as any subparts, (d) materials that are required to conduct the exercise, (e) physical setting properties necessary to facilitate the activities involved (e.g., movable chairs), (f) specific process steps the group leaders will need to take to move through the exercise, and (g) evaluation planned to discover process and outcomes.

STANDARDS CLUSTER 3

Teaching Therapeutic Dynamics and Leader Skills in Psychoeducation Groups

In psychoeducation groups, no less than in counseling or psychotherapy groups, attention must be paid to the development of therapeutic dynamics and leader skills. Five standards define the competencies required of psychoeducation group leaders:

- K-3: Enumerate principles of instruction relevant to psychoeducation groups.

- K-8: Discuss principles of structure as related to guidance/psychoeducation groups.

- K-9: Discuss the concept of empowerment in guidance/psychoeducation groups.

- S-3: Conduct a personally selected psychoeducation group model appropriate to the age and clientele of the group leader's specialty area (e.g., student personnel education).

- S-5: Present information in a psychoeducation group.

- S-6: Use environmental dynamics to the benefit of the psychoeducation group.

- S-7: Conduct skill training in psychoeducation groups.

Issues in Skill Training

Specific considerations include maintaining group process while imparting information, attending to the experiential learning cycle in experiential groups, and using known principles of behavioral skill training. Each is sufficiently important to warrant separate discussion.

Maintaining group process emphasis while presenting information. Group processes are critically important for all group work. Group leaders need to be aware of human factors in group work and must be able to facilitate positive dynamics. Therefore, attention to such group processes as communication patterns, decision-making procedures, seating arrangements, norms, and interpersonal relations are all germane.

In contrast to the attention paid to group process issues in group counseling and group psychotherapy, in psychoeducation and task groups, attention to group process too frequently gets short shrift or is forgotten. When either occurs, the quality of work suffers and group members are not well served. Maintaining an ongoing balance of attention to content and process is necessary.

Because of their emphasis on teaching content or skills, psychoeducation groups are especially susceptible to ignoring process. The leaders can find themselves getting trapped in designing and delivering informational presentations related to the topical focus of the group—whether it be pregnancy prevention, substance abuse prevention, developing social skills, or academic survival skills—while minimizing attention given to group processes.

Using experiential learning cycle. Consistent with the group plan, each psychoeducation group session is carefully organized to promote specific goals, following a planned structure, within a set time limit. Structured exercises for use in psychoeducation groups are plentiful. They are available through the annual publications of University Associates (e.g., in its "structured experiences kit," which contains some 400 structured exercises, each of which is categorized and rated), and in other sources, such as 52 exercises for groups (Dossick & Shea, 1988), and the clearinghouse abstract catalog for structured thematic groups and innovative programs in mental health (Masters, 1988).

A psychoeducation group follows a general series of steps within each group session. Morganett/Smead (1994), in her book on group counseling activities for elementary students, identifies these steps as ice breaking, working, and processing. Others have used similar descriptions.

An especially pertinent way to structure each psychoeducation group session is found in the "experiential learning cycle" (Pfeiffer & Jones, 1980b). This interdependent series of five steps includes (a) experiencing of a structured activity, such as an exercise or skill training; (b) publishing, through sharing, of observations, reactions, ratings taken, etc.; (c) processing events and dynamics that occurred during the activity; (d) generalizing what was learned and its meaning; and (e) applying learnings to specific situations outside the group.

Using psychological and behavioral skill training processes. During the working or experiential phases of a psychoeducaton group session, it may be desirable to include skill training. A number of social skills and problem-solving training programs have been developed which are very appropriate for inclusion within psychoeducation groups. An example of a social skills program is Structured Learning (Goldstein, Sprafkin, Gershaw, & Klein, 1986), from which students learn beginning social skills, skills for dealing with feelings, skill alternatives for aggression, skills for dealing with stress, and planning skills. Another example of a social skills training program is Active Parenting Today (Popkin, 1993), a video-based small group prevention program aimed at building a strong parent–child relationship, helping parents teach their children positive self-esteem and social skills, and teaching parents how to discuss drug use with their children. An example of a problem-solving program is the Social Problem-Solving Curriculum (Weissberg & Gesten, 1982). It is a highly structured preventive program for children used to develop skills in problem identification, generating alternative solutions, considering consequences, and integration of problem-solving behavior. In all of these programs that include skill training, the same general behavioral and psychological processes are used: modeling, shaping, coaching, guided rehearsal, and generalization (Knoff, 1988). Or, stated in a slightly different sequence but just as usefully, in psychoeducation groups skills are defined, taught, practiced, observed, and processed (Langer, 1994).

Examples of Training in Psychoeducation Group Work

Our review of psychoeducation group work training indicates that it seems to occur in tandem with training in the core group work competencies. Separating training components into the psychoeducation standards clusters is premature at this point. For instance, at Southern Illinois University at Carbondale, the courses Theory and Practice of Group Counseling and Career Group Practicum are intended to provide the content to meet both the core competencies and those in psychoeducation groups. The practicum course then immerses students in supervised leadership of two psychoeducational groups. The training at Governors State University, the University of Cincinnati, and other programs we were able to review also generally follow this approach.

Returning to the Southern Illinois—Carbondale approach to psychoeducation group work training, curriculum content in the initial course is presented to meet all knowledge competencies identified in the standards for psychoeducational groups. In addition, students are required to examine the research and create a structured psychoeducation group design for a selected topic and population. Because of their experience in creating a structured and focused group design, students in the second (group practicum) course are able to focus on specific skills related to psychoeducation group leadership.

During the group practicum, students lead a psychoeducation group twice a week for 9 weeks under intensive supervision. Each skill is systematically shaped as students increase the complexity of their leadership abilities.

The process of teaching the career group practicum is unusual. A task group format is used in teaching. This format includes a team of leaders that implements the roles of observation group facilitator, supervisor, instructor, gate keeper, and so on. Leadership roles with the practicum task group are distributed across leaders on the basis of previous training and opportunities to learn new leadership or instructional skills. Members and leaders support each other as they all mutually explore new skills and strategies to improve the practicum.

Although they are assigned one primary supervisor, students have access to all team leaders for modeling and support. Team leaders are accessible to each other in order to receive support, learn new skills, and share responsibilities. As the semester continues, students assume more responsibility in the practicum task group for helping each other and for self-correction within supervision. For the leaders, new skills are developed, research is conducted on the class, and ideas emerge for new trials.

What is significant to this instructional model is that students are *with* and *in* groups at the same time. That is, the students are learning about groups, observing them, participating in a task group, and facilitating their own psychoeducation group.

A different teaching model embeds psychoeducation design and delivery competencies within courses and elements of the school counseling sequence. This model is consistent with group guidance, which is part of a larger developmental guidance framework. In this model, instruction and experience are treated separately but adjunctively to any existing group work courses. Because this is not a group work training model per se, we will not focus on it, although much could be learned from how school counseling students are taught to design and deliver group guidance activities.

STANDARDS CLUSTER 4

Teaching Research and Evaluation in Psychoeducation Groups

The unique research and evaluation factor in psychoeducation group work is ecological validity of interventions. As the sole standard in this section indicates, psychoeducation group workers must be skilled in conducting environmental assessment.

- K-7: Discuss environmental assessment as related to psychoeducation groups.

Instructional Methods

Needs assessment, program development, and research and evaluation all are important in psychoeducation group work. We have noted already the centrality of a specific group plan emerging from real-world collaboration with members of a setting. Moreover, because psychoeducation groups with a prevention orientation seek to help members to increase their repertoire of competencies in dealing with future challenges, it is important to consider context; that is, psycho-

education groups are most effective when content and skills are addressed in relation to actual environmental situations that group members face or may face. The ecological context surrounding the
application of knowledge and skills is of considerable practical benefit.
Leaders want to design group experiences that target real-world issues
for members and to assist members to learn how to apply newly gained
competencies in the real world. Thus, for instance, when working with
young fathers in a preventively oriented psychoeducation group, the
group leaders work to actively include role play situations that are
drawn from the life experience of the members. Because these kinds
of environmental data are included, the learning experience comes
alive for the members, and they are motivated to grow toward responsible parenthood.

Evaluation is a particularly knotty concern in those psychoeducation groups which seek prevention goals. How does one measure
something that has not occurred? That is, if the group intends to lessen
the incidence of academic failure in its members, is the reduced failure
rate that was attained due to the group experience? Effects of treatment (remedial) groups can be evaluated with regard to reductions in
identified behaviors. However, in prevention-oriented psychoeducation groups, evaluation takes a different tack, such as measuring reductions in the rate of increase of a target behavior (e.g., Botvin &
Tortu, 1988) or, as a midrange approach, measuring competencies
learned (Conyne, 1987). Students need to develop good evaluation
skills and how to apply them in measuring preventive effects (Price,
Cowen, Lorion, & Ramos-McKay, 1988).

STANDARDS CLUSTER 5

Teaching the Ethical Practice of Psychoeducation Groups

In psychoeducational groups, as in all other specializations, particular
ethical difficulties arise. The psychoeducational group worker must
have clear understanding of these special ethical considerations. The
standard for ethical practice of psychoeducational group work is this:

• K-10: Identify specific ethical considerations unique to psychoeducation groups.

Instructional Methods

In addition to the array of ethical considerations applicable to all groups, leaders of psychoeducation groups with a preventive orientation must be especially cognizant of privacy issues. Privacy concerns are endemic at the point of determining an appropriate at-risk target group. Potential invasion of privacy may occur if group leaders independently decide to bring their psychoeducation group to a target population without sanction or formative participation. It is tempting for prospective group leaders, armed with expertise, a commitment to the prevention of dysfunction, and a well-designed psychoeducation group, to decide that a particular target population could really benefit from participating in the group and then to set out recruiting their involvement. For instance, social indicator statistics suggest that single, unemployed parents living in public housing are vulnerable to child abuse. With this information, prospective group leaders design a psychoeducation group reflective of the very best in current research information and based on sound psychoeducation group work principles. They then randomly contact 30 unemployed, single parents living in a local public housing setting to invite them for an initial selection interview for potential membership in the child abuse prevention group. If you were on the receiving end of such a contact, how might you react?

Such an autonomous process can lead to unintended invasion of privacy. Advisable ethical practice suggests that prospective psychoeducation group leaders work collaboratively with setting managers, administrators, and target population members themselves in the earliest practical stages of program development. Such a collaborative approach reflects Patton's (1978) concept of "user" participation. Enlisting member involvement and special expertise in the process of developing the group plan and identifying potential group members will enhance the group experience and its chances for success.

SUMMARY

Task and Psychoeducation Group Work Training

In this extended chapter, we have combined the emerging group work in counseling specializations of task groups and psychoeducation groups. As we have pointed out, these curricula are only now being developed in counseling programs to educate and train students in these two developing areas. We have cited training examples wherever appropriate and have taken the liberty of drawing from the literature to provide professors and students alike with relevant material that could be used to implement the ASGW Training Standards in the areas of task and psychoeducation group work training. We hope this information will prove to be useful in stimulating and guiding creative activity necessary to support future training in these emerging specializations of group work.

6 CHAPTER

Group Psychotherapy

Separate standards for the training of group psychotherapists were developed and promulgated to sharpen the distinction between group counseling with essentially normal clients facing developmental difficulties and the provision of remedial or reconstructive work for persons with chronic mental or emotional disorders. Specifically, the ASGW Training Standards (ASGW, 1991b) for group psychotherapy identify group psychotherapy as one of the four possible group work specializations. The group worker who specializes in group psychotherapy is described in the standards as seeking to

> help individual group members to remediate their in-depth psychological problems. Because the depth and extent of the psychological disturbance is significant, the goal is to aid each individual to reconstruct major personality dimensions. (pp. 14–15)

Discussion of training for prospective group psychotherapists must, of necessity, consider sources outside the ASGW Training Standards. Psychotherapy, group or individual, typically involves work with persons who have been diagnosed as having a mental or emotional disorder; thus, the training of the group psychotherapist must take into account general standards for the training of mental health practitioners and the standards for training group psychotherapists from other disciplines (e.g., psychiatry, psychology, psychiatric nursing, and social work). To begin this chapter, we will present a brief review of training models for group psychotherapists drawn from the writings of Mullan and Rosenbaum (1962), Yalom (1970), Levine (1979), Fenster and Colah (1991), and Gallagher (1994). Next we will review the standards for accreditation of mental health counseling training programs promulgated by the Council for Accreditation of Counseling and Related Educational Programs (CACREP) and will note portions of those standards which prescribe specific instructional content. Finally, before beginning a direct discussion of the ASGW Training Standards, we will discuss counselor licensure standards and will note specifically the requirements for clinical endorsement for independent practice of diagnosis and treatment of mental and emotional disorders in various states. With these considerations as a backdrop, we will then begin our discussion of the ASGW standards for training group psychotherapists and a cluster-by-cluster presentation of curricular suggestions.

Training Models for Group Psychotherapists

Contextually, the ASGW Training Standards fit into a rich history of models for the training of group psychotherapists. Nearly three decades ago, Mullan and Rosenbaum (1962) outlined a basic model for the training of a group psychotherapist. Though focused on psychoanalytic group psychotherapy, much of Mullan and Rosenbaum's model is applicable today.

Mullan and Rosenbaum's training model. Mullan and Rosenbaum divided their training model into four clusters: (a) didactic instruction in the fundamentals of group psychotherapy, (b) clinical workshops to facilitate the study of group psychotherapy, (c) personal work in a psychotherapy group, and (d) supervised experience in coleading or leading psychotherapy groups. Each of these clusters will be described in turn.

- *Didactic instruction in fundamentals.* In Mullan and Rosenbaum's view, didactic instruction should include a number of discrete topics. Prospective group psychotherapists should know of the history, development, and philosophy of group psychotherapy. They should also be instructed regarding administrative problems of group psychotherapy, pregroup preparation, recruitment and selection of members, therapeutic factors in a psychotherapy group, introduction of new members to an ongoing group, and termination of the group. Mullan and Rosenbaum also recommended didactic instruction in specific leader skills. This instruction should include techniques for management of a therapeutic group atmosphere; psychophysiological and personality factors in group psychotherapy; interventions with group member resistances; dealing with transference and countertransference; and dealing with medical, social, and intrapsychic emergencies.

- *Clinical workshops.* Mullan and Rosenbaum recommended that group psychotherapy students work in year-long training groups of 7–10 members. These training groups, according to Mullan and Rosenbaum, should be moderately unstructured, yet not so unstructured as to become a therapy group. When clearly articulated protocols are adhered to, an optimal balance of task activity and intra- and interpersonal introspection may be achieved. Such training groups often embody many of the characteristics of a therapeutic group and therefore offer the opportunity for participants to experience and analyze the phenomena and dynamics characteristic of psychotherapy groups. The accreditation committee of the American Group Psychotherapy Association has recommended a minimum requirement of 60 hours as a participant in a training group.

- *Personal work.* Personal work in a therapy group setting was recommended by Mullan and Rosenbaum as the third facet of the group psychotherapist's training. As they said, "entering and participating in his [or her] own group as [client] allows him [or her] to experience the anxiety, hopefulness, helplessness, and the pulls and tugs, which are so common and so unlike the one-to-one binding of individual therapy" (p. 309).

- *Supervised experience.* The final component in the Mullan and Rosenbaum model is practicing one's therapy skills as cotherapist or therapist under supervision. They suggested supervision on a weekly basis for at least 50 sessions. Consistent with most theories of supervision, Mullan and Rosenbaum noted that the supervisor's approach must vary with the sophistication of the supervisee—providing support and technical training for the beginning group therapist, promoting personal introspection for those who are wrestling with countertransference issues, and providing more abstract and philosophical analysis for those with more advanced skills.

Mullan and Rosenbaum's model has held up well over time. Yalom (1985) articulated a training model markedly similar to that of Mullan and Rosenbaum. Yalom's model features (a) a T-group experience at the onset of training, (b) 4–6 months of student observation of an experienced group therapist, (c) a series of content seminars on the theory and practice of group therapy, (d) a supervised group therapy experience with a nonfaculty therapist, and (e) supervised leadership of therapy groups.

Fenster and Colah's model. Even more recently, Fenster and Colah (1991) reaffirmed the proposition that group therapy has its own history, literature, and specialized skills which should be taught separate from individual therapy. As was seen in the Mullan and Rosenbaum model, Fenster and Colah's training model includes (a) a didactic course in theory and technique in which the prospective group therapist gains a sense of the history of group therapy and is exposed to current thinking in the field, (b) opportunities to observe experienced group therapists at their work, (c) a professional training group experience in which students can experience and analyze group phenomena and dynamics, (d) personal group therapy to enhance personal awareness and interpersonal sensitivity, and (e) one or more supervised clinical experiences doing group therapy, preferably in the company of a cotherapist.

Gallagher's model. Gallagher (1994) proposed a briefer, hierarchical, three-stage model for training the modern group psychotherapist. In the first stage, technical development, prospective group psychotherapists are taught fundamental skills and techniques. The second stage, enrichment, focuses learners on group phenomena, including theory of group dynamics. Then in the third, or final, stage, students attend to personalization of learnings, exploring countertransference issues, and learning about the termination process. Though only three stages are identified, their content mirrors the earlier models of Mullan and Rosenbaum (1962), Yalom (1985), and Fenster and Colah (1991).

Summary of the historical models. Perhaps the philosophy behind these various training models was best summarized by Levine (1979), who said:

> To be effective, group therapists must know about themselves in the helping role, about dynamics of individual dysfunction and amelioration, and about dynamics of therapy groups. When therapists approach groups without either knowledge of or readiness to learn about all three areas, consequences for the group, individual members, and perhaps the therapist as well are unfortunate. (p. 51)

As will be seen, the ASGW Training Standards are consistent with these historical recommendations.

The CACREP Standards for Mental Health Counelors

Given the relationship between the ASGW Training Standards for group psychotherapists and the broader issue of training for mental health counseling, it is important to attend to the 1994 CACREP Accreditation Standards for mental health counselors. Of particular importance are the standards relating to the knowledge and skills viewed as necessary for the mental health worker. Specifically, CACREP Standards for mental health counseling assert that the student must acquire knowledge and skills for the practice of mental health counseling, including the following:

- general principles of etiology, diagnosis, treatment, and prevention of mental and emotional disorders and dysfunctional behavior, and general principles and practices for the promotion of optimal mental health;
- specific models and methods for assessing mental status; identification of abnormal, deviant, or psychopathological behavior, and the interpretation of findings in current diagnostic categories;
- application of modalities for maintaining and terminating counseling and psychotherapy with mentally and emotionally impaired clients, including crisis intervention, brief, intermediate, and long-term approaches;

• basic classifications, indications, and contraindications of commonly prescribed psychopharmacological medications for the purpose of identifying effects and side effects of such medications;
• principles of conducting an intake interview and mental health history for planning and managing of client caseload.

Though these CACREP Standards for accredited mental health programs do not speak directly to the training of group psychotherapy skills, they are an important backdrop for considering the variety of skills viewed as important for persons intending to work with clients diagnosed with mental or emotional disorders, as is the case for prospective group psychotherapists.

Counselor Licensure Requirements

As of April, 1995, the District of Columbia and 41 states have passed some form of counselor credentialing legislation. Whether or not a state's counselor license permits practice in the area of diagnosis and treatment of mental and emotional disorders varies among the states. In states which permit counselors to engage in psychotherapeutic work, licensure regulations may also prescribe training requirements (e.g., required curriculum, required practicum experiences) and require passage of an advanced clinical or mental health counseling examination.

For example, in Illinois, clinical professional counselors are permitted to provide clinical counseling and psychotherapy with individuals, couples, families, groups, and organizations as a treatment for emotional disorders. To qualify for this Illinois license, an applicant must hold a master's or doctoral degree in counseling, rehabilitation counseling, psychology, or a related field and must document 2 years of full-time supervised experience as a clinical professional counselor. In Virginia, a licensed professional counselor, whose scope of practice includes identification and remediation of mental, emotional, or behavioral disorders, must complete coursework in nine content areas, including four specifically related to psychopathology and psychotherapy: (a) theories of counseling and psychotherapy; (b) counseling and psychotherapy techniques; (c) appraisal, evaluation, and diagnostic procedures; and (d) abnormal behavior. The counselor must also document supervised practice in appraisal, evaluation, diagnosis, treatment planning, and treatment implementation. The scope of practice for Massachusetts licensed mental health counselors includes individual, family, and group treatment using counseling and psychotherapeutic techniques for prevention, treatment, and resolution of mental and emotional dysfunction.

Currently, Massachusetts license applicants must complete some course work in counseling theories, human development, and psychopathology. Massachusetts standards may soon be strengthened to include the competency areas defined in the standards for CACREP-accredited mental health counseling programs. Licensed professional counselors in Ohio may obtain clinical endorsement which permits them to diagnose and treat mental and emotional disorders by completing 30 quarter hours of instruction beyond the counseling master's degree in five content areas: (a) clinical psychopathology, personality, and abnormal behavior; (b) evaluation of mental and emotional status; (c) diagnosis of mental and emotional disorders; (d) methods of intervention and prevention of mental and emotional disorders; and (e) treatment of mental and emotional disorders. Prospective group psychotherapists should refer to the counselor licensure laws in the state in which they intend to practice in order to determine what course work is required for the practice of group psychotherapy. Other states which permit counselors to practice diagnosis and treatment of mental and emotional disorders have similar training requirements.

The ASGW Standards for Group Psychotherapists

The ASGW Training Standards for group psychotherapy include 13 knowledge standards and 16 skill competencies. All of the standards established for group counseling are applicable to the group psychotherapy setting and are therefore included. Five additional knowledge standards and four additional skill standards focus specifically on the study, assessment, and clinical management of abnormal behavior and psychopathology. Persons interested in the group psychotherapy specialization are encouraged to complete "course work in the areas of group psychotherapy, abnormal psychology, psychopathology, and diagnostic assessment to assure capabilities in working with more disturbed populations" (ASGW, 1991b, p. 21). As with the specialization in group counseling, persons specializing in group psychotherapy are required to obtain a minimum of 45 clock hours of supervised practice in leading or coleading a psychotherapy group in a field practice setting.

As with other group work specializations, the group psychotherapy standards can be divided into five clusters: (a) Cluster 1: defining group psychotherapy; (b) Cluster 2: pregroup preparation; (c) Cluster 3: therapeutic dynamics and leader skills; (d) Cluster 4: research and evaluation; and (e) Cluster 5: ethical practice.

STANDARDS CLUSTER 1

Teaching the Definition of Group Psychotherapy

The individual standards in this cluster include the same requirement for definitional understanding of the specialization that is required for group counselors (Standards K-1 and K-3). In addition, specialists in psychotherapy are required to possess foundational knowledge of abnormal behavior, psychopathology, and personality theory (Standards K-9, K-10, K-11). Standards unique to the training of group psychotherapists will be set in italics for emphasis.

- K-1: State for at least three major theoretical approaches to group psychotherapy the distinguishing characteristics of each and the commonalities shared by all.

- K-3: List advantages and disadvantages of group psychotherapy and the circumstances for which it is indicated or contraindicated.

- K-9: *Identify and describe abnormal behavior in relation to group psychotherapy.*

- K-10: *Describe psychopathology as related to group psychotherapy.*

- K-11: *Describe personality theory as related to group psychotherapy.*

These standards recognize the CACREP requirement for mental health counselors to complete foundational studies covering (a) the social, cultural, economic, and political dimensions of mental health counseling; (b) the roles and functions of mental health counselors; and (c) training standards pertaining to the practice of group psychotherapy. They also require knowledge of and skills pertaining to psychopathology and personality development as required under

CACREP Accreditation Standards for mental health counselors. Thus, for example, in the University of Georgia model for training group psychotherapists, students complete at least one course in group counseling or in group dynamics (and are encouraged to take both) and an advanced course in group counseling and therapy.

Instructional Methods

The methods used for training group counseling specialists in definitional competence are equally applicable to group psychotherapy specialists; however, much more extensive training regarding abnormal human behavior and psychopathology is required. The major categories previously mentioned will be reviewed below, and additional methods will be discussed in depth:

- field interviews
- presentations
- readings, lecturettes, and discussion
- specific content courses

Field interviews. As is required at the University of Nebraska at Kearney for group counseling students, students of group psychotherapy could be required to conduct interviews with group psychotherapists in the field about the nature of group work in general and the nature of group psychotherapy in particular. It would be especially instructive for prospective group psychotherapists to gain an early perspective on the benefits and limitations of group psychotherapy, the kinds of psychotherapy groups led by the respondent, and the kinds of training experiences the respondent found to be most beneficial, personally and professionally.

Presentations. Following the model provided by Montana State University (for group counselors), prospective group psychotherapy students could be required to make an oral presentation with supplementary handout materials on the nature of group psychotherapy. Key ingredients in this presentation might include (a) the purpose of a psychotherapy group, (b) screening prospective members, (c) a typical group psychotherapy meeting (under the presenter's chosen therapy model), (d) common difficulties in psychotherapy groups and skills required to handle them, (e) common emergency situations in psychotherapy groups and skills required to handle them, and (f) assessing member progress.

Readings, lecturettes, and discussion. As was seen in our earlier discussion of task and work groups, psychoeducational groups, and group counseling, student awareness of the nature of psychotherapy and group leadership may be heightened by readings, lecturettes, and class discussion. Videotaped recordings of psychotherapy groups in action may be used in lieu of *in vivo* observation. For example, Yalom's (1990) videotaped discussion and demonstration of psychotherapeutic group work are particularly useful.

Specific content courses. Eastern Washington University, for example, makes specific comparisons between group counseling and group therapy to sharpen students' conceptualization. The ASGW Training Standards clearly state that, at minimum, the prospective group psychotherapist should complete course work in abnormal behavior, psychopathology, and personality theory. Of key importance is the development of an understanding of how various kinds of abnormal intrapsychic process and interpersonal behavior manifest themselves in group interactions.

STANDARDS CLUSTER 2

Teaching Pregroup Preparation in Group Psychotherapy

Just as pregroup preparation was important for the group counseling specialization, so pregroup preparation is crucial for practitioners of group psychotherapy. Because clients are expected to experience long-standing dysfunction, proper pregroup selection and preparation are vital to the success of the psychotherapy group. In addition to the general competencies regarding interpersonal assessment (Standard K-6), principles of group formation (Standard K-8), and skills in recruitment (Standard S-1), practitioners of group psychotherapy need additional knowledge of methods for assessing and diagnosing individual psychopathology (Standards K-13 and S-16). For emphasis, the competencies unique to group psychotherapy training are set in italics.

- K-6: Discuss interpersonal assessment and intervention in group psychotherapy.

- K-8: Describe group formation principles in group psychotherapy.

- K-13: *Specify diagnostic and assessment methods appropriate for group psychotherapy.*

- S-1: Recruit and screen prospective psychotherapy group members.

- S-16: *Assess and diagnose mental and emotional disorders of psychotherapy group members.*

These standards include the knowledge of and skill in assessment and diagnosis of mental and emotional disorders required under CACREP standards for mental health counselors.

Instructional Methods

Again, as with training for work in counseling groups, methods for teaching pregroup preparation include

- specific content courses
- implementing selection and screening criteria
- developing detailed plans for a psychotherapy group

Specific content courses. Because of the necessity for group psychotherapists to demonstrate competence in assessment and diagnosis of psychopathology, prospective group psychotherapists should take advanced course work in specific assessment tools and techniques to be used in assessment and diagnosis. Group psychotherapy students should have exposure to typical instrumentation and methods used in mental health assessment, including broad-spectrum instruments such as the California Psychological Inventory, the Minnesota Multiphasic Personality Inventory, the Millan Clinical Multiaxial Inventory; symptom assessment inventories such as the Symptom Checklist or Mooney Problem Checklist; and specific symptom instruments like the Beck Depression Inventory or the Fear Survey Schedule. In addition to comprehensive mental health assessment, training in group psychotherapy also should include assessment strategies for identifying client skills which may be useful in the group therapy setting. Consistent with the counseling profession's value of focusing on health and development, Kleinberg (1991), for example, suggests that the training and supervision of group psychotherapists are enhanced by focusing on group member's empathic capacity. Kleinberg presents a model using the

Empathy Assessment Scale for assessing the client's level of empathic ability.

Implementing selection and screening procedures. Course work for prospective group psychotherapists should include opportunities to demonstrate competence in assessment and diagnosis and the use of assessment data in screening and selection of group members. It is typical for students in testing and assessment courses to complete a variety of assessment instruments and to either develop a written analysis of their test results or to interpret the test results for a student partner. To fulfill the training standards in this section, it is important that the students of group psychotherapy have the opportunity to study and practice interpreting a variety of mental health assessment instruments. Further, to provide group psychotherapy students with the opportunity to receive supervision in the interpretation of mental health assessment with clients, those who prepare prospective group psychotherapists may need to arrange for their students to obtain such experience during individual counseling practica and internship activities. Finally, instruction and practice in evaluating client's suitability for group psychotherapy are required. Meadow (1988) integrated theoretical assumptions underlying member preparation for group psychotherapy and developed and field-tested a pregroup interview protocol which has proved to help clients gain a realistic perception of group membership.

Developing detailed plans for a psychotherapy group. Although some psychotherapy groups are structured as time-limited, theme-oriented groups, it is somewhat more common for psychotherapy groups to be less structured, scheduled for a longer period of time, and tolerant of thematic shifts as group members become more therapeutically accessible. Thus, the group plan for an open-ended, dynamically oriented, psychotherapy group may focus more on expected developmental growth across time and may have less in common with a lesson plan than can be true for a time-limited, theme-oriented counseling group. However, both counseling groups and psychotherapy groups share common pregroup preparation issues. Several programs (e.g., Rollins College, East Tennessee State, University of Cincinnati, Indiana University, Indiana University–Purdue University at Fort Wayne, and Montana State University) require group counseling students to develop detailed plans for a counseling group which typically include, in a section on pregroup preparation, discussion of the nature of the population with which they want to work, leadership characteristics shown to be valuable in working with the targeted population, individual member characteristics shown to be important for screening group applicants, and conformance of the plan to ethical standards of practice.

Perhaps a modification of the assignment given to group counseling students at Montana State University would be beneficial for prospective group psychotherapists. As noted earlier, Montana State students write a proposal for a counseling group which includes four elements pertinent to pregroup preparation. In the group counseling course, students develop plans for a theme-oriented group and, thus, are concerned with identifying populations that can profit from a group with the targeted thematic content. Students of group psychotherapy may need to plan a bit differently. For the population-and-concerns section of the group plan, students might address the following:

- With what kinds of client problems (diagnostic categories) do you intend to work?
- Describe the client population in some depth addressing relevant culture, gender, and developmental issues.
- Use theory to explain these clients' intrapsychic and interpersonal concerns and to identify goals for remediating their difficulties.
- With this population of clients, what kinds of medical or psychological emergencies might be anticipated?

The second element of the Montana State group counseling pregroup preparation assignment is leadership. This section could be expanded and refocused to fit with planning for group psychotherapy, as follows:

- What personal characteristics will be important for leaders working with clients having these characteristics?
- What pregroup training and supervision will be needed by the leader?
- What special skills will be needed by the leader to work with clients from this population?

- As you know yourself as a person and a counselor, what leadership difficulties do you anticipate?
- Discuss your own personal emotional reactions to clients from this client population.

The third element, membership, also may be modified to permit prospective group psychotherapists to practice their learnings. Here, students may be asked to consider the following:

- How will group members be recruited and what effects might be anticipated from this recruitment process?
- What is the optimal and acceptable number of group members?
- What roles and behaviors will be expected of group members?
- What are their rights and responsibilities?
- What risks are there to members for participating in the group?
- What criteria and methods will be used for screening out and screening in group members?
- What kinds of assessment devices might be used?
- What would be the ideal group composition?
- To what extent will this group be homogeneous or heterogeneous?
- How will data be interpreted, and how will the decision on membership be communicated to the group applicants?

The final element of the Montana State assignment which focuses on pregroup preparation is a discussion of ethics. As in the assignment for prospective group counselors, group psychotherapy students should review the "Ethical Guidelines for Group Counseling (ASGW, 1991a) and should evaluate their proposal's conformance to professional ethical guidelines.

STANDARDS CLUSTER 3

Teaching Therapeutic Dynamics and Leader Skills in Group Psychotherapy

There are many similarities between the within-group dynamic forces found in counseling groups and those found in psychotherapy groups. Further, many group leader techniques are equally applicable in group counseling and in group psychotherapy. Thus, the 4 knowledge competencies and 13 skill competencies required of group counselors also are required of group psychotherapists. In addition to these, group psychotherapists must have knowledge of and skill in crisis intervention techniques (Standards K-12 and S-14), skill in working with a broader range of developmental tasks (Standard S-13), and skill in effecting client hospitalization when required (Standard S-15). The competencies required for leadership of psychotherapy groups are enumerated below. Competencies unique to group psychotherapy training are set in italics for emphasis.

- K-4: Specify intrapersonal and interpersonal dynamics in group psychotherapy.

- K-5: Describe group problem-solving approaches in relation to group psychotherapy.

- K-7: Identify referral sources and procedures in group psychotherapy.

- K-12: *Detail crisis intervention approaches suitable for group psychotherapy.*

- S-2: Recognize self-defeating behaviors of psychotherapy group members.

- S-3: Describe and conduct a personally selected group psychotherapy model appropriate to the age and clientele of the group leader's specialty area (e.g., mental health counseling).

- S-4: Identify and develop reasonable hypotheses about nonverbal behavior among psychotherapy group members.

- S-5: Exhibit appropriate pacing skills involved in stages of a psychotherapy group's development.

- S-6: Identify and intervene effectively at critical incidents in the psychotherapy group process.

- S-7: Work appropriately with disruptive psychotherapy group members.

- S-8: Make use of the major strategies, techniques, and procedures of group psychotherapy.

- S-9: Provide and use procedures to assist transfer and support of changes by group psychotherapy members in the natural environment.

- S-10: Use adjunct group psychotherapy structures such as psychological homework (e.g., self-monitoring, contracting).

- S-11: Work cooperatively and effectively with a psychotherapy group coleader.

- S-13: *Assist individual change along the full range of development, from "normal" to "abnormal" in the psychotherapy group.*

- S-14: *Handle psychological emergencies in the psychotherapy group.*

- S-15: *Institute hospitalization procedures when appropriate and necessary in the psychotherapy group.*

These standards include knowledge of and skill in the provision of therapeutic treatment, coping with psychological emergencies, and instituting restraint when necessary, as required under the CACREP standards for mental health counselors.

Instructional Methods

The goals for training group psychotherapists are generally congruent with the goals for training group counselors. Thus, many of the methods used for group counselor training in therapeutic dynamics and leadership skills apply directly to group psychotherapy training. The training methods drawn from curricular submissions in group counseling and group psychotherapy and from literature on group psychotherapist training fit into the following general categories:

- classroom training exercises and laboratory experiences
- observation and critiquing of a group
- participation in a therapy or training group as a member
- supervised practice as a group leader or coleader

Classroom training exercises and laboratory experiences. As was noted in the earlier chapter on group counseling, Rollins College uses a Multiple-T activity in group leadership skills. In this minimum structure activity, participants (a) describe problems the therapist might face in leading a psychotherapy group, (b) identify strategies for coping with the problem, (c) design simulated experiences in which to practice coping with the targeted problem, (d) enact the simulated experiences in small groups (6–10 persons) to explore trial solutions to the problem, and (e) critique the small group's process and outcomes. The groups recycle their activities to permit various members to try various strategies. A case example of the Multiple-T method at Rollins College was provided earlier. This laboratory experience can be readily adapted to meet the needs of group psychotherapy training.

Cohen and Smith (1976a) developed a set of critical incidents occurring in early, middle, and late stages of group development for use in stimulating group leaders to develop their intervention repertoire. The vignettes may be used as the basis for group role plays or as stimuli to prompt conceptualization and development of written intervention responses. Watkins and Vitanza (1993) described how the case study method using clinical vignettes can supplement other clinician training methods. Watkins and Vitanza organized case study material into four discrete components: a clear description of the problem, the challenge presented to the therapist, key issues to be considered, and suggested reading materials. Although their approach was designed for training therapists to work with individual clients, it is reminiscent of the Cohen and Smith (1976a, 1976b) critical incident method and can clearly be adapted for use in training group psychotherapists. Stone and Klein's (1989) method also uses prepared clinical vignettes, graded to match the level of sophistication of the therapy students. Student evaluation of the data contained in the vignette is guided by a two-dimensional model of analysis: (a) Students are encouraged to identify client and therapist contributions to the dynamic process of the group, and (b) students are instructed in conceptualizing intrapsychic, interpersonal, and group-as-a-whole phenomena. The "Here and Now Response Practice Sheet" used at the University of Louisville is an example of the utilization of brief clinical vignettes to stimulate skill practice. In this University of Louisville activity, individuals are presented with individual group member statements constructed to provide an opportunity for the leader to practice immediacy skills. The learner writes out a response which brings the group member into the here-and-now of the group. Learner responses may then be critiqued by the instructor or by the group as a whole.

Observation and critiquing of a group. Theorists of group psychotherapy training such as Fenster and Colah (1991) have underscored the importance of student observation of both seasoned group psychotherapists and fellow students in the process of leading psychotherapy groups. As with the training of group counselors, one might view prerecorded examples of therapy group leadership, such as have been provided by Yalom (1985), or contemporary groups which have given permission to be observed live or recorded for later observation and analysis. The results of a questionnaire study of members of the American Group Psychotherapy Association (Kadis, Krasner, Weiner, Winick, & Foulkes, 1974) yielded the recommendation that experience as an observer of a group conducted by an experienced group therapist was an especially desirable part of the training process.

At the University of Louisville, group counselors use a "Group Observation Critique Form" to guide their analysis of 10 videotaped group counseling sessions prerecorded by the instructor. Because of its direct applicability to group psychotherapy, we will restate the content in summary form. The University of Louisville critique form requires the learner to respond to categories such as (a) the stage of the group development, (b) therapeutic factors present (cf. Yalom, 1985), (c) group norms observed, (d) evidence of resistance, (e) evidence of trust or mistrust, (f) evidence of challenges to the leader(s), (g) evidence of here-and-now focus. Depending on the group leader's theoretical orientation, additional categories such as use of interpretation, use of self, use of Gestalt experiments, or assignment of homework might be added to provide a more complete picture of the group psychotherapist's work.

University of Georgia group therapy students are encouraged to view live group interactions and/or review sets of tapes of model group leaders (e.g., Peg Carroll, Rex Stockton, Merle Ohlsen, William Glasser, Carl Rogers). In addition, tapes of faculty are available, and students are encouraged to observe faculty conducting a variety of group experiences.

Rose (1988) described a program for training in empirical group work. This novel training program uses systematic, ongoing collection of data for making decisions and for evaluating short-term and long-term shifts in individual and group phenomena. Rose uses a multi-stage shaping strategy for training group leaders. At first, students participate in a simulated training group which mirrors the type of group for which the students are preparing. Initially, the instructor models leader behavior; then students take over the leadership and rotate leadership periodically. After each student's leadership period, feedback is provided by observers. Students are then trained as observers, and they rotate taking responsibility for observation and data coordination. A postsession questionnaire is administered after each simulated session; then the data coordinator collates the observations and postsession data and reports the findings at the next group meeting. Pretreatment and posttreatment testing is conducted by using tests appropriate to the theme of the group, and group members discuss their response to the assessment process and the potential usefulness of the assessment data in the training seminar. Throughout the training process, the students receive feedback on their leadership and data management role enactment.

During his 16-week course, Schwartz (1981) holds class in a viewing room equipped with a TV monitor on which the student therapists can observe a live therapy group in progress. The session is also taped for subsequent review by the students. When the therapy group ends, the therapist/instructor joins the student therapists. For the next 75 minutes, the class discusses the session of the previous week. Each student distributes his or her typewritten process notes in which the student has described, critiqued, and commented on the previous week's session.

Participation in a training or therapy group as a member. Levine (1979) persuasively argued:

> Self-awareness is one of the major facets of the therapist's role in the group. Therapists are entitled to the same range of human emotions and reactions as any one else. But the two major questions are these: Are those reactions based on perception of the group or clouded by phenomena the therapist brings to the meeting? Is the therapist prepared to recognize the difference in order to facilitate accurate assessment and appropriate therapeutic action for the members and group? (p. 55)

In order that students understand the power of the group to harm or to heal, most theoreticians who have studied the training of group psychotherapists stress the importance of participatory experience in some form of training or therapy group. It is argued that only through personal self-exploration in a group setting can participants learn the fullness of self-disclosure; the power of resistances and defenses; the depth and strength of one's sadness, anger, and vulnerability; and the nature of one's preferred role in a group (Yalom, 1970).

But whether to require participation in a training group, a therapy group, or both is a matter of long-standing debate. Hearst (1990) pointed out that there is a clear difference between therapy groups, in which participants are usually clients attending sessions for relief of symptoms, and professional training "experiential" groups, in which participants are professionals attending sessions to increase their professional competence. Therapeutic processes, especially transference, countertransference, and projective processes, differ across these settings.

In the Mullan and Rosenbaum (1962) model, for example, group psychotherapy students are advised to work in year-long, moderately unstructured, training groups with clearly articulated training protocols to facilitate experiencing and analyzing the phenomena and dynamics characteristic of therapy groups. Yalom's (1985) avowed preference was to offer students an opportunity to participate in a human relations T group to allow students to learn at an emotional level that they had previously comprehended only intellectually. Yalom observed that such training groups are most effective when they are voluntary and are focused on here-and-now phenomena to the exclusion of past or outside-the-group, private matters. Alonso (1984) also argued that the training group (T group) provided a better vehicle for training group psychotherapists than did the historically recommended therapy group. Alonso believed that because the T-group model focused on aspects of contractual clarity and management of learning regression, it provided a better holding environment for professional development and helped foster the student's emergent identity as a group therapist. Alonso suggested that participation in the T group facilitates development of the student's capacity to conceptualize and process group stimuli. Further, Alonso suggested that the T-group structure protects students from unanticipated regressive experiences, often part of a traditional therapy group experience, which may be difficult to assimilate and may prove frightening to the student. Finally, Alonso observed that the opportunity to bond with other group therapy students may help the student develop an identification with the group therapy methodology. Mullan and Rosenbaum (1962) specifically advised against allowing the training group to become so unstructured as to become a therapy group.

Still, there is a persuasive argument for engaging in personal therapy work, either in an individual or a group modality. Kadis et al. (1974) recommended that group psychotherapy students should have the experience of being a participant in individual psychotherapy. Yalom (1970) recommended that group therapy students engage in some self-exploratory venture to help the student recognize countertransference responses, recognize personal distortions, to heighten awareness of one's own motivations, and to use feelings and fantasies as information sources. Yalom resisted, however, prescribing how much and what type of personal work the student group therapist requires. And Fenster and Colah (1991) recommended both a training group experience and an experience of personal work in a therapy group.

At the University of Georgia, students are expected to explore their own issues related to facilitating client growth. As in most counselor training programs, they struggle with achieving a balance between providing opportunities for student growth and development and developing dual-role relationships that provide faculty with too much knowledge of the student's personal issues.

Supervised practice as a group leader or coleader. Yalom (1985) referred to the supervised clinical experience as a sine qua non in the education of the group psychotherapist, and every writing on the subject of group therapist training has emphasized the crucial nature of the supervised clinical experience. Mullan and Rosenbaum (1962) emphasized practicing therapy skills as cotherapist or therapist under weekly supervision for at least 50 sessions. Mullan and Rosenbaum's recommendation was echoed by Yalom (1985), Kadis et al. (1974), Zaslav (1988), Rose (1988), and Fenster and Colah (1991).

University of Missouri—Columbia group therapy students who are judged to have succeeded in their first semester's preparatory work colead therapy groups composed of clients from the University Counseling Center with a member of the Counseling Center staff or a Counseling Center intern. The groups are audio- or videotaped, live supervision is employed, and follow-up supervision is extended to more than a single session per week and may involve the cotherapist on a regular basis. At the University of Georgia, doctoral students of group therapy lead personal growth groups for master's students and participate as leaders and as coleaders of their own groups. Students are expected to seek supervision actively. Sessions are videotaped and reviewed by a peer using a structured format which yields a written evaluation prior to being evaluated by a supervisor.

In Rose's (1988) empirical group work method, students who are successful in their initial training experience (learning group observation and basic group leadership skills) are promoted to working as a cotherapist with a more experienced therapist in a client group. Between sessions, leader and coleader meet in a planning session to evaluate data collected in their group and to determine the directions to be taken in the next group. As the student becomes more skillful, he or she assumes greater responsibility for planning and leadership. Summative feedback is provided. Students who are successful in this coleadership experience with clients are then assigned to work as a coequal leader with another student; they follow the same format as just described. Finally, the seasoned student is promoted to a solo leadership experience, with consultation from the supervising clinician available on request.

STANDARDS CLUSTER 4

Teaching Research and Evaluation in Group Psychotherapy

Although crucial to the implementation of best practice in group psychotherapy, this cluster is represented by a single standard. However, this single standard captures an essential value in the practitioner-scientist view of best practice:

- S-12: Use assessment procedures in evaluating effects and contributions of group psychotherapy.

Instructional Methods

Relatively little attention was paid to addressing formal research literature in the group counseling curricula. Rather, attention was focused on qualitative analysis of ongoing group counseling activities. The methods employed for ongoing group analysis in counseling groups have direct application to psychotherapy groups. Instructional methods for teaching evaluation of group psychotherapy process and outcome include:

- research literature review
- ongoing assessment of group psychotherapy
- the empirical group work approach

Research literature review. At the University of Georgia, doctoral students of group psychotherapy develop a specific research proposal to be carried out during practicum. For this assignment, students provide a proposal describing the background and rationale for the study, an extensive literature review, and a methodology (qualitative or quantitative) for examining the question being researched. In their literature review, students provide an extensive description of the theory and application of a specific group model, including a step-by-step discussion of the group (e.g., intake procedures, session-by-session outlines, methods for assessing effectiveness, ethical issues). Examples of topics explored include "the viability of adding moral development components to skills training groups for incarcerated adolescents" and "the interactional components of group supervision when provided by experienced and inexperienced supervisors." At completion, students write up their project in publishable form for submission and critique at the end of the practicum.

At Montana State University, group counseling students are required to prepare a formal critique of a group counseling research study. Students are provided with a set of questions, abstracted from Gazda (1989), to guide them in their critique. (See the chapter on group counseling for a listing of the questions used.) Although such an exercise would certainly be of value for the prospective group psychotherapist, the group psychotherapist needs thorough grounding in the research literature because of the seriousness of the difficulties faced by his or her clients.

Beyond the Montana State University assignment, we recommend that prospective group psychotherapists immerse themselves in the research literature on both individual and group treatment of the populations of clients with whom the student intends to work. The group therapy student might, for example, prepare a series of research papers, each attempting to identify the best practice in working with clients who have been diagnosed with various specific disorders.

Ongoing assessment of group psychotherapy. As important as ongoing assessment of group process is for the counseling group, it is critical for the therapy group. As will be noted below, avoidance of malpractice claims is partly dependent on providing reasonable and customary care for the clients of the therapy group. It is crucial for the group psychotherapist to be aware, on a session-by-session basis, of what has occurred for each member of the group and to analyze whether each member is receiving reasonable and customary care for the difficulties which prompted that client to enter treatment. The intervention critiques and session-by-session process analysis described for group counseling clearly apply.

(a) Intervention critique. A variety of methods may be used to encourage students to evaluate the consequences of interventions made and the consequences of failing to intervene when an intervention was needed. At the initial stage of training, several authors have recommended using clinical vignettes to facilitate student skill acquisition (Cohen & Smith, 1976a; Stone & Klein, 1989; Watkins & Vitanza, 1993). Each of these authors has provided a framework to help the student evaluate the consequences of interventions. Cohen and Smith's critical incident model focuses the learner on the developmental stage of the group, the antecedents to the critical incident, the specific events or verbalizations that constitute the critical incident, the leader's intentions for the intervention, the actual intervention made, and the consequences within the group following the intervention. Watkins and Vitanza (1993), taking a similar tack, sequence the learner activities through identification of the problem, identification of the challenge presented to the therapist, and key issues to which the therapist must attend. Stone and Klein's two-dimensional model requires learners to identify client and therapist contributions to the dynamic process of the group and to conceptualize them as being intrapsychic, interpersonal, or group-as-a-whole.

As described in the group counseling section, at Indiana University students examine their own behavior in a group they are coleading, write a detailed narrative, and discuss the consequences of three interventions they made and of three opportunities for intervention which they now regret having missed. The Indiana University method appears to be similar to the Cohen and Smith (1976a) critical incident methodology for examining the triggers for and consequences of leader's interventions or failures to intervene when needed. The Cohen and Smith method also has been used at the University of Cincinnati in supervision of student leaders of a personal development group for counseling master's students. Following the example of videotape examination used by the group counseling training program at the University of Louisville, students of group psychotherapy could be provided with an opportunity to critique videotapes of the coleadership work of other students and to critique their own work as a leader of a psychotherapy group. Because the examination of leader intentions is a generic issue in group work, the University of Louisville "Group Counseling Leader Intentions Critique" could be used for study of group psychotherapy process in its present form: Students would record their actual intervention along with what members were saying or doing just before the intervention, what the leader was thinking about prior to the intervention (what the leader's intention was for the intervention), the group members' response to the leader's intervention, and what the leader would say or do differently now (if the intervention did not accomplish the intention). Additional ideas for critiquing are found in the Governors State examples: (a) observing and analyzing at least two group sessions led by another student or a professional; (b) identifying, describing, and critiquing a 20-minute videotape segment that the student considers an example of his or her best work; (c) identifying, describing, and critiquing a full group meeting that the student regards as an example of his or her best work; and (d) completing and submitting a "Group Analysis Form" on request.

(b) Session-by-session process analysis. As in the leadership of any group, session-by-session process analysis can be facilitated by the regular completion of journals (logs, diaries, or other structured writing assignments). In the section on group counseling, examples were provided from the University of Missouri, East Tennessee State University, the University of Cincinnati, and Idaho State University of different methods for structuring session-by-session journal writing assignments. In addition, a number of instruments have been developed to facilitate the recording of session by session impressions. For example, brief questionnaires and scales have been developed to measure general leadership behaviors (Group Leader Behavior Instrument,

DiPalma, Gardner, & Zastowny, 1984); between-member affiliation (Group Climate Questionnaire, Hurley & Brooks, 1987); and core elements in therapeutic group process, skill development and insight into professional role and responsibility, and receipt of guidance from group processes. Simple frequency counts of observed leader intervention behavior based on a leadership theory such as Cohen and Smith's (1976b) three-dimensional leader intervention analysis system can help leaders identify their typical style.

(c) Self-assessment paper. The Idaho State University self-assessment paper, used in their group counseling course, is directly applicable to group psychotherapy leadership. Students are required to discuss their perception of (a) their current level of group membership and leadership skills and how their skill level has changed over the time of the course; (b) the process of their learning (e.g., critical incidents, significant personal work); and (c) their differentiation of the roles of member and leader and management of boundaries. This method could be expanded to include additional topics critical to the development of group psychotherapy skills such as the leader's significant emotional reactions to group members, the leader's perception of his or her own stimulus value for group members, and difficulties the leader has encountered in working with resistance.

The empirical group-work method. Rose (1988) described a methodology in which data are collected for two purposes: (a) to describe ongoing group processes to permit adjusting intervention strategies to facilitate goal attainment and (b) to describe group member behavior at two different times in the life of the group in order to evaluate change following group treatment. Tests, self-rating scales, and inventories are administered before treatment begins, at the conclusion of the group, and perhaps at one or more points during the life of the group. In addition, postsession questionnaires are filled out by the clients and group leaders after each group session. Homework assignments are given, completed, and evaluated. Clients are assigned responsibility for self-monitoring ongoing behavior or cognitions. Finally, systematic observations of group members may be conducted by trained observers using observation protocols such as the multidimensional observer schedule developed by Budman, Demby, Feldstein, and Redondo (1987). As described earlier, Rose uses a multistage shaping strategy for training in which a key facet is training in systematic observation of group process phenomena and group leadership behavior.

Summative group evaluation. The examples of summative evaluation in the Indiana University–Purdue University at Fort Wayne and the University of Cincinnati group counseling courses use member and leader perceptions of the process and outcomes of the group experience as the key data. The Indiana University–Purdue University at Fort Wayne summary evaluation guidelines focus on the leader's experience of the counseling group by asking questions about the leader's personal beliefs about counseling and group work, perceptions of the members, perception of the group process, and judgment of the group's effectiveness. The University of Cincinnati approach combines leader perceptions and formal participant-generated data. In addition to these methods, direct measurement of the effects of group psychotherapy may be undertaken. As noted earlier, group psychotherapists are to receive training in the use of mental health assessment techniques which may be employed in evaluating the effects of therapy (e.g., behavior change, personality change, symptom relief).

STANDARDS CLUSTER 5

Teaching the Ethical Practice of Group Psychotherapy

As in the standards for group counseling, for group psychotherapy, this cluster consists of a single, encompassing standard:

- K-2: Identify specific ethical problems and considerations unique to group psychotherapy.

Because group psychotherapy involves working with individuals who may have chronic debilitating symptoms and chronic impairment of intrapsychic and interpersonal functioning, attention to ethical issues needs to be a substantial concern for the group psychotherapist. Group psychotherapists must know and attend to recognized treatment protocols for the various disorders with which they work. If a client suffers actual damage as a result of a professional's failure to meet reasonable and customary standards of care, that is grounds for malpractice. Areas of particular concern to the group psychotherapist include diagnosis, informed consent, group composition, confidentiality, written records, reevaluation, techniques employed, observing the duty to warn or restrain, and client abandonment (Weiner, 1984).

Instructional Methods

As was seen in the techniques for teaching other group work specializations, a number of programs include a specific instructional unit on professional ethics which might be directly applied to training group psychotherapists (Rollins College, University of Cincinnati). However, simple didactic instruction may be insufficient to help prospective group psychotherapists become sensitive to ethical problems as they arise in the heat of group life. At the University of Georgia, as is true at many institutions, group work ethics are incorporated within all aspects of the training. Throughout the curriculum, students are frequently presented with the necessity of explaining the ethical and professional issues involved in their group work. The University of Georgia faculty take the position that there is an inherent relationship between a student's development as an active moral agent and the social context surrounding the ethical dilemmas being confronted. As a consequence, the faculty stimulate classroom discussions of ethical and moral dilemmas in group work.

Since group psychotherapy is rarely conducted in a time-limited, theme-oriented format, addressing anticipated ethical issues in a written, pregroup plan, as is required of group counselors at Montana State University, may not be appropriate or practical. Still, group therapy students could be required to write an "expectations" paper in which they systematically identify and discuss ethical difficulties which could arise as a result of (a) the population(s) with which they intend to work, (b) the student's chosen theory of therapy, (c) the methods to be used in recruitment and screening of prospective group members, (d) emergency situations which might arise, and (e) the therapist's response to persons who fail to make progress or who are harmed in the course of treatment.

Written vignettes could be used instructionally to stimulate the processing of ethical dilemmas in group psychotherapy. Any of the vignette methodologies presented earlier (cf. Cohen & Smith, 1976a; Stone & Klein, 1989; Watkins & Vitanza, 1993) can be focused on ethical issues in group psychotherapy. Vignettes may be constructed by drawing on one's own or a colleague's professional experience, from student contributions of expected ethical dilemmas, or from professional literature (Corey, Corey, & Callanan, 1993; Herlihy & Golden, 1990). The Cohen and Smith (1976a, 1976b) critical incident framework may be especially useful in that in helps to place the critical incident in the context of group developmental stage, and focuses the learner on the antecedents of the incident, the specific events which constitute the incident, and the consequences of the leader's behavior during the incident.

SUMMING UP GROUP PSYCHOTHERAPY

Contributions from the field for this group work specialization were sparse. Although there are clear indicators that some programs have established a group psychotherapy curriculum for their group work students and that others are engaged in the development of such a curriculum, these programs are rare rather than common. Thus, much of the material discussed in this chapter was drawn from published reports of programs and curricular approaches used in ancillary disciplines such as psychiatry, psychology, and social work.

That such is the case is not surprising. Only recently and only in some states have counselors been licensed to practice diagnosis and treatment of mental and emotional disorders. Again, only recently did CACREP offer specific accreditation for programs in mental health counseling. But despite its recency, there is a clear movement within the counseling profession to recognize the contribution that counselors have made and are making in work with clients who have more serious and chronic mental health concerns.

Assuming that this trend continues, we anticipate that an increasing number of counselors will be trained for and practice in the area of mental health counseling. It is certain that mental health counselors will complete course work and supervised experience in individual assessment, diagnosis, and treatment planning and delivery. It seems likely that mental health counselors will need and will request course work and supervised experience in group approaches to working with their mental health clients. Our findings indicate that the challenge for counselor educators with an interest in group work is to sharpen the identification of knowledge and skills required of a group psychotherapist and to formulate and disseminate well-articulated, counseling-based curricular models for imparting that knowledge and those skills.

Meaning and Action

INTRODUCTION

Our primary intent in this book is to provide material that can be used to advance group work training, consistent with the ASGW Training Standards. In this final section we intend to extract and summarize general training principles suggested by the exemplary methods described earlier (Chapter Seven) and then to translate these general principles into concrete action steps that can be taken by faculty, students, and practitioners (Chapter Eight).

The training descriptions contained in preceding chapters clearly indicate that many existing approaches can be emulated or adapted. Both cutting-edge and solid work is already in place in selective programs across the country. Extensive approaches exist for training in core and in group counseling. Emergent models are appearing for training in task groups, psychoeducation groups, and group psychotherapy. Exemplary training sequences, ranging across knowledge, skills, and supervised experiences, are developing from isolated, stand-alone experiences and from a curriculum restricted to didactic presentations.

The combination of general training principles and specific action steps, which follows in this section, may help to guide programs toward more effective and comprehensive training. Such training will help our students to better anticipate and respond to the increasing need for more diverse group work in the future.

7 CHAPTER

Learning from the Examples: What Principles Emerge?

Group workers are often confronted with helping members make sense of mounds of information and data produced through multiple interactions of members. The question they help members (and themselves) to answer is "So, what does all this mean?"

We ask a similar question in this chapter. Many examples of excellent group work training regimens have been described throughout the previous chapters on core training and the four group work specializations. Perhaps you have been able to identify some concrete approaches that could be adapted within your group work training program. Maybe you are searching for some general principles that could be used to guide successful training vehicles and to make group work preparation more comprehensive.

The purpose of this chapter is to identify a number of principles that emerge from the exemplary programs. In this way, we seek to help answer the question "So, what does all this mean?" We hope that these principles will provide you with helpful guidance as you consider designing or adapting the group work training offered within your program.

PROGRAM CONTENT

The first set of principles which emerge from our examination of exemplary group work training programs center on program content. Exemplary programs appear to have evolved a central organizing vision of the essence of group work, what we are calling a philosophical framework. Within these programs, there is a balance between attention paid to content (e.g., the content of member communications and interactions, the content of knowledge and skill instruction) and process (e.g., the interpersonal dynamics among group members, the process of integration and contextualization of knowledge and skills learned). The exemplary programs strive to help students move beyond simple learnings to create meaning from their experience. Multiplicity and diversity are stressed. Effective personal functioning, intrapersonally and interpersonally, is viewed as mandatory. Finally, instruction involves the use of multiple training methods and is hierarchically sequenced so that learnings build from simple to complex, from molecular to molar.

Adopt a Philosophical Framework for Training

Group work training can be viewed as an extension of the strong foundation students receive in individual counseling knowledge and skills. Critically important, however, is the necessity of group work training to include specific knowledge, skills, and supervised experiences.

Exemplary group work training involves more than adding specific knowledge, skills, and supervised experiences to the foundations of counseling training, however. The best training efforts generally are those that integrate these general and particular curricular experiences within an overarching philosophical framework. Such frameworks vary across counseling programs, and perhaps they need to do so in order to match the philosophical orientation of the total counseling training program of which the group training is a part.

We have identified from the exemplary programs a particular framework that offers many advantages for group work training. We call it the "group viewpoint." In short, this group viewpoint involves perceiving the group as a dynamic entity with a varied set of complex dynamics. This viewpoint holds that groups are dynamic, interactive, interdependent units of people who mutually influence one another. This notion presumes that the group cannot be completely understood solely from the perspective of identifying and describing the separate activity of each member and leader nor by the straightforward addition of these separate activities. The skilled group worker attempts to maximize the development of the group so that a strong, cooperative atmosphere of collaborative effort—a sense of team work—will become normative in order to increase the quality and quantity of effort and outcome.

One implication of the group viewpoint is that training programs can help students to realize that their competencies generally can be best employed when they view leadership as a cooperative and collaborative function to be developed and discharged with members. Leaders who work in coordination with members to accomplish tasks can increase productivity beyond individually directed or uncoordinated efforts.

Moreover, the group viewpoint holds that the groups with which counselors work consist of, and are themselves part of, systems within systems. To increase any group's effectiveness, well-trained group leaders must be helped to understand that the groups with which they work exist within the political-social-cultural world of larger systems. Acknowledging the importance of these dynamics within the training philosophy enables the curriculum to address the rich collection of social influence—interpersonal and systemic factors available in group interaction—and thus to strengthen individual, interpersonal, and group level outcomes.

Help Students Develop Meaning

Training in group work amounts to far more than simply mastering knowledge and skills. The best programs help their students to create meaning from their experiences. This is similar to how good group leaders help members make sense of their group participation. The creation of meaning is associated with constructivism, an increasingly central concept to many disciplines in postmodernist thought, and it captures a very critical perspective long-valued by many counselors and group workers. The essential meaning of constructivism is that people create their self-concepts and world views from internal pre-dispositions and experiences, as well as from their interaction with other people and the external world. This concept is consistent with the phenomenological perspective that most modern counseling and group work theories have at least partially espoused for many years.

Emphasize Multiplicity and Diversity

Training programs that challenge students to view the group through a lens of multiplicity assist them to become increasingly aware of how combinations of intragroup and extragroup factors interact to mutually influence the group and its members. This broader perspective is especially relevant for a richer understanding of how diversity variables affect group functioning.

Enhance Effective Personal/Interpersonal Functioning

Modern group work theory and training philosophy was heavily influenced by Kurt Lewin, his colleagues, and his students. The development of the T group (i.e., training group) model and the subsequent exploration of its many applications emphasized the critical importance of personalized learning of group participants and the personal and interpersonal functioning of group leaders. Bennis, Benne, Chin, and Corey (1976), Bradford, Gibb, and Benne (1964), and Yalom (1995) provide excellent descriptions of the origination and evolution of the T-group model.

The T-group model and its variations provided a primary foundation for group work training practices that were enthusiastically adopted by counselor educators of the 1960s. These early courses centered their training emphasis on experiential learning, in many cases to the exclusion of traditional didactic, academic approaches. Students typically participated in one or more training groups and reflected on their experience by journal writing. Reading assignments, academic papers, and examinations were rarely required. The apparent neglect of scholarly activity arose partly because group work literature was relatively scarce and partly because of the Lewinian training philosophy that experience was paramount. Following initial exposure to group process phenomena in a training group, a student might participate in an advanced course which featured supervised coleadership of a group of counseling students enrolled in the initial group work course, again without required reading or examinations.

Although the group work training methods have changed to include didactic and academic components, the emphasis on experiential learning and on the exploration and development of effective personal and interpersonal functioning is one of the strongest trends across virtually all modern training programs. Experience in groups is generally positioned as a central part of the learning process. Further, modern training programs stress the importance of developing and maintaining personal mental health and skillful interpersonal functioning in order to provide effective leadership in the complex context of group work.

Invariably, then, counseling students are required to participate in groups during the group work training process to enhance their learning of group phenomena and to advance their personal and interpersonal growth. The evolution of professional ethics in counseling has caused counselor educators to exercise caution regarding such group participation. To lessen potential dual relationship conflicts, for example, various safeguards have been applied; these include the provision of group facilitators from outside the training program and the practice of not grading group participation. In fact, some widespread and well-meaning experiential group work training practices common a generation ago are now considered obsolete. At the same time, perhaps the most basic tenet of the modern group training movement, growing out of Lewin's original work, is that personal and professional realms of training cannot and should not be totally separated if potential group leaders are to learn to conduct effective groups.

Emphasize the Content–Process Balance

Effective training programs demonstrate to students that much more of import occurs in groups than simply the content of the verbal behavior expressed. Balancing content with process is one of the most significant challenges facing group workers. Likewise, it is a fundamentally important principle for guiding group work training. Exemplary programs balance the necessary presentation of knowledge and skills with an attention to the student's process of learning and, as noted earlier, the students' derivation of meaning from their experience.

This principle, however, may seem "old hat," even easily accomplished in training. After all, process and content emphases run through all training counseling interventions. Yet, many counseling programs are able to offer only one group work course to their students. As a result, the curriculum only partially addresses both content and process. The best curricular experiences in group work incorporate effectively how content and process can be observed, understood, and considered in relation to group leader interventions.

Clearly, one way in which the exemplary programs help their students to attend to the process by which things happen in groups is by their attention to the process by which growth and development occur in the students themselves. Exemplary programs encourage students to reflect on their experience, integrate their learnings, and note not only what they are learning but also how they are learning it.

Plan Sequenced Training

Quality group work training clearly involves planned sequences of curricular experiences. Ideally, this sequenced training involves the development of focused knowledge and skills that are integrated through carefully selected supervised experiences. Complete articulation of such integrated sequences is not yet widely realized in present training efforts, although progress is being made.

Use Multiple Training Methods

The work of another prominent figure in the field of group work, Irvin Yalom, helped to identify and legitimize the critical importance of integrating cognitive factors with affective-experiential factors in the ideal change process created through group work. In a departure from previous typological theories, Lieberman, Yalom, and Miles (1973) focused on leadership functions (i.e., providing meaning attribution, demonstrating caring, stimulating emotion, and executive management) deemed necessary for positive growth and development of a group and its members. This functional perspective was maintained throughout several editions of Yalom's (1970) classic textbook on group psychotherapy, now used by many counselor educators. It helped to validate the intuitive sense of many in the field that the purely experiential approach to group worker training was inadequate. Since that time, considerable energy has been expended to identify, synthesize, and describe cognitive knowledge and skills necessary to ensure adequate training for prospective group workers.

Counselor educators who teach group work in the exemplary programs submitted for review universally use a variety of training methods and materials to help students to develop the competencies necessary to conduct successful group work. Some of the most commonly used methods and materials include the use of reading assignments, including books, journals, and other print materials; lectures; discussion; speakers; student projects and presentations; observations, both live and filmed or taped; simulations; proposals; group membership participation; supervised group leadership practice, often as a coleader of a group of students; and supervised group leadership with real-world group member-clients.

These varied components or modules used in group work training recognize the multiple learning styles of individuals and stress the integration of the cognitive-analytical and experiential-intuitive for prospective group workers. This inclusion of multiple methods is also consistent with the modern trend toward applying constructivist thought to counseling and group work processes. If group work itself can be conceptualized as a process in which the group worker helps to establish a cooperative learning/working environment in which members can be assisted to extract meaning from their interpersonal experience and to revise old, inadequate meaning systems and world views, the teaching of group work can be viewed as a parallel process. Counselor educators who submitted program descriptions appear to recognize and endorse this position by using a broad variety of materials and training experiences to help group work students extract meaning from their training experiences and to construct a personalized, integrated, working model.

Enhance Instruction With Print, Film/Video, and Internet Resources

At the height of the almost exclusively experiential approach to group work training for counselors (ca. 1969), there were few books (e.g.,

Bradford, Gibb, & Benne, 1964; Gazda, 1968a, 1968b; Otto, 1967; Thelen, 1954; Yalom, 1970) and virtually no films (with the exception of Rogers's *Journey into Self*, 1968) to serve as resources in counselor education. Beginning in the early 1970s, increased recognition of the importance of cognitive factors to balance experiential and intuitive processes led to the production of group counseling textbooks outlining applications of individual counseling theory to group practice and summarizing a growing body of research on group leadership, membership, development, and dynamics. In fact, so many excellent resources are now in print that a brief listing would fail to do justice to this large body of scholarly work. However, frequently cited sources include the various editions of Yalom's *Theory and Practice of Group Psychotherapy* (1970, 1975, 1985, and 1995) and a number of books (in multiple editions) on group work by Gazda (e.g., 1989), Gladding (1991, 1995), Corey (1990), Corey and Corey (e.g., 1992), and Trotzer (1989) that well represent this evolving body of printed materials. Although the logistics of producing visual representations of group work are daunting, several experts have produced major film/videotape products that have been widely and enthusiastically used as part of group work training programs. These include the demonstration tapes of Peg Carroll (1985), Rex Stockton (1992), and Irvin Yalom (1990).

The ASGW Professional Standards for the Training of Group Workers (1983, 1991) has begun to influence writing about group work. More authors are including consideration of competencies described in the standards, and both content and organization of articles and books increasingly reflect the use of the schematic structure of the standards.

Originally, authors attended to core competencies. This trend assisted faculty and supervisors seeking to teach and supervise students and group workers to clarify the specific foundation-level knowledge and skill competencies which learners were working to develop. More recently, articles and books are giving specific differential treatment to the group work specialties described in the standards. Therefore, teachers, supervisors, students, and practitioners are able to read materials and organize their efforts toward mastery of specific skills in the areas of task/work groups, psychoeducation groups, counseling groups, or psychotherapy groups. In its editorial policy and review process, the *Journal for Specialists in Group Work* encourages authors to identify the specific types of group work specializations their work emphasizes according to the ASGW Training Standards model.

In the last 2 years, there has been a virtual explosion of resources available through World Wide Web and other Internet information sources. Mail lists have arisen for an increasing variety of counseling special interests (e.g., mental health, rehabilitation, substance abuse, child neglect and abuse). Recently Dr. Rex Stockton at Indiana University launched *groupstuff*, a mail list for and about group work, and ASGW gained presence on the World Wide Web with the establishment of an ASGW home page. Using Internet and World Wide Web search capabilities (e.g., Archie, Veronica, Yahoo), students of group work have access to global information sources and databases.

This increased activity in the development and production of printed, visual, and electronic media resources has helped to strengthen the group work training process. The increased quantity, quality, and variety of targets allow faculty and supervisors flexibility in the types of materials they assign to meet the special needs of their specific programs and curricula. In addition, these varied resources have helped to reduce the overgeneralization of approaches developed for specific types of group work and specific types of members or clients. It is now less likely that well-trained group workers will attempt to apply knowledge and skills developed solely for work with T groups to psychotherapy groups, or for psychotherapy groups to psychoeducational work. This trend toward differential application has momentum and thus is likely to continue.

PROGRAM ISSUES

To achieve these curricular ends, faculty in the exemplary programs appear to exert strong influence over their group work curriculum. Achievement of this desirable end suggests that the group work faculty were effective in negotiation within their programs, departments, colleges, and the university community. Three ideas emerge from the descriptions of their programs. The ASGW Training Standards form a coherent platform from which to launch negotiations for strengthening the group work curriculum. But appealing to external standards is rarely sufficient in a negotiation. The exemplary programs evidence success at blending group work training with the overarching mission of their academic unit and the needs of their community. Finally, the faculty in the exemplary group work programs contribute to increasing the visibility of group work by having a presence in professional and public venues.

Exercise Curriculum Influence and Control

Exemplary group work training is more possible in programs where the group work curriculum is shaped by the faculty responsible for group work training. Multiple demands to cover a variety of content areas and practice modalities in counseling programs obviate dedication of many resources to any one curricular area, including group work. Therefore, the overall counseling curriculum is often carefully designed to include infusion of group-work knowledge and skills in broader content courses, such as career development, practica, and internships.

Group work courses often attend to more than one type of group work, such as core and group counseling in the same course. In some cases, students may gain skills in the planning, preparation, and practice of group work through supervised coleadership of career exploration groups. Careful coordination of curriculum and integration of group work training is a hallmark of exemplary programs.

Use the ASGW Training Standards

The 1990 version of the *ASGW Professional Standards for the Training of Group Workers* (1991b) has strongly influenced group work training objectives and approaches, as is reflected in the descriptions of group work training contained in virtually all of the exemplary programs. Many faculty are finding that the standards provide reference points to guide the development of training emphases. Moreover, the standards have served to provide consistency in group work training across counseling programs and thus have helped to stabilize a field that always has been quite variable.

Blend Training Needs With Program Context

Related to the already-identified principle of curriculum influence and control is how group work training experiences can be tailored to blend with existing situations and resources. That is, training needs to be contextualized and integrated within the overall counselor education program.

In many cases, an initial group work course emphasizing core and some of the group counseling and psychoeducation and/or task group work competencies is required of all students. More advanced and specialized courses are often required of specific majors, such as a course in group guidance for school counseling majors, or for particular degree levels, such as one or two additional courses emphasizing group work at the doctoral level. One potential difficulty is that some programs seem to require only one course dedicated to group work in the entry-level master's degree counseling program. This trend may be more prevalent in programs that are not CACREP approved. Although students may take additional group work courses as electives in most cases, it is very difficult to guarantee that all entry-level counseling practitioners graduating with a single group work course are even minimally competent to conduct quality group work. Requiring only one group work course may also influence counselor educators to attempt to treat this initial course as a stand-alone training experience in which depth is sacrificed for gain in breadth of coverage. Under such circumstances, it is unlikely that learners will develop true competency in the delivery of group work services so necessary in the field.

Increase the Visibility of Group Work

To garner the resources needed to support quality group work training, members of the group work faculty within the exemplary programs proactively participate in national, regional, state, and local group work organizations. Further, they make the benefits of group work available to the community through placing student group workers at field placement sites, by providing community workshops, and by providing group work consultative services. To borrow a concept from the field of marketing, they create and expand their market share by working to create a demand for their service and product.

THE BROADER PERSPECTIVE

One area in which the group work training practice lags behind the expectations identified in the ASGW Training Standards (1991b) is the extent to which all counseling students are *required* to complete sufficient course work and experiential and supervised practice activities. This deficiency results in a failure to insure that all entry-level counseling practitioners are at least minimally competent in the general group work core and are able to plan, design, and deliver effective group work services appropriate to their work setting in at least one of the specialties (e.g., task/work groups, psychoeducation groups, counseling groups, or psychotherapy groups).

It is unfortunate that many counselor education programs across the United States, including some with CACREP accreditation, may *require* only one group work course. It is very unlikely that a single course experience can build the kind of professional competence in group work that the standards imply is ideal for every counselor in practice, let alone skills in the practice of specific group work specializations. Although the 1994 CACREP Standards identify group work as one of eight core curricular areas and require supervised experiential hours as a group leader during the practicum, these standards can still be met with but one required course in group work and through general practicum and internship experiences. In most exemplary programs, additional group work courses allowing for the development of advanced and specialization training are available, recommended, and included in the programs of many students. However, we remain concerned that some entry-level counselors still enter the profession with inadequate training in group work.

Recent trends in group worker preparation appear to have reduced this gap between ideal and actual practice. We hope that the revised ASGW Training Standards (1991b), the 1994 CACREP Accreditation Standards, and ASGW education and training activities will continue to stimulate efforts toward further reduction of this discrepancy.

THE COMPLEAT TRAINING PROGRAM

How can we summarize all of what has been learned through this examination of comprehensive group work preparation? To borrow Isaac Walton's archaic spelling of the term, what constitutes the "compleat" training program?

First and foremost, the compleat training program is concerned that both faculty and students are effectively functioning human beings. They are comfortable with themselves, able to interact well with others, and are generally healthy. The single best source for group training success is traceable to the personal and interpersonal qualities and functioning level of the people involved with it.

Compleat training programs must be able to develop in students the knowledge, skills, attitudes, and practices that are peculiar to group work. These elements are addressed concretely by the Training Standards of ASGW. Emerging group workers need to learn through their training programs how to define the nature and scope of their group work practice, how to conduct appropriate pregroup preparation, how to attend to therapeutic dynamics and use leader skills effectively, how to appreciate and draw from research and evaluation data in their work, and how to employ ethical decision making and professional judgment.

The compleat group work training program has set training in personal development, knowledge, skills, and attitudes within a coherent philosophical framework that is in tune with the total counseling program and with professional standards. We have described the group viewpoint, with its focus on interdependent functioning, as one attractive example of such a framework.

The development of professional judgment is fundamentally important in the compleat group work training program. It is necessary to help students to differentially apply competencies within an integrated, effective group work approach that specifically responds to the situational context. Offering a psychotherapy group to generally well-functioning elementary students whose needs center on problem solving demonstrates questionable professional judgment. The kind of group should match the needs and situation. Students need to learn how to make such decisions so that they can design, implement, and conduct a group which provides a best fit for the context.

The compleat group work training program helps students to put together all the above—personal development, competencies and positive attitude, a philosophical framework, and professional judgment. Providing students with effective clinical supervision of appropriate group work practica and internship experiences is an important way to promote such mastery. Successful integration of these dimensions allows group workers to generate and apply specific strategies to meet the challenges, intervention choices, and potential threats inherent within group work.

Describing the compleat group work training program can lead to concern that such a program is nearly impossible to reach. In fact, many of the methods and materials currently in use by exemplary group work training programs—those that we have featured in this book—already demonstrate that the goal is achievable.

8 CHAPTER

Suggested Actions for Enhancing the Preparation of Group Workers

In the chapters of this book, we have presented a framework for understanding the training of group workers (the baker's dozen), presented examples of group work core and specialization training methods from exemplary programs in comprehensive group work from across the United States, and distilled from these examples a set of abstract principles of curricular excellence. What remains is for faculty, students, and community practitioners to take action. Drawing from the examples of excellence in comprehensive group work training, we will close with suggestions intended to stimulate thought and action. It is, of course, in the interest of our growing profession for all programs to provide core training which meets ASGW Training Standards. Programs with limited resources may be able to seek modest improvements in core training. Programs with more extensive resources may be stimulated to broader program enhancements. We hope these suggestions prove to be thought provoking and empowering.

PROGRAM CONTENT

The developmental principles reported in Chapter Seven help to give focus to efforts needed in the development of a comprehensive group work curriculum, especially in the emerging specializations. However, for curriculum to grow, group work faculty, students, and community practitioners must gather energy and take action. In this section we offer suggestions, drawn from our studies of exemplary group work training programs, to assist persons with interest in group work to enhance specific group work curricular offerings and group work educational programs in general.

Adopt a Philosophical Framework for Training

To organize discrete knowledge and skills acquired during one's training in group work, the exemplary programs teach us that an overarching philosophical framework is essential. One such framework that emerged from the materials submitted we have termed the group viewpoint. What can faculty, students, and practitioners do to insure that a comprehensive, interdependent view of the complexity of group dynamics is framed, learned, and maintained? From the exemplary programs studied during the preparation of this book, we have gathered the following suggestions.

FACULTY ACTION

- Focus instruction on the interactive, interpersonal, and group-level social influences within groups to a greater extent than on the individual, intrapsychic phenomena which are the common focus of courses in individual counseling.
- Engender a broad-perspective appreciation of the powerful forces which may result in a well functioning, curative community or a poorly functioning, destructive one.
- Instill a cooperative, collaborative outlook among prospective group workers by intentionally encouraging students to integrate and apply learnings from diverse areas of the curriculum to group work.

STUDENT ACTION

- Read beyond basic group work textbooks. While reading novels, attending movies or plays, listening to news broadcasts, participating in committee meetings, church functions, and recreational activities, strive to develop personal awareness of how groups develop, change, manage conflict, solve problems. Be in tune with the rhythm of the group and notice how activity pacing is accomplished. Stretch your awareness in the direction of apprehending the bigger picture.

- Add courses from outside the counseling program that bear on group work from an interdisciplinary perspective.
- As important as it is to obtain skill in working with individual, intrapsychic phenomena, assess the extent to which you are also learning to identify, interpret, and intervene in the interpersonal, interactional, systemic phenomena which characterize developing groups. In cases where you find such content lacking, request faculty to add the content to the program's curriculum.

PRACTITIONER ACTION

- Ask faculty at neighboring universities to design courses or continuing education workshops focusing on the interactive, interpersonal aspects of group work.
- When supervising group work students, insure that supervisory efforts focus on the interactional, interpersonal dynamics of student-led groups, as well as on the intrapsychic and personal knowledge and skill issues of the individual group members.

Emphasize the Content–Process Balance

The exemplary programs consistently emphasized the importance of attending to both the content of group member interactions and the process of group dynamics and development. Several suggestions follow from their examples.

FACULTY ACTION

- Periodically ask students and program graduates if there was an acceptable balance between theory and practice. Although program content may appear balanced when viewed from the faculty point of view, students may have a different viewpoint and thus may make a different judgment of the balance.
- Insure that course work provides *both* theory/research-based group work content *and* experiential time as a member and as a leader of a group. Realize that personal growth group work is not just for persons with mental or emotional disorders—all can benefit from

the healing and enhancing forces which operate in well-run personal growth groups.

STUDENT ACTION

- Involve yourself in multiple curricular and extracurricular courses, workshops, and group experiences.
- Notice whether the group work curriculum at your university provides a balanced treatment of theory, research, experience, and practice. If you find a lack of balance, ask faculty to provide the missing curricular elements.

PRACTITIONER ACTION

- Become familiar with the group work curriculum at your nearby university. Examine the curriculum offerings for balance and provide the counseling faculty with your observations.

Help Students Develop Meaning

Students in the exemplary group work training programs are encouraged to grow beyond the rote learning of facts, theories, and skills. The exemplary programs help their students extract meaning from their experience. Suggestions for enhancing constructive education follow.

FACULTY ACTION

- Demonstrate your own efforts at personal creation of meaning by "reporting out" your personal attempts to integrate internal predispositions with current, here-and-now experiences.
- Encourage students to integrate readings and experiences internally. Assign journal writing and ask students to prepare papers integrating personal data recorded in their journals with theoretical writings and research findings.

STUDENT ACTION

- Become a student of the "self-in-the-world." Become as fully aware as you can of how your personal construction of the world guides your perceptions and your behavior. Test your personal construction of the world by systematic data gathering and broad reading.

- Take moderate risks. Realize that this is the best way to maximize your benefit from group experiences.
- Be an active engager of your learnings rather than a passive recipient of them. Strive to make connections between learnings from diverse classes, teachers, resource materials, and clients. Test inner assumptions and experiences against current learnings and strive for integration.

PRACTITIONER ACTION

- As a supervisor of group work students, encourage supervisees to examine their personal constructions of the world and of their individual and group clients. Encourage systematic collection and analysis of data which could confirm or disconfirm the students' personal construction of the world.
- As a supervisor of group work students, demonstrate how you use data from personal experiences and readings about the human condition to test your predispositions to view the world. Share personal examples of how groups have challenged or changed your assumptions.

Emphasize Multiplicity and Diversity

Challenging students to embrace multiplicity and diversity is another hallmark of the exemplary training programs. Faculty, students, and practitioners alike can contribute to a program's efforts to increase the breadth of diversity encouraged and accepted within a group work training program.

FACULTY ACTION

- Think of diversity in as broad a context as possible (i.e., not just racial or ethnic differences but differences in values, family dynamics, ability, social class, financial background, gender, sexual orientation, philosophical orientation, etc.).
- Actively support the recruitment and retention of students with diverse backgrounds (interpreted broadly).
- Actively support the recruitment and retention of faculty with diverse backgrounds (interpreted broadly).

- Insure that students experience diversity in the faculty and students with whom they study, the curriculum which guides their study, the clients with whom they work, and the settings in which they work.
- Insure that students are at least exposed to each of the four group work specializations (e.g., task/work, psychoeducational, counseling, and psychotherapy).

STUDENT ACTION

- Intentionally move beyond your comfort zone. Seek out opportunities to experience the diversity of humankind. Accept that at times this process may be painful but rewarding.
- Seek opportunities to study with diverse faculty and students. For key concepts in counseling (e.g., empathy, regard, authenticity), read broadly to find what writers from diverse disciplines have to say.
- Resist premature specialization with a single type of client, a single presenting problem, or a single theoretical orientation.

PRACTITIONER ACTION

- Insure that group work students have the opportunity to work with clients from diverse ethnic, cultural, sexual identity, and economic groups with diverse presenting problems.
- Respect and encourage differences between your theoretical orientation and preferred methods and those of your students.
- Encourage student exposure to the community's diversity. Introduce students to the variety of ethnic, cultural, sexual identity, and economic backgrounds present in your school or agency and your community.

Enhance Personal Functioning

The exemplary programs follow the Lewinian lead in emphasizing the personalized learning and the development of personal and interpersonal competence. Faculty, students, and community practitioners alike can be instrumental in assuring that graduates of group work training programs achieve the level of personal and interpersonal functioning necessary for effective group work.

FACULTY ACTION

• Assess the level of personal functioning of students in your Counselor Education program. As required by CACREP, determine the student's capacity for forming and sustaining interpersonal relationships. Make appropriate interventions when deficiencies are identified.

• Provide multiple opportunities for counseling students to engage in personalized, experiential learning.

• Provide avenues for group work students to secure personal counseling or therapy when needed.

• Faculty who teach group work also need training and experience in group work. Examine your own personal credentials and take action to enhance your level of personal and professional development if needed.

STUDENT ACTION

• Conduct a personal assessment of your own level of personal functioning. Are you aware of personal difficulties in forming and maintaining interpersonal relationships? For chronic interpersonal difficulties, consider personal counseling.

• Seek multiple opportunities to participate as a member of a task/work, psychoeducational, counseling, or psychotherapy group. Engage in intentional activity to synthesize and integrate your experience, perhaps through journal writing. Be an active rather than a passive participant.

PRACTITIONER ACTION

• Offer psychoeducational or personal growth group experiences to students in counseling on a for-fee or pro bono basis.

• Take advantage of continuing education offerings to enhance your own personal effectiveness.

Plan Sequenced Training

With a group viewpoint and sufficient influence over curricular design, the faculty responsible for group work training have the necessary platform for curricular design. One common characteristic among the exemplary group work training programs reviewed in this book is their presentation of sequenced training. The following suggestions are offered to help faculty, students, and practitioners achieve a curriculum design which sequentially shapes student knowledge and skill development.

FACULTY ACTION

- Examine the group work curriculum for sequencing of knowledge to be acquired and skills to be learned. Be sure that competencies are presented in an order in which new learnings build on previous learnings.
- Be available to students as they work through the training sequence to help them be aware of their own process of skill acquisition.

STUDENT ACTION

- Provide feedback to faculty on the sequencing of group work program content. Notice when you have a "now they tell me!" kind of experience.
- Talk with faculty about your own process of learning, especially when feeling frustrated, confused, or lost. Use your faculty to learn more about your own process of learning. Your frustration may arise from a missed step or a misunderstood concept. It may also arise from an unintentional error in instructional sequencing.

PRACTITIONER ACTION

- Assess supervisees' skill deficiencies. If the relevant learnings are presented within the student's academic program, the faculty may profit from feedback about the timing of the learnings relative to the student's participation in supervised practice.
- Encourage students to develop their skills beyond the minimum competency level. Help them become aware of the next steps in their process of learning.

Use Multiple Training Methods and Media

The use of a variety of training methods and materials is an essential key to success in the exemplary training programs reviewed. Specific suggestions drawn from their examples include the following.

FACULTY ACTION

- Use multiple resources and practices to enhance learning and mastery of group work competencies. Insure that quality resources continue to increase for both core and group work specialty training.
- Increase your active involvement in the Association for Specialists in Group Work. It is inexpensive, popular, inclusive, egalitarian, and receptive to new contributors and their ideas. Encourage your students to do so as well—point out that student membership is quite inexpensive.

STUDENT ACTION

- Make use of the multiple resources now available. Read in the growing body of group work literature. Do not limit yourself only to assigned reading. Search out and absorb professional books, journal articles, films, and audio- and videotape recordings. Watch for relevant programs on commercial or public television stations.
- Seek additional learning experiences beyond those required in the training program to enhance your knowledge and skills. Become involved with research projects and actively seek a variety of group leadership experiences during your practica, internships, and other student activities.
- Attend presentations, conferences, and conventions at which group work programs are featured. Such presentations often represent the cutting edge of the status and progress in the field.
- Begin developing an area of expertise; participate as a presenter at local conferences or professional meetings. Start locally and build toward presenting at regional or national meetings. Start as part of a student/faculty team and build toward assuming the role of an individual presenter.

PRACTITIONER ACTION

- Identify the resources which have helped you grow and develop as a professional. Share these resources with your supervisees and colleagues.

PROGRAM ISSUES

Because this book has concentrated on enhancing the development of group work curricula, its audience will be individuals who are interested in group work and group work training. As with all such books, it preaches to the converted. Any program faculty faces stiff challenges in their attempts to secure greater resources to support their emphasis area. Thus, faculty with interest in group work compete for resources with faculty who most likely have different interests. In this section we will make suggestions to enhance ability to negotiate for support and enhancement of group work training at their institutions. Included are suggestions to exercise curriculum influence and control, use the ASGW Training Standards, blend training needs within the overall program context, and increase the visibility of group work.

Exercise Curriculum Influence and Control

To be effective in establishing a group viewpoint with prospective group workers, it appears to be essential that the program faculty who have responsibility for provision of group work training also have control or influence in the development of the program curriculum. The following suggestions may help faculty responsible for group work training to gain greater influence in the curriculum planning process.

FACULTY ACTION

- Consult and collaborate with other faculty who have group work interest, including faculty from other programs, departments, and colleges.
- Lobby within the program or department to shape the overall curriculum in the direction of high-quality group work instruction. Demonstrate for colleagues how group work might provide value-added outcomes for the entire department, as well as for specific courses and programs within the department.
- Knowledge is power—stay abreast of current developments in group work theory, research, and practice. Help other faculty become aware of emergent trends and the importance of keeping the group work curriculum apace with the times.
- Think proactively with regard to your own department, program, and faculty. Envision ways in which your skill in group work can facilitate the programmatic needs of other faculty. Encourage students to apply group work learnings in assignments for other classes.

• Conduct community needs assessment to determine what community needs might be served by a strengthened program in group work.

STUDENT ACTION

• Encourage faculty membership and participation in the Association for Specialists in Group Work.
• Encourage faculty to request library subscriptions for the major group work journals, including the *Journal for Specialists in Group Work.*
• Be aware of your personal power as a student as universities become more and more consumer-driven institutions.
• Form a group work special-interest network of students and ask the group work faculty member(s) to serve as its faculty advisor.
• If you think that offerings in group work training are insufficient for your needs, ask faculty to provide special topics courses on group work themes, perhaps by using community practitioners as adjunct instructors.
• Keep yourself focused on obtaining the learning as opposed to obtaining the diploma.

PRACTITIONER ACTION

• Request the counseling program in a neighboring university to provide group-work-oriented continuing education. When such offerings are made, sign up and participate. Continuing education offerings of counseling programs are market driven. Help the program to know there is a market for group work training.
• Volunteer to be a member of the community advisory committee of the counseling program at a neighboring university. Use the community advisory as a vehicle for providing feedback about community needs for group work training.

Use the ASGW Standards

In some programs and departments, the political work of lobbying for increasing the prominence of group work within an overall counseling curriculum may be difficult. The ASGW Training Standards may provide some leverage in negotiations undertaken by group work faculty with faculty from other interest areas.

FACULTY ACTION

- Obtain, study, and disseminate the ASGW Training Standards (1991b).
- Use the ASGW Standards as a diagnostic tool to evaluate your mastery of the knowledge and skills you need in order to teach the areas of group work which are your responsibility.
- Assess your current program against the Standards and identify its current strengths and weaknesses. Inform other program faculty of your findings.
- Argue for using the ASGW Training Standards (1991b) as part of the basis for curriculum design. Point out that the Standards are an external criterion for documenting program excellence.

STUDENT ACTION

- Become familiar with the ASGW Professional Standards for the Training of Group Workers (1991b) yourself.
- Use the ASGW Standards as a diagnostic check to evaluate your mastery of the knowledge and skills you need in the area of group work.
- If specific group work curricular elements outlined in the ASGW Standards are missing from your studies, ask faculty to provide them.
- Discuss ASGW Standards with faculty to get an idea of how the program meets or could meet the standards. Such discussions may help you, the student, understand and make connections between the various courses you have completed or will complete. Such discussions may also serve to raise faculty awareness of how your needs for group work training are not being met.
- Seek admission to programs or departments that give attention to ASGW Training Standard competencies in the group work core and in the group work specialization areas that are likely to be most applicable in your projected professional work setting and with the specific types of members and clients with whom you will work.

• Envision the big picture of your professional development. Think about how individual courses or experiences within courses fit within this personal big picture.

PRACTITIONER ACTION

• Become familiar with the ASGW Professional Standards for the Training of Group Workers (1991b).
• Use the ASGW Standards as a diagnostic instrument with which to conduct a self-evaluation of your present mastery of critical knowledge and skills at the core level and in the specialty or specialties relevant to your work.
• Use the ASGW Standards in diagnostic evaluation of supervisees. Provide the group work training program with feedback about the group work preparation of students and mention your use of the ASGW Standards as the basis for your assessment.

Blend Training Needs With Program Context

The exemplary group work programs are integrated within the overall program and departmental thrust. Rather than being an appendage to the whole, the exemplary group work programs feature infusion of group work principles in diverse courses. They are contextualized, so that their group work emphases enhance the overall vision and mission of the program. From these exemplary programs, we derive the following suggestions.

FACULTY ACTION

• Design the group work training sequence to meet the specific needs and resources of your department, program, degrees offered, students, and the counseling settings and the types of group members whom your graduates will serve.
• Seek the help and feedback of other professionals in the department. This will serve to generate new insights, as well as encourage faculty to see the benefit of group work.

STUDENT ACTION

• If group work training does not appear to blend with the rest of the program, talk with faculty to determine how the fit can be improved.

Engage faculty with a positive focus and helping attitude. Resist assuming that because you are a student you cannot effect change.

PRACTITIONER ACTION

- Keep programs abreast of students' readiness to work with groups *and* individuals. Students should be receiving training in both facets of counseling.
- Provide input to the group work training program regarding how you perceive the fit between student and community needs and current program offerings.

Increase the Visibility of Group Work

Key to the acceptance of any point of view is the creation of widespread appreciation for the viewpoint. Faculty from the exemplary programs are consistent contributors to professional and public awareness of the importance of group work in the profession of counseling. Faculty, students, and practitioners can all contribute to the creation of a broad support base for group work theory, research, and practice. Ideas for increasing the visibility of group work within the profession of counseling and across the breadth of the public sector are drawn from their example.

FACULTY ACTION

- In addition to incorporating your increased knowledge and skills into your own classes and curriculum, share your work through inservice, convention, and conference presentations. Particularly valuable are presentations related to specific specialization areas and target client populations.
- Share your expertise through writing and submitting your ideas for review for publication. The *Journal for Specialists in Group Work* in particular welcomes well-constructed manuscripts related to particular specialty areas and client populations.
- Contribute material on group work to newspapers and to state and local school and agency newsletters.
- Offer local workshops on topics related to group work.

STUDENT ACTION

- Volunteer to work with a faculty member, supervisor, or field practitioner to write for publication. The majority of articles in the *Journal for Specialists in Group Work* are written by more than one author.
- Join and become involved in the Association for Specialists in Group Work. For student members, it is even less expensive to add this divisional membership to membership in the American Counseling Association. ASGW welcomes new members. Each year ASGW hosts a special reception for new members, student members, and first-time convention attenders in the ASGW suite at the ACA national convention. ASGW membership provides excellent quarterly copies of the journal and newsletter, as well as opportunities to become involved in ASGW committees, projects, and the graduate student group.

PRACTITIONER ACTION

- Share your knowledge in areas of group work in which you regularly work and have developed expertise through in-service presentations, or program presentations at local, state, and national conventions and conferences.
- Write about and submit for publication your ideas about practice in the group work specialty areas in which you have experience and expertise. Well-written articles by practitioners who are working on the firing line of service delivery are often the most welcome and most well-read articles in the ACA journals. This is especially true of the *Journal for Specialists in Group Work*.
- Join and/or increase your participation level in the activities of the ASGW. It is a comfortable home and source of identity, camaraderie, information, and stimulation to over 6,000 members who believe in the importance and efficacy of group work.

THE BROADER PERSPECTIVE

Although both the CACREP Accreditation Standards and the ASGW Training Standards provide clear direction for program efforts to improve their offerings in group work training, they are not mandates.

Compliance is voluntary, and, with diminishing resources, programs are often in the uncomfortable position of not being able to provide the level of quality they desire across the full range of their curriculum. We recognize the dilemma. However, as proponents of group work, we urge faculty, students, and practitioners to take the following steps.

FACULTY ACTION

- Provide and require sufficient training in group work core and basic specialty training to insure that all graduates will be able to provide quality group work services appropriate to the clients they will serve.
- Provide additional and advanced specialty training in group work in those areas which are most consistent with the philosophy and resources of your program and which will best meet the needs of your students and their prospective clients. Few programs can or should attempt to provide intensive advanced training in all of the specialty areas.
- Organize your own professional development by extending your expertise to specific specialty areas.
- Choose to take the courses in the group work area that are necessary to insure that you develop the competencies that you will need for effective group work practice, including elective courses where necessary.

STUDENT ACTION

- Set a personal goal to gain competency in core group work skills and at least one specialization area. Seek supervision of work in this specialization area until you have demonstrated your competency.
- Become a regular reader of the *Journal for Specialists in Group Work* to be familiar with general trends in the field and trends in your interest areas.
- Seek training from programs that provide quality training in the group work specialization areas consistent with your goals.

PRACTITIONER ACTION

- Read the *Journal for Specialists in Group Work* or other journals which focus on group work to expand your awareness of emerging trends in the field. The *Journal for Specialists in Group Work*, in particular, contains articles focused on group work practice.

- Read, take formal course work, or avail yourself of continuing education opportunities to expand your knowledge and skills in specific areas of group work. Emphasize group work in your seeking of CEUs to renew your professional licensure, certification, or registration.
- Seek supervision to expand your knowledge and skills. Sometimes veteran practitioners have enough background and experience to expand their expertise by working under the supervision of someone who is already competent in new areas of group work.

In Conclusion

C hange is in the air around us as we hurtle toward the 21st century, and the pace of change grows more rapid with passing time. Certainly, group work training is affected by this climate of change.

The use of groups for therapeutic and educational purposes is accelerating across diverse sectors of American society. Schools, mental health agencies, social service units, business and industry, religious centers, managed care, and community centers represent just some of the places where professionally led group work is taking hold as a preferred course of intervention. In addition, millions of people in this country meet regularly in thousands of informal support groups of various kinds to find help and personal meaning in their lives.

Those who are and will be members of these groups also are becoming increasingly diverse. Rapid multicultural expansion is the obvious wave of the future. An important immediate need is to link training in group work competence with the multicultural counseling competencies that have been developed by the Association for Multicultural Counseling and Development (AMCD) (Association for Multicultural Counseling & Development, 1995). Although such a collaborative effort between ASGW and AMCD has begun and is under way, much remains to be accomplished in this important endeavor.

Group work itself is undergoing metamorphosis. It has become comprehensive. Once confined to group counseling and group psychotherapy, group work now means much more; it is a figurative rainbow of services, as we have emphasized. The ASGW Training Standards reflect this broad understanding of group work and identify competencies and supervision necessary to produce effective group workers.

We think that all counselors of the 21st century will need to be effective group workers. Moreover, they will need to exercise their competencies flexibly, as they seek to provide a range of services compatible with their training and expertise and matching target needs. Appropriate group work training approaches that themselves are comprehensive and flexible will need to be created.

We intended this book to offer practical information about such group work training to counselor educators, supervisors, and students. This book defines group work in comprehensive terms, reflecting the image of a "group work rainbow," and is entirely consistent with the ASGW Training Standards. It contains a wealth of excellent examples that show how some counseling programs are presently teaching group work according to this perspective. It presents a number of design principles and courses of specific action that readers may find helpful in any redesign efforts they may wish to make.

There is much yet to do in the design, dissemination, and delivery of comprehensive group work preparation. May this book be of aid to colleagues involved with this effort.

References

Alonso, A. (1984). T Groups: An essential model in the training of group therapists. *Group, 8*(2), 45–50.

American Counseling Association. (1995). *Code of ethics and standards of practice.* Alexandria, VA: Author.

Anderson, J. (1984). *Counseling through group process.* New York: Springer.

Argyris, C., Putnam, R., & Smith, D. (1985). *Action science.* San Francisco: Jossey-Bass.

Association for Multicultural Counseling and Development (1995). Multicultural counseling competencies: Counselor awareness of own cultural values and biases. *Counseling Today, 38,* 28, 29, 32.

Association for Specialists in Group Work. (1983). *ASGW professional standards for group counseling.* Alexandria, VA: Author.

Association for Specialists in Group Work. (1989). *Ethical guidelines for group counselors.* Alexandria, VA: Author.

Association for Specialists in Group Work. (1991a). *Ethical guidelines for group counselors.* Alexandria, VA: Author.

Association for Specialists in Group Work. (1991b). *Professional standards for the training of group workers.* Alexandria, VA: Author.

Authier, J., & Gustafson, K. (1976). The application of supervised and non-supervised microcounseling paradigms in the training of registered and licensed practical nurses. *Journal of Consulting and Clinical Psychology, 44,* 704–709.

Bednar, R., & Kaul, T. J. (1985). Experiential group research: Results, questions, and suggestions. In S. L. Garfield & A. Bergin (Eds.), *Handbook for psychotherapy and behavior change* (3rd ed., pp. 671–714). New York: Wiley.

Bennis, W., Benne, K., Chin, R., & Corey, K. (Eds.). (1976). *The planning of change* (3rd ed.). New York: Holt.

Botvin, G., & Tortu, S. (1988). Preventing substance abuse through life skills training. In R. Price, E. Cowen, R. Lorion, & J. Ramos-McKay (Eds.), *14 ounces of prevention: A casebook for practitioners* (pp. 98–110). Washington, DC: American Psychological Association.

Bradford, L. (1976). *Making meetings work: A guide for leaders and group members.* San Diego, CA: University Associates.

Bradford, L., Gibb, J., & Benne, K. (Eds.). (1964). *T-group theory and laboratory method.* New York: Wiley.

Budman, S. H., Demby, A., Feldstein, M., & Redondo, J. (1987). Preliminary findings on a new instrument to measure cohesion in group psychotherapy. [Special Issue: Integration of research in the field of group psychotherapy.] *International Journal of Group Psychotherapy, 37*(1), 75–94.

Budman, S., & Gurman, A. (1988). *Theory and practice of brief therapy.* New York: Guilford.

Capuzzi, D., & Gross, D. R. (1992). *Introduction to group counseling.* Denver, CO: Love.

Carkhuff, R., & Berenson, B. (1967). *Beyond counseling and therapy.* New York: Holt, Rinehart & Winston.

Carr, C. (1992). Planning priorities for empowered teams. *Journal of Business Strategy, 13,* 43–47.

Carroll, M. (1987). *Group work: Leading in the here and now (I, II, & III)* [Videotape]. Alexandria, VA: American Counseling Association.

Christensen, E. (1983). Study circles: Learning in small groups. *Journal for Specialists in Group Work, 8,* 211–217.

Clack, R. J. (1985). Skill development: Human relations skills training groups. In R. Conyne (Ed.), *The group workers' handbook: Varieties of group experience* (pp. 63–85). Springfield, IL: Charles C Thomas.

Cohen, A. M., & Smith, R. D. (1976a). *The critical incident in growth groups: A manual for group leaders.* La Jolla, CA: University Associates.

Cohen, A. M., & Smith, R. D. (1976b). *The critical incident in growth groups: Theory and technique.* La Jolla, CA: University Associates.

Conyne, R. (Ed.). (1985). *The group workers' handbook: Varieties of group experience.* Springfield, IL: Charles C Thomas.

Conyne, R. (1987). *Primary preventive counseling: Empowering people and systems.* Muncie, IN: Accelerated Development.

Conyne, R. (1989). *How personal growth and task groups work*. Newbury Park, CA: Sage.

Conyne, R. (1994a, January). *Core Group Work Training Method: Personal-Learning Group*. Materials presented at the Second National Group Work Conference, St. Petersburg Beach, FL.

Conyne, R. (1994b). Preventive counseling [Whole issue]. *Counseling and Human Development, 27.*

Conyne, R., & Rapin, L. (1994, January). Task group workshop. Workshop presented at the Second Group Work Conference of the Association for Specialists in Group Work, St. Petersburg Beach, FL.

Conyne, R., & Rapin, L. (in press). Group skills workshop: Developing core and task group work skills. *The 1996 annual: Developing human resources.* San Diego, CA: Pfeiffer.

Conyne, R., Rapin, L., & Rand, J. (1995, January). *Critical incident training in task group leadership*. Workshop presented at the Third National Conference of the Association for Specialists in Group Work, University of Georgia, Athens, GA.

Conyne, R., Rapin, L., & Rand, J. (in press). A model for leading task groups. In H. Forester-Miller & J. Kottler (Eds.), *Issues and challenges for group practitioners*. Denver, CO: Love.

Conyne, R., Sturm, P., Fishbach-Goodman, E., Rand, J., & Brown, R. (1995). Ideal–real discrepancies for the group work student. *Journal for Specialists in Group Work, 20,* 200–206.

Conyne, R. K., Wilson, F. R., Kline, W. B., Morran, D. K., & Ward, D. E. (1993). Training group workers: Implications of the new ASGW Training Standards for training and practice. *Journal for Specialists in Group Work, 18*(1), 11–23.

Corey, G. (1990). *Theory and practice of group counseling* (3rd ed.). Pacific Grove, CA: Brooks/Cole.

Corey, M., & Corey, G. (1992). *Groups: Process and practice* (4th ed.). Pacific Grove, CA: Brooks/Cole.

Corey, G., Corey, M. S., & Callanan, P. (1982). *A casebook of ethical guidelines for group leaders*. Monterey, CA: Brooks/Cole.

Corey, G., Corey, M. S., & Callanan, P. (1990). Role of group leader's values in group counseling. *Journal for Specialists in Group Work, 15,* 68–74.

Corey, G., Corey, M. S., & Callanan, P. (1993). *Issues and ethics in the helping professions* (4th ed.). Pacific Grove, CA: Brooks/Cole.

Corey, G., Corey, M. S., Callanan, P., & Russell, J. M. (1982). Ethical considerations in using group techniques. *Journal for Specialists in Group Work, 7,* 140–148.

Cormier, W., & Cormier, L. S. (1991). *Interviewing strategies for helpers: Fundamental skills and cognitive behavioral interventions*. Pacific Grove, CA: Brooks/Cole.

Council for Accreditation of Counseling and Related Educational Programs. (1993). *CACREP accreditation standards and procedures manual: 1994.* Alexandria, VA: Author.

Craig, D. (1978). *HIP pocket guide to planning & evaluation.* Austin, TX: Learning Concepts.

DeLucia, J., Coleman, V., & Jensen-Scott, R. (1992). Group counseling and multicultural populations [Special issue]. *Journal for Specialists in Group Work, 17.*

DiPalma, D. M., Gardner, K. G., & Zastowny, T. R. (1984). The development of an instrument for measuring leadership behaviors in therapy groups. *Group, 8*(3), 3–16.

Donigian, J., & Hulse-Killacky, D. (1995, January). *Effective group leadership: Balancing process and content.* Workshop presented at the Third National Conference of the Association for Specialists in Group Work, University of Georgia, Athens, GA.

Dossick, J., & Shea, E. (1988). *Creative therapy: 52 exercises for groups.* Sarasota, FL: Professional Resource Exchange.

Drum, D., & Knott, E. (1977). *Structured groups for facilitating development: Acquiring life skills, resolving life themes, and making life transitions.* New York: Human Sciences Press.

Dye, A. (1994, January). *ASGW Training Standards.* Presentation at the Second National Group Work Conference, St. Petersburg Beach, FL.

Ettin, M., Heiman, M., & Kopel, S. (1988). Group building: Developing protocols for psychoeducational groups. *Group, 12,* 205–225.

Fatout, M., & Rose, S. (1995). *Task groups in the social services.* Thousand Oaks, CA: Sage.

Fenster, A., & Colah, J. (1991). The making of a group psychotherapist: Needs and goals for graduate and postgraduate training. [Special Issue: Group methods for enhancing the training of mental health professionals.] *Group, 15*(3), 155–162.

Forester-Miller, H., & Davis, T. (1996). *A practitioner's guide to ethical decisionmaking.* Alexandria, VA: American Counseling Association.

Forester-Miller, H., & Duncan, J. A. (1990). The ethics of dual relationships in the training of group counselors. *Journal for Specialists in Group Work, 15,* 88–93.

Forsyth, D. (1990). *An introduction to group dynamics* (2nd ed.). Monterey, CA: Brooks/Cole.

Frey, D. H. (1972). Conceptualizing counseling theories: A content analysis of process and goal statements. *Counselor Education and Supervision, 11,* 143–250.

Gallagher, R. E. (1994). Stages of group psychotherapy supervision: A model for supervising beginning trainees of dynamic group therapy. *International Journal of Group Psychotherapy, 44*(2), 169–183.

Gazda, G. (Ed.). (1968a). *Basic approaches to group psychotherapy and group counseling.* Springfield, IL: Charles C Thomas.

Gazda, G. (1968b). *Innovations in group psychotherapy.* Springfield, IL: Charles C Thomas.

Gazda, G. (1984). *Group counseling: A developmental approach* (3rd ed.). Boston: Allyn & Bacon.

Gazda, G. (1989). *Group counseling: A developmental approach* (4th ed.). Englewood Cliffs, NJ: Prentice-Hall.

Gazda, G., & Pistole, M. C. (1986). Life skills training: A model [Whole issue]. *Counseling and Human Development, 19.*

Gladding, S. (1991). *Group work: A counseling specialty* (1st ed.). New York: Macmillan.

Gladding, S. (1995). *Group work: A counseling specialty* (2nd ed.). Englewood Cliffs, NJ: Merrill.

Goldstein, A., Sprafkin, R., Gershaw, N., & Klein, P. (1986). The adolescent: Social skills training through structured learning. In G. Cartledge & J. Milburn (Eds.), *Teaching social skills to children: Innovative approaches* (2nd ed., pp. 303–336). New York: Pergamon.

Goodman, M. (1995). From the outgoing President: A blue print for the future (or my personal wish list). *The Group Psychologist, 5,* 2.

Gumaer, J. (1982). Ethics and the experts: Insight into critical incidents. *Journal for Specialists in Group Work, 7,* 154–161.

Gumaer, J., & Scott, L. (1985). Training group leaders in ethical decision making. *Journal for Specialists in Group Work, 10,* 198–204.

Hackman, J. (1987). The design of work teams. In J. Lorsch (Ed.), *Handbook of organizational behavior* (pp. 315–342). Englewood Cliffs, NJ: Prentice-Hall.

Hansen, J. C., Warner, R. W., & Smith, E. J. (1980). *Group counseling: Theory and process.* (2nd ed.). Chicago: Rand McNally.

Hanson, P. (1969). *What to look for in groups.* Alexandria, VA: National Training Labs.

Harvill, R., Masson, R. L., & Jacobs, E. (1983). Systematic group leader training: A skills development approach. *Journal for Specialists in Group Work, 8,* 226–232.

Harvill, R., West, J., Jacobs, E., & Masson, R. L. (1985). Systematic group leader training: Evaluating the effectiveness of the approach. *Journal for Specialists in Group Work, 10,* 2–13.

Hearst, L. E. (1990). Transference, countertransference, and projective processes in training course block sessions. *Group Analysis, 23*(4), 341–346.

Herlihy, B., & Golden, L. B. (1990). *Ethical standards casebook.* Alexandria, VA: American Counseling Association (Formerly the American Association for Counseling and Development).

Hill, W. F. (1965). *HIM: Hill interaction matrix*. Los Angeles, CA: University of Southern California, Youth Studies Center.

Hill, W. F. (1969). *Learning through discussion: Guide for leaders and members of discussion groups* (2nd ed.). Beverly Hills, CA: Sage.

Hollis, J. W., & Wantz, R. A. (1994). *Counselor preparation: Volume 2. Status, trends and implications*. Muncie, IN: Accelerated Development.

Horne, A., & Hayes, R. (1995). *The University of Georgia Model*. Athens, GA: University of Georgia.

Hoyt, M. (1995). *Brief therapy and managed care: Readings for contemporary practice*. San Francisco: Jossey-Bass.

Hurley, J., & Brooks, L. J. (1987). Group climate's principal dimension: Affiliation. *International Journal of Group Psychotherapy, 37*(3), 441–448.

Insel, P., & Moos, R. (1974). Psychological environments: Expanding the scope of human ecology. *American Psychologist, 29*, 179–188.

Ivey, A., & Authier, J. (1978). *Microcounseling: Innovations in interviewing, counseling, psychotherapy, and psychoeducation*. Springfield, IL: Charles C Thomas.

Jacobs, E., Harvill, R., & Masson, R. (1994). *Group counseling: Strategies & skills*. Pacific Grove, CA: Brooks/Cole.

Jacobsohn, R. (1994). *The reading group handbook: Everything you need to know from choosing members to leading discussions*. New York: Hyperion.

Johnson, D., & Johnson, F. (1994). *Joining together: Group theory and group skills* (5th ed.). Boston: Allyn & Bacon.

Jones, J. (1973). A model of group development. In J. Jones & J. Pfeiffer (Eds.), *The 1973 annual handbook for group facilitators* (pp. 127–129). La Jolla, CA: University Associates.

Kadis, A. L., Krasner, J. D., Weiner, M. F., Winick, C., & Foulkes, S. H. (1974). *Practicum of group psychotherapy* (2nd ed.). New York: Harper & Row.

Kaplan, J. (1989). Efficacy: The real bottom line in health care. *HMO Practice, 3*, 108–110.

Katzenbach, J., & Smith, D. (1993). The discipline of teams. *Harvard Business Review, 71*, 111–120.

Kitchener, K. S. (1984). Intuition, critical evaluation, and ethical principles: The foundation for ethical decisions in counseling psychology. *Counseling Psychologist, 12*(3), 43–55.

Kitchener, K. S. (1988). Dual role relationships: What makes them so problematic? *Journal of Counseling & Development, 67*, 217–221.

Klein, R. (1985). Some principles of short-term group therapy. *International Journal of Group Psychotherapy, 35*, 309–330.

Kleinberg, J. L. (1991). Teaching beginning group therapists to incorporate a patient's empathic capacity in treatment planning. [Special Issue: Group methods for enhancing the training of mental health professionals.] *Group*, *15*(3), 141–154.

Knoff, H. (1988). Effective social interventions. In J. Graden, J. Zins, & M. Curtis (Eds.), *Alternative educational delivery systems: Enhancing instructional options for all students* (pp. 431–453). Washington, DC: National Association of School Psychologists.

Kottler, J. A. (1982). Unethical behaviors we all do and pretend we do not. *Journal for Specialists in Group Work, 7*, 182–186.

Kottler, J. A. (1995). Struggling to see through the tears. *Counseling Today, 38*, 38.

Lacoursiere, R. (1980). *The life cycle of groups.* New York: Human Sciences Press.

Langer, G. (1994). *Group learning in college classrooms.* Workshop presented at Eastern Michigan University, Ypsilanti, MI.

Levine, B. (1979). *Group psychotherapy: Practice and Development.* Englewood Cliffs, NJ: Prentice-Hall.

Lewin, K. (1936). *Principles of topological psychology.* New York: McGraw-Hill.

Lewin, K. (1951). *Field theory in social science.* New York: Harper.

Lieberman, M., Yalom, I., & Miles, M. (1973). *Encounter groups: First facts.* New York: Basic Books.

Lippitt, R., Watson, J., & Westley, B. (1958). *The dynamics of planned change.* New York: Harcourt, Brace, & World.

Lloyd, A. P. (1990). Dual relationships in group activities: A counselor education/accreditation dilemma. *Journal for Specialists in Group Work, 15*, 83–87.

London, P. (1964). *The modes and morals of psychotherapy.* New York: Holt, Rinehart, & Winston.

MacNeil, K. (1993). *What a school psychologist needs to know in order to offer psychoeducation/guidance groups.* In-class paper for Group Theory and Process course, Counseling Program, University of Cincinnati.

Masters, J. (Ed.). (1988). *The clearinghouse abstract catalogue: 1988.* Austin: University of Texas at Austin.

Meadow, D. (1988). Preparation of individuals for participation in a treatment group: Development and empirical testing of a model. *International Journal of Group Psychotherapy, 38*(3), 367–385.

Miller, H. F., & Rubenstein, R. L. (1992). Group counseling: Ethics and professional issues. In D. Capuzzi & D. R. Gross (Eds.), *Introduction to group counseling* (pp. 307–323). Denver, CO: Love.

Morganett, R. (1993). Empowering school personnel through group work principles [Whole issue]. *Counseling and Human Development, 26*.

Morganett/Smead, R. (1994). *Skills for living: Group counseling activities for elementary students.* Champaign, IL: Research Press.

Moyse-Steinberg, D. (1990). A model for adolescent pregnancy prevention through the use of small groups. *Social Work with Groups, 13,* 57–68.

Mullan, H., & Rosenbaum, M. (1962). *Group psychotherapy.* New York: Free Press.

Muriel, A. (1993). Facilitating effective work teams. *SAM Advanced Management Journal, 58,* 22–27.

Oliver, L. (1987). *Study circles: Coming together for personal growth and social change.* Cabin John, MD: Seven Locks.

Otto, H. (1967). *Guide to developing your potential.* New York: Scribner.

Patterson, C. (1966). *Theories of counseling and psychotherapy.* New York: Harper & Row.

Patton, M. Q. (1978). *Utilization-focused evaluation.* Beverly Hills, CA: Sage.

Pearson, R. E. (1985). A group-based training format for basic skills of small-group leadership. *Journal for Specialists in Group Work, 10,* 150–156.

Pfeiffer, J., & Jones, J. (1980a). Group development graph. In J. Pfeiffer & J. Jones (Eds.), *Structured experience kit* (GC-PO/A-6-ii). San Diego, CA: University Associates.

Pfeiffer, J., & Jones, J. (1980b). User's guide. In J. Pfeiffer & J. Jones (Eds.), *Structured experience kit* (pp. 1–16). San Diego, CA: University Associates.

Pierce, K. A., & Baldwin, C. (1990). Participation versus privacy in the training of group counselors. *Journal for Specialists in Group Work, 15,* 149–158.

Popkin, M. (1993). *Active parenting today.* Atlanta, GA: Active Parenting.

Price, R., Cowen, E., Lorion, R., & Ramos-McKay, J. (Eds.). (1988). *14 ounces of prevention: A casebook for practitioners.* Washington, DC: American Psychological Association.

Rabow, J., Charness, M., Kipperman, J., & Radcliffe-Vasile, S. (1994). *William Fawcett Hill's Learning through discussion* (3rd ed.). Thousand Oaks, CA: Sage.

Reddy, W. (1994). *Intervention skills: Process consultation for small groups and teams.* San Diego, CA: Pfeiffer.

Rice, K., & Meyer, A. (1995). Preventing depression among young adolescents: Preliminary process results of a psycho-educational intervention program. *Journal of Counseling & Development, 73,* 145–152.

Robbins, D. (1993). The dark side of team building. *Training and Development, 47,* 17–21.

Rogers, C. R. (1968). *Journey into self* [Videotape]. La Jolla, CA: Western Behavioral Sciences Institute.

Rose, S. D. (1988). Training for empirical group work. *Social Work with Groups, 11*(1–2), 43–51.

Schindler-Rainman, E. (1981). Training task group leaders. *Journal for Specialists in Group Work, 6,* 171–174.

Schutz, W. (1973). Encounter. In R. Corsini (Ed.), *Current psychotherapies* (pp. 401–443). Itasca, IL: Peacock.

Schwartz, B. D. (1981). An eclectic group therapy course for graduate students in professional psychology. *Psychotherapy: Theory, Research, & Practice. 18*(4), 417–423.

Schwartz, R. (1994). *The skilled facilitator: Practical wisdom for developing effective groups.* San Francisco: Jossey-Bass.

Shaffer, J., & Galinsky, M. (1974). *Models of group therapy and sensitivity training.* Englewood Cliffs, NJ: Prentice-Hall.

Slezak, E. (1993). *The book group book: A thoughtful guide to forming and enjoying a stimulating book discussion group.* Chicago: Chicago Review Press.

Smaby, M. H., & Tamminen, A. W. (1983). Helping while learning: A skilled group helper training program. *Journal for Specialists in Group Work, 8,* 159–168.

Stockton, R. (1992). *Developmental aspects of groups: Process, leadership, and supervision (I, II, & III)* [Videotape]. Alexandria, VA: American Counseling Association.

Stone, W. N., & Klein, L. D. (1989). The clinical vignette: Use in teaching and evaluation of group therapists. *Group, 13*(1), 3–9.

Study Circles Resource Center. (1990). *Portfolio starter kit: An introduction to study circles and guidelines for organizing and leading a study circle.* Pomfret, CT: Topsfield Foundation.

Study Circles Resource Center. (1993). *The study circle handbook: A manual for study circle discussion leaders, organizers, and participants.* Pomfret, CT: Topsfield Foundation.

Thelen, H. (1954). *Dynamics of groups at work.* Chicago: University of Chicago Press.

Toseland, R., & Rivas, R. (1994). *An introduction to group work practice* (2nd ed.). New York: Macmillan.

Trotzer, J. (1979). Group counseling and the dynamic of structure [Special issue]. *Journal for Specialists in Group Work, 4.*

Trotzer, J. (1980). Develop your own guidance group: A structural model for planning and practice. *The School Counselor, 27,* 341–349.

Trotzer, J. (1989). *The counselor and the group* (2nd ed.). Muncie, IN: Accelerated Development.

Tuckman, B., & Jensen, M. (1977). Stages of small group development revisited. *Group and Organizational Studies, 2,* 419–427.

Watkins, C. E. (1985). Psychoeducational training in counseling psychology programs: Some thoughts on a training curriculum. *The Counseling Psychologist, 13,* 295–302.

Watkins, C. E., & Vitanza, S. A. (1993). Using the case study method in the training of psychotherapists. *Clinical Supervisor, 11*(2), 145–157.

Weiner, M. F. (1984). *Techniques of group psychotherapy.* Washington, DC: American Psychiatric Press.

Weissberg, R., & Gesten, E. (1982). Considerations for developing effective school-based social problem-solving (SPS) training programs. *School Psychology Review, 11*, 56–63.

Wheelan, S. (1994). *Group processes: A developmental perspective.* Boston: Allyn & Bacon.

Wilson, F. R., Conyne, R. K., & Ward, D. (1994). The general status of group work training in accredited counseling programs. *Journal for Specialists in Group Work, 19*(3), 140–154.

Winston, R., Bonney, W., Miller, T., & Dagley, J. (1988). *Promoting student development through intentionally structured groups.* San Francisco: Jossey-Bass.

Yalom, I. D. (1970). *The theory and practice of group psychotherapy* (1st ed.). New York: Basic Books.

Yalom, I. D. (1975). *The theory and practice of group psychotherapy* (2nd ed.). New York: Basic Books.

Yalom, I. D. (1985). *The theory and practice of group psychotherapy* (3rd ed.). New York: Basic Books.

Yalom, I. D. (1990). *Understanding group psychotherapy: Outpatient group and inpatient group* (Vol. I & II) [Videotape]. Berkeley, CA: University of California Extension Media Center.

Yalom, I. D. (1995). *The theory and practice of group psychotherapy* (4th ed.). New York: Basic Books.

Zaslav, M. R. (1988). A model of group therapist development. *International Journal of Group Psychotherapy, 38*(4), 511–519.

ASGW Professional Standards for the Training of Group Workers (1991)

Association for Specialists in Group Work; Professional Standards for the Training of Group Workers

All counselors should possess a set of core competencies in general group work. These basic knowledge and skills provide a foundation which specialty training can extend. Mastery of the core competencies does not qualify one to independently practice any group work specialty. Specialists in group work must possess advanced competencies relevant to a particular group work type.

The Association for Specialists in Group Work (ASGW) advocates the incorporation of core group competencies as part of the master's level training required in all counselor education programs. The Association also supports preparation of group work specialists at the master's level. ASGW further supports the continued preparation of group work specialists at the post-master's level (Ed.S. or Certificate, Doctoral, Continuing Education, etc.), and recognizes that recommended levels of group work specialty training in many programs will need to be accomplished following completion of the master's degree.

This revision of the *Professional Standards for Training of Group Workers* contains two levels of competencies and related training that have been identified by the ASGW Standards Committee: (1) core group competencies: the minimum core of group worker competencies and related training necessary for all counselors, including knowledge, skills, and practice (minimum: 10 clock hours; recommended: 20 clock hours); and (2) competencies for group work specialists: advanced competencies that build on the generalized core in the following four identified group work specialties:

- *Task/work groups*, including knowledge, skills, and supervised practice beyond core group training. (Additional minimum: 30 clock hours; recommended: 45 clock hours);

- *Guidance/psychoeducation groups*, including knowledge, skills and supervised practice beyond core group training. (Additional minimum: 30 clock hours; recommended: 45 clock hours);
- *Counseling/interpersonal problem-solving groups*, including knowledge, skills, and supervised practice beyond core group training. (Additional minimum: 45 clock hours; recommended: 60 clock hours);
- *Psychotherapy/personality reconstruction groups*, including knowledge, skills, and supervised practice beyond core group training. (Additional minimum: 45 clock hours; recommended: 60 clock hours).

Definitions

Group work. "Group work" is a broad professional practice that refers to the giving of help or the accomplishment of tasks in a group setting. It involves the application of group theory and process by a capable professional practitioner to assist an interdependent collection of people to reach their mutual goals, which may be personal, interpersonal, or task related in nature.

Core training in group work for all counselors. All professional counselors should possess basic, fundamental knowledge and skills in group work. Moreover, this set of competencies provides a basic foundation upon which specialization training in group work is built.

Core training group work competencies do not prepare a counseling professional to independently assume responsibility for conducting any of the specialty groups to be defined in these Standards. Additional focused training is required for independent practice in a specialty, as detailed below.

Group work specializations. The student may proceed beyond core training in group work to specialize in one or more advanced areas of practice. It is expected that all counseling programs would provide core training in group work to all students, and most would offer additional training in at least one of the other specializations. Definitions of each specialization follow.

- *Task/work groups.* Much work in contemporary Western society is accomplished through group endeavor. The task/work group specialist is able to assist groups such as task forces, committees, planning groups, community organizations, discussion groups, study circles, learning groups, and other similar groups to correct or develop their functioning. The focus is on the application of group dynamics principles and processes to improve practice and the accomplishment of identified work goals.
- *Guidance/psychoeducation groups.* Education and prevention are critically important goals for the contemporary counselor. The guidance/psychoeducation group specialist seeks to use the group medium to educate group participants who are presently unaffected by a potential threat (such as AIDS), a developmental life event (such as a transition point), or an immediate life crisis (such as suicide of a loved one), with the goal of preventing an array of educational and psychological disturbances from occurring.

- *Counseling/interpersonal problem-solving groups.* The group worker who specializes in counseling/interpersonal problem-solving seeks to help group participants to resolve the usual, yet often difficult, problems of living through interpersonal support and problem solving. An additional goal is to help participants to develop their existing interpersonal problem-solving competencies so that they may be better able to handle future problems of a similar nature. Nonsevere career, education, personal, social, and developmental concerns are frequently addressed.
- *Psychotherapy/personality reconstruction groups.* The group worker who specializes in psychotherapy/personality reconstructions seeks to help individual group members to remedy their in-depth psychological problems. Because the depth and extent of the psychological disturbance is significant, the goal is to aid each individual to reconstruct major personality dimensions.

Training Standards for
Core Group Work Training for All Counselors
Knowledge Competencies

All counselors can effectively

1. State for the four major group work specializations identified in this document (task groups, guidance groups, counseling groups, psychotherapy groups) the distinguishing characteristics of each, the commonalities shared by all, and the appropriate instances in which each is to be used.
2. Identify the basic principles of group dynamics.
3. Discuss the basic therapeutic ingredients of groups.
4. Identify the personal characteristics of group workers that have an impact on members: knowledge of personal strengths, weaknesses, biases, values, and their effect on others.
5. Describe the specific ethical issues that are specific to group work.
6. Discuss the body of research on group work and how it relates to one's academic preparation in school counseling, student personnel education, community counseling, or mental health counseling.
7. Define the process components involved in typical stages of a group's development (i.e., characteristics of group interaction and counselor roles).
8. Describe the major facilitative and debilitative roles that group members may take.
9. State the advantages and disadvantages of group work and the circumstances for which it is indicated or contraindicated.
10. Detail therapeutic factors of group work.
11. Identify principles and strategies for recruiting and screening prospective group members.
12. Detail the importance of group and member evaluation.

13. Deliver a clear, concise, and complete definition of group work.
14. Deliver a clear, concise, and complete definition of each of the four group work specialties.
15. Explain and clarify the purpose of a particular form of group work.

Skill Competencies

All counselors are able to effectively
 1. Encourage participation of group members.
 2. Observe and identify group process events.
 3. Attend to and acknowledge group member behavior.
 4. Clarify and summarize group member statements.
 5. Open and close group sessions.
 6. Impart information in the group when necessary.
 7. Model effective group leader behavior.
 8. Engage in appropriate self-disclosure in the group.
 9. Give and receive feedback in the group.
10. Ask open-ended questions in the group.
11. Empathize with group members.
12. Confront group members' behavior.
13. Help group members attribute meaning to the experience.
14. Help group members to integrate and apply learnings.
15. Demonstrate ASGW ethical and professional standards in group practice.
16. Keep the group on task in accomplishing its goals.

COURSE WORK

Core training in group work should include a minimum of one course. Contained in this course should be attention to competencies in the knowledge and in the skills domains.

SKILLS THROUGH SUPERVISED PRACTICE

The practice domain should include observation and participation in a group experience, which could occur in a classroom group.

Minimum amount of supervised practice: 10 clock hours.

Recommended amount of supervised practice: 20 clock hours.

Training Standards for Group Work Specializations

The counselor student, having mastered the core knowledge and skill domains displayed above, can specialize in one or more advanced areas of group work practice. These advanced specialty areas are task/work groups, guidance/ psychoeducation groups, counseling/interpersonal problem-solving groups, and psychotherapy/personality reconstruction groups. The advance knowledge and skill competencies associated with each of these specialties are presented below.

TASK/WORK GROUPS

Knowledge Competencies

In addition to core knowledge, the qualified task/work group specialist can effectively
1. Identify organizational dynamics pertinent to task/work groups.
2. Describe community dynamics pertinent to task/work groups.
3. Identify political dynamics pertinent to task/work groups.
4. Describe standard discussion methodologies appropriate for task/work groups.
5. Identify specific ethical considerations in working with task/work groups.
6. Identify program development and evaluation models appropriate for task/work groups.
7. List consultation principles and approaches appropriate for task/work.

Skills Competencies

In addition to core skills the qualified task/work group specialist is able to effectively
1. Focus and maintain attention on task and work issues.
2. Obtain goal clarity in a task/work group.
3. Conduct a personally selected task/work group model appropriate to the age and clientele of the group leader's specialty area(s) (e.g., school counseling).
4. Mobilize energies toward a common goal in task/work groups.
5. Implement group decision-making methods in task/work groups.
6. Manage conflict in task/work groups.
7. Blend the predominant task focus with appropriate attention to human relations factors in task/work groups.
8. Sense and use larger organizational and political dynamics in task/work groups.

Course Work

Course work should be taken in the broad area of organization development, management, and/or sociology so that the student understands organizational life and how task groups function within it. Course work also should be taken in consultation.

Skills Through Supervised Practice

In addition to core training acquired through observation and participation in a group (10 clock hours minimum; 20 clock hours recommended), practice should include a minimum amount of 30 clock hours in coleading or leading a task/work group in a field practice setting supervised by qualified faculty or staff personnel.

GUIDANCE/PSYCHOEDUCATION GROUPS

Knowledge competencies

In addition to core knowledge, the qualified guidance/psychoeducation group specialist can effectively
1. Identify the concepts of primary prevention and secondary prevention in guidance/psychoeducation groups.
2. Articulate the concept of "at risk" in guidance/psychoeducation groups.
3. Enumerate principles of instruction relevant to guidance/psychoeducation groups.
4. Develop a knowledge base relevant to the focus of a guidance/psychoeducation group intervention.
5. List principles involved in obtaining healthy and/or at risk members for guidance/psychoeducation groups.
6. Describe human development theory pertinent to guidance/psychoeducation groups.
7. Discuss environmental assessment as related to guidance/psychoeducation groups.
8. Discuss principles of structure as related to guidance/psychoeducation groups.
9. Discuss the concept of empowerment in guidance/psychoeducation groups.
10. Identify specific ethical considerations unique to guidance/psychoeducation groups.
11. List advantages of guidance/psychoeducation groups and where indicated or contraindicated.

Skills Competencies

In addition to core skills, the qualified guidance/psychoeducation group specialist can effectively
1. Plan a guidance/psychoeducation group in collaboration with "target" populations members or representatives.
2. Match a relevant guidance/psychoeducation topic with a relevant (and currently "unaffected") target group.
3. Conduct a personally selected guidance/psychoeducation group model appropriate to the age and clientele of the group leader's specialty area (e.g., student personnel education).
4. Design a guidance/psychoeducation group plan that is developmentally and practically sound.
5. Present information in a guidance/psychoeducation group.

6. Use environmental dynamics to the benefit of the guidance/psychoeducation group.
7. Conduct skill training in guidance/psychoeducation groups.

Course Work

Course work should be taken in the broad area of community psychology, health promotion, marketing, consultation, and curriculum design.

Skills Through Supervised Practice

In addition to core training acquired through observation and participation in a group (10 clock hours minimum; 20 clock hours recommended), practice should include the following:

Minimum amount of 30 clock hours should be obtained in coleading or leading a guidance/psychoeducation group in a field practice setting supervised by qualified faculty or staff personnel.

Recommended amount of 45 clock hours should be obtained in coleading or leading a guidance/psychoeducation group in a practice setting supervised by qualified faculty or staff personnel.

COUNSELING/INTERPERSONAL PROBLEM-SOLVING GROUPS

Knowledge Competencies

In addition to core knowledge, the qualified counseling/interpersonal problem-solving group specialist can effectively
1. State for at least three major theoretical approaches to group counseling the distinguishing characteristics of each and the commonalities shared by all.
2. Identify specific ethical problems and considerations specific to group counseling.
3. List advantages and disadvantages of group counseling and the circumstances for which it is indicated or contraindicated.
4. Describe interpersonal dynamics in group counseling.
5. Describe group problem-solving approaches in relation to group counseling.
6. Discuss interpersonal assessment in group counseling.
7. Describe group formation principles in group counseling.

Skills Competencies

In addition to core skills, the qualified counseling/interpersonal problem-solving group specialist can effectively
1. Recruit and screen prospective counseling group members.

2. Recognize self-defeating behaviors of counseling group members.
3. Conduct a personally selected group counseling model appropriate to the age and clientele of the group leader's specialty area(s) (e.g., community counseling).
4. Develop reasonable hypotheses about nonverbal behavior among counseling group members.
5. Exhibit appropriate pacing skills involved in stages of a counseling group's development.
6. Intervene effectively at critical incidents in the counseling group process.
7. Work appropriately with disruptive counseling group members.
8. Make use of the major strategies, techniques, and procedures of group counseling.
9. Use procedure to assist transfer and support of changes by group counseling members in the natural environment.
10. Use adjunct group counseling structures such as homework (e.g., goal setting).
11. Work cooperatively and effectively with a counseling group coleader.
12. Use assessment procedures in evaluating effects and contribution of group counseling.

Course Work

As much course work in group counseling as possible is desirable, but at least one course beyond the generalized is necessary. Other courses in the counseling program should provide good support for the group counseling specialty.

Skills Through Supervised Practice

In addition to core training acquired through observation and participation in a group (10 clock hours minimum; 20 clock hours recommended), practice should include the following:

Minimum amount of 45 clock hours should be obtained in coleading or leading a counseling/interpersonal problem-solving group in a field practice setting supervised by qualified faculty or staff personnel.

Recommended amount of 60 clock hours should be obtained in coleading or leading a counseling/interpersonal problem-solving group in a field practice setting supervised by qualified faculty or staff personnel.

PSYCHOTHERAPY/PERSONALITY RECONSTRUCTION GROUPS

Knowledge Competencies

In addition to core knowledge, the psychotherapy/personality reconstruction group specialist can effectively

1. State for at least three major theoretical approaches to group psycho-therapy the distinguishing characteristics of each and the commonalities shared by all.
2. Identify specific ethical problems and considerations peculiar to group psychotherapy.
3. List advantages and disadvantages of group psychotherapy and the circumstances for which it is indicated or contraindicated.
4. Specify intrapersonal and interpersonal dynamics in group psychotherapy.
5. Describe group problem-solving approaches in relation to group psycho-therapy.
6. Discuss interpersonal assessment and intervention in group psychother-apy.
7. Identify referral sources and procedures in group psychotherapy.
8. Describe group formation principles in group psychotherapy.
9. Identify and describe abnormal behavior in relation to group psychother-apy.
10. Identify psychopathology as related to group psychotherapy.
11. Describe personality theory as related to group psychotherapy.
12. Detail crisis intervention approaches suitable for group psychotherapy.
13. Specify diagnostic and assessment methods appropriate for group psycho-therapy.

Skill Competencies

In addition to core skills, the qualified psychotherapy/personality reconstruc-tion group specialist can effectively

1. Recruit and screen prospective psychotherapy group members.
2. Recognize self-defeating behaviors of psychotherapy group members.
3. Describe and conduct a personally selected group psychotherapy model appropriate to the age and clientele of the group leader's specialty area (e.g., mental health counseling).
4. Identify and develop reasonable hypotheses about nonverbal behavior among psychotherapy group members.
5. Exhibit appropriate pacing skills involved in stages of a psychotherapy group's development.
6. Identify and intervene effectively at critical incidents in the psychotherapy group process.
7. Work appropriately with disruptive psychotherapy group members.
8. Make use of the major strategies, techniques, and procedures of group psychotherapy.
9. Provide and use procedures to assist transfer and support of changes by group psychotherapy members in the natural environment.
10. Use adjunct group psychotherapy structures such as psychological home-work (e.g., self-monitoring, contracting).
11. Work cooperatively and effectively with a psychotherapy group coleader.

12. Use assessment procedures in evaluating effects and contributions of group psychotherapy.
13. Assist individual change along the full range of development, from normal to abnormal in the psychotherapy group.
14. Handle psychological emergencies in the psychotherapy group.
15. Institute hospitalization procedures when appropriate and necessary in the psychotherapy group.
16. Assess and diagnose mental and emotional disorders of psychotherapy group members.

Course Work

Course work should be taken in the areas of group psychotherapy, abnormal psychology, psychopathology, and diagnostic assessment to assure capabilities in working with more disturbed populations.

Skills Through Supervised Practice

In addition to core training acquired through observation and participation in a group (10 clock hours minimum; 20 clock hours recommended), practice should include the following:

Minimum amount of 45 clock hours should be obtained in coleading or leading a psychotherapy/personality reconstruction group in a field practice setting supervised by qualified faculty or staff personnel.

Recommended amount of 60 clock hours should be obtained in coleading or leading a psychotherapy/personality reconstruction group in a field practice setting supervised by qualified faculty or staff personnel.

The Group Work Rainbow

WELCOME TO
THE RAINBOW CAFE

ASGW

TASK

PSYCHOED

COUNSELING

THERAPY

CORE

THE GROUP WORK RAINBOW

Rainbow Café

Home of the world famous "Pittsburgher"

The staff of the Rainbow Cafe invite you to enjoy a unique and diverse dining experience. Group work specialists have created a variety of recipes, derived from the foundational ingredients of the basic Core Group Work and Specialty Training Standards. Each course has a distinct group work flavor of its own, reflecting the skill, knowledge, and practice domains of each specialty. We at the Rainbow Cafe pride ourselves in serving group work specialists with the highest quality training in knowledge, skill, and supervised practice domains. Bon appetit!

APPETIZERS

Group leader gumbo
Problem behavior tonic
Self disclosure consommé

Group member rolls
Feedback wafers served
  with garlic butter

SAMPLE ENTREES

All entrees come with a serving of 1 knowledge and 1 skill competency, plus a helping of clock hours of supervised experience.

"Core" Sampler:
A clear, concise and complete definition of group work marinated in methods of giving and receiving feedback and served on a bed of 20 hours of supervised practice.

House Special-"Group Work" Sampler:
Enjoy our world famous 1/4 lb. Confluence Pittsburgher served with a side of collaboration cocktail and scoop of rainbow sherbet for dessert.

"Task Group Specialty" Sampler:
A colorful combination of organizational dynamics pertinent to task groups seasoned with the ability to focus and maintain attention on task issues, atop 45 hours of supervised experience.

"Psychoeducational Group Specialty" Sampler:
A discussion of principles of structure sautéed in a psychoed group planned in collaboration with target population members accompanied by 45 hours of supervised practice.

"Counseling Group Specialty" Sampler:
A description of interpersonal dynamics combined with
cooperative and effective work with a group co-leader, topped
with a saucy 60 hours of supervised practice.

"Psychotherapy Group" Sampler:
Psychopathology as related to group psychotherapy served with
60 hours of supervised practice, smothered in appropriate work
with disruptive group members.

BEVERAGES

Psychoeducational soda	Counseling cooler
Task group tea	Psychotherapy sparkling wine
Iced Confluence cafe	

DESSERTS

Interaction Matrix mud pie
Critical incident custard
Interpersonal Problem Matrix pudding
Basic skills soufflé
Therapeutic factors love Potient #9
Here and now cafe au lait
Johari Window Gelatin
Group development delight

Special thanks to Laura Carol Haas and the intrepid band of U.C.
ASGW students who worked with me on this project!

-Bob Conyne

MORE PROCESS FOR THE PRICE

conceptualized by Laura C. Haas
and
professionally typeset by Nick Haas

APPENDIX C

Group Work Survey

University of Cincinnati

College of Education
**Department of School Psychology
and Counseling**
522 Teachers College
P.O. Box 210002
Cincinnati, OH 45221-0002

January 26, 1993
Informant
University
Address
City, State, Zip Code

Dear Salutation

As you may know, the Association for Specialists in Group Work (ASGW) has established training standards for core and specialization training in group work. As members of the ASGW Training Standards Committee, my colleague, Dr. Wilson, and I participated in the development of these training standards, and we are invested in how they are being used.

To facilitate the implementation of the ASGW Training Standards, Dr. Wilson and I are conducting this survey of key informants who are active in group work training. You have either identified yourself or have been identified by others as an individual who is responsible for or invested in the provision of group work training for counselors and/or group work specialists in your counseling program at University~ you are the key informant for your counseling program, your participation in our study is of the utmost importance and value.

Purpose of the Study. The purpose of this study is three-fold: (a) to describe group work training nationally and by region, (b) to identify exemplary programs for core and/or specialist level training in group work, and (c) to assemble a reference material library for core and specialist level training.

Method. Each key informant is being asked to complete a brief questionnaire about group work training in his/her counseling program. At the end of this questionnaire, the key informant will be asked to consider nominating his/her group work training (core and/or specialization training) as *exemplary.* Key informants who nominate their group work training (core and/or specialization training) as an exemplar will be asked to describe the relevant training components and supply source materials (e.g., course lists, course syllabi, field-placement manuals, training workshops). These materials will be placed in a reference file at the University of Cincinnati Research Center for Group Work Training and Practice which we are establishing. With your permission, your materials will be disseminated to interested parties.

Training standards have value in their implementation. The information you provide will aid in making curriculum materials available to counselor educators, trainees, and group workers to advance training and practice. We hope, Salutation, that you will be willing to donate your time to this effort.

Please complete and return the enclosed questionnaire. Because you are so familiar with group work training in your counseling program at University~, it should not take you more than half an hour to complete the questions. Naturally, should you nominate one or more of your group work training components as an exemplar, completion of the nomination form and collection of the reference materials will take additional time. Our experience with surveys has shown us that if we do not receive your questionnaire within the next three weeks, it has likely been mismailed or misplaced. Therefore, we will make our first follow-up contact in about three weeks' time.

Sincerely,

R. K. Conyne, Ph.D., Head   F. R. Wilson, Ph.D., Director
Dept. School Psychology & Counseling   Counseling Program

GENERAL QUESTIONNAIRE

University:

Department:

Program:

Key Informant:

In the sets of questions which follow, various aspects of group work training are described including; scope of practice, populations served, coursework objectives, and clinical instruction objectives. In responding to the questions, please indicate whether or not the program(s) of study in your counselor training program provide training for each practice area and population and whether each of the coursework and clinical instruction objectives are met. Note: Though all programs are expected to provide core training in group work, there is no expectation in the ASGW Training Standards that each counselor training program will be able to provide specialization training in any (or all) areas.

Scope of Practice

Below are listed five *scope of practice* definitions. Please indicate for each *scope of practice* whether your program provides (or does not provide) training.

Level	Practice Area	Is training provided?
Core	**CORE** Understand the basic fundamentals of group work and possess the foundational skills necessary for subsequent development of a group work specialization.	Provided [ ] Not Provided [ ]
Specialization	**Task/Work Group Work:** Assist task/work groups to correct or develop their functioning by applying group dynamics principles and processes to improve practice and the accomplishment of identified work goals.	Provided [ ] Not Provided [ ]
	Psychoeducational Group Work: Educate group participants with the goals of preventing an acute or chronic dysfunctionality and developing life skills.	Provided [ ] Not Provided [ ]

Counseling Group Work: Help group participants resolve the usual, yet often difficult, problems of living through interpersonal support and problem-solving; help participants to develop existing interpersonal problem-solving competencies that they may be better to handle future problems of a similar nature.

Provided [ ]
Not Provided [ ]

Psychotherapeutic Group Work: Help group participants remediate serious acute or chronic intrapersonal and interpersonal problems; to aid group participants reconstruct major personality dimensions.

Provided [ ]
Not Provided [ ]

Populations Served

Below are listed four descriptions of *populations served* by counselors. Please indicate for which populations students may be trained within your counselor training program.

Population	Is training provided?
Normally functioning persons who are participants in task forces, committees, planning groups, community organizations, discussion groups, study circles, learning groups.	Provided [ ] Not Provided [ ]
Normally functioning persons who are presently unaffected by a potential threat (e.g., AIDS), who are approaching or facing a developmental life event (e.g., midlife transition), or are having to cope with an immediate life crisis (e.g., suicide of a loved one).	Provided [ ] Not Provided [ ]
Normally functioning persons who are presently experiencing non-severe career, educational, personal, social, and/or developmental concerns.	Provided [ ] Not Provided [ ]
Persons experiencing severe (acute or chronic) career, intrapersonal, interpersonal, and/or developmental concerns.	Provided [ ] Not Provided [ ]

Group Work Competencies

Below are listed a set of *knowledge competencies* and *skill competencies*. For each competency, please indicate whether the objective is met within your group work training program.

Core Training

Knowledge Competency	Is this objective met?
CORE-K1. State for the four major group work specializations identified in this document (task groups, psychoeducational groups, counseling groups, psychotherapy groups) the distinguishing characteristics of each, the commonalities shared by all, and the appropriate instances in which each is to be used.	Met [ ] Not Met [ ]
CORE-K2. Identify the basic principles of group dynamics.	Met [ ] Not Met [ ]
CORE-K3. Discuss the basic therapeutic ingredients of groups.	Met [ ] Not Met [ ]
CORE-K4. Identify the personal characteristics of group workers that have an impact on members; knowledge of personal strengths, weaknesses, biases, values, and their effect on others.	Met [ ] Not Met [ ]
CORE-K5. Describe the specific ethical issues that are unique to group work.	Met [ ] Not Met [ ]
CORE-K6. Discuss the body of research on group work and how it relates to one's academic preparation in either school counseling, student personnel education, community counseling, or mental health counseling.	Met [ ] Not Met [ ]
CORE-K7. Define the process components involved in typical stages of a group's development (i.e., characteristics of group interaction and counselor roles).	Met [ ] Not Met [ ]
CORE-K8. Describe the major facilitative and debilitative roles that group members may take.	Met [ ] Not Met [ ]
CORE-K9. State the advantages and disadvantages of group work and the circumstances for which it is indicated or contraindicated.	Met [ ] Not Met [ ]

	Is this objective met?
CORE-K10. Detail therapeutic factors of group work.	Met [ ] Not Met [ ]
CORE-K11. Identify principles and strategies for recruiting and screening prospective group members.	Met [ ] Not Met [ ]
CORE-K12. Detail the importance of group and member evaluation.	Met [ ] Not Met [ ]
CORE-K13. Deliver a clear, concise, and complete definition of group work.	Met [ ] Not Met [ ]
CORE-K14. Deliver a clear, concise, and complete definition of each of the four group work specialties.	Met [ ] Not Met [ ]
CORE-K15. Explain and clarify the purpose of a particular form of group work.	Met [ ] Not Met [ ]

Skill Competency

	Is this objective met?
CORE-S1. Encourage participation of group members.	Met [ ] Not Met [ ]
CORE-S2. Observe and identify group process events.	Met [ ] Not Met [ ]
CORE-S3. Attend to and acknowledge group member behavior.	Met [ ] Not Met [ ]
CORE-S4. Clarify and summarize group member statements.	Met [ ] Not Met [ ]
CORE-S5. Open and close group sessions.	Met [ ] Not Met [ ]
CORE-S6. Impart information in the group when necessary.	Met [ ] Not Met [ ]
CORE-S7. Model effective group leader behavior.	Met [ ] Not Met [ ]
CORE-S8. Engage in appropriate self-disclosure in the group.	Met [ ] Not Met [ ]
CORE-S9. Give and receive feedback in the group.	Met [ ] Not Met [ ]
CORE-S10. Ask open-ended questions in the group.	Met [ ] Not Met [ ]

	Is this objective met?
CORE-S11. Empathize with group members.	Met [ ] Not Met [ ]
CORE-S12. Confront group members' behavior.	Met [ ] Not Met [ ]
CORE-S13. Help group members attribute meaning to their experience.	Met [ ] Not Met [ ]
CORE-S14. Help group members to integrate and apply learnings.	Met [ ] Not Met [ ]
CORE-S15. Demonstrate ASGW ethical and professional standards in group practice.	Met [ ] Not Met [ ]
CORE-S16. Keep the group on task in accomplishing its goals.	Met [ ] Not Met [ ]

Specialization: Task/Work Groups

Knowledge Competency	Is this objective met?
WORK-K1. Identify organizational dynamics pertinent to task/work groups.	Met [ ] Not Met [ ]
WORK-K2. Describe community dynamics pertinent to task/work groups.	Met [ ] Not Met [ ]
WORK-K3. Identify political dynamics pertinent to task/work groups.	Met [ ] Not Met [ ]
WORK-K4. Describe standard discussion methodologies appropriate for task/work groups.	Met [ ] Not Met [ ]
WORK-K5. Identify specific ethical considerations in working with task/work groups.	Met [ ] Not Met [ ]
WORK-K6. Identify program development and evaluation models appropriate for task/work groups.	Met [ ] Not Met [ ]
WORK-K7. List consultation principles and approaches appropriate for task/work groups.	Met [ ] Not Met [ ]

Skill Competency		Is this objective met?
WORK-S1.	Focus and maintain attention on task and work issues.	Met [ ] Not Met [ ]
WORK-S2.	Obtain goal clarity in a task/work group.	Met [ ] Not Met [ ]
WORK-S3.	Conduct a personally selected task/work group model appropriate to the age and clientele of the group leader's specialty area(s) (e.g., school counseling).	Met [ ] Not Met [ ]
WORK-S4.	Mobilize energies toward a common goal in task/work groups.	Met [ ] Not Met [ ]
WORK-S5.	Implement group decision-making methods in task/work groups.	Met [ ] Not Met [ ]
WORK-S6.	Manage conflict in task/work groups.	Met [ ] Not Met [ ]
WORK-S7.	Blend the predominant task focus with appropriate attention to human relations factors in task/work groups.	Met [ ] Not Met [ ]
WORK-S8.	Sense and use larger organizational and political dynamics in task/work groups.	Met [ ] Not Met [ ]

Specialization: Psychoeducational Groups

Knowledge Competency		Is this objective met?
PEDU-K1.	Identify the concepts of primary prevention and secondary prevention in guidance/psychoeducation groups.	Met [ ] Not Met [ ]
PEDU-K2.	Articulate the concept of "at risk" in guidance/psychoeducation groups.	Met [ ] Not Met [ ]
PEDU-K3.	Enumerate principles of instruction relevant to guidance/psychoeducational groups.	Met [ ] Not Met [ ]
PEDU-K4.	Develop a knowledge base relevant to the focus of a guidance/psychoeducational group intervention.	Met [ ] Not Met [ ]
PEDU-K5.	List principles involved in obtaining healthy and/or at risk members for guidance/psychoeducational groups.	Met [ ] Not Met [ ]

Skill Competency	Is this objective met?
PEDU-K6. Describe human development theory pertinent to guidance/psychoeducational groups.	Met [ ] Not Met [ ]
PEDU-K7. Discuss environmental assessment as related to guidance/psychoeducational groups.	Met [ ] Not Met [ ]
PEDU-K8. Discuss principles of structure as related to guidance/psychoeducational groups.	Met [ ] Not Met [ ]
PEDU-K9. Discuss the concept of empowerment in guidance/psychoeducational groups.	Met [ ] Not Met [ ]
PEDU-K10. Identify specific ethical considerations unique to guidance/psychoeducational groups.	Met [ ] Not Met [ ]
PEDU-K11. List advantages of guidance/psychoeducational groups and where indicated or contra-indicated.	Met [ ] Not Met [ ]
PEDU-S1. Plan a guidance/psychoeducational group in collaboration with "target" population members or representatives.	Met [ ] Not Met [ ]
PEDU-S2. Match a relevant guidance/psychoeducational topic with relevant (and currently "unaffected") target group.	Met [ ] Not Met [ ]
PEDU-S3. Conduct a personally selected guidance/psychoeducation group model appropriate to the age and clientele of the group leader's specialty area (e.g., student personnel education).	Met [ ] Not Met [ ]
PEDU-S4. Design a guidance/psychoeducational group plan that is developmentally and practically sound.	Met [ ] Not Met [ ]
PEDU-S5. Present information in a guidance/psychoeducational group.	Met [ ] Not Met [ ]
PEDU-S6. Use environmental dynamics to the benefit of the guidance/psychoeducational group.	Met [ ] Not Met [ ]
PEDU-S7. Conduct skill training in guidance/psychoeducational groups.	Met [ ] Not Met [ ]

Specialization: Counseling Groups

	Knowledge Competency	Is this objective met?
COUN-K1.	State for at least three major theoretical approaches to group counseling the distinguishing characteristics of each and the commonalities shared by all.	Met [ ] Not Met [ ]
COUN-K2.	Identify specific ethical problems and considerations unique to group counseling.	Met [ ] Not Met [ ]
COUN-K3.	List advantages and disadvantages of group counseling and the circumstances for which it is indicated or contra-indicated.	Met [ ] Not Met [ ]
COUN-K4.	Describe interpersonal dynamics in group counseling.	Met [ ] Not Met [ ]
COUN-K5.	Describe group problem-solving approaches in relation to group counseling.	Met [ ] Not Met [ ]
COUN-K6.	Discuss interpersonal assessment in group counseling.	Met [ ] Not Met [ ]
COUN-K7.	Identify referral sources and procedures in group counseling.	Met [ ] Not Met [ ]
COUN-K8.	Describe group formation principles in group counseling.	Met [ ] Not Met [ ]

	Skill Competency	Is this objective met?
COUN-S1.	Recruit and screen prospective counseling group members.	Met [ ] Not Met [ ]
COUN-S2.	Recognize self-defeating behaviors of counseling group members.	Met [ ] Not Met [ ]
COUN-S3.	Conduct a personally selected group counseling model appropriate to the age and clientele of the group leader's specialty area(s) (e.g., community counseling).	Met [ ] Not Met [ ]
COUN-S4.	Develop reasonable hypotheses about nonverbal behavior among counseling group members.	Met [ ] Not Met [ ]
COUN-S5.	Exhibit appropriate pacing skills involved in stages of a counseling group's development.	Met [ ] Not Met [ ]
COUN-S6.	Intervene effectively at critical incidents in the counseling group process.	Met [ ] Not Met [ ]

COUN-S7. Work appropriately with disruptive counseling group members.	Met [ ] Not Met [ ]
COUN-S8. Make use of the major strategies, techniques, and procedures of group counseling.	Met [ ] Not Met [ ]
COUN-S9. Use procedures to assist transfer and support of changes by group counseling members in the natural environment.	Met [ ] Not Met [ ]
COUN-S10. Use adjunct group counseling structures such as homework (e.g., goal setting).	Met [ ] Not Met [ ]
COUN-S11. Work cooperatively and effectively with a counseling group co-leader.	Met [ ] Not Met [ ]
COUN-S12. Use assessment procedures in evaluating effects and contributions of group counseling.	Met [ ] Not Met [ ]

Specialization: Psychotherapy Groups

Knowledge Competency	Is this objective met?
PSYX-K1. State for at least three major theoretical approaches to group psychotherapy the distinguishing characteristics of each and the commonalities shared by all.	Met [ ] Not Met [ ]
PSYX-K2. Identify specific ethical problems and considerations unique to group psychotherapy.	Met [ ] Not Met [ ]
PSYX-K3. List advantages and disadvantages of group psychotherapy and the circumstances for which it is indicated or contra-indicated.	Met [ ] Not Met [ ]
PSYX-K4. Specify intrapersonal and interpersonal dynamics in group psychotherapy.	Met [ ] Not Met [ ]
PSYX-K5. Describe group problem-solving approaches in relation to group psychotherapy.	Met [ ] Not Met [ ]
PSYX-K6. Discuss interpersonal assessment and intervention in group psychotherapy.	Met [ ] Not Met [ ]
PSYX-K7. Identify referral sources and procedures in group psychotherapy.	Met [ ] Not Met [ ]

Competency		Met [ ] Not Met [ ]
PSYX-K8.	Describe group formation principles in group psychotherapy.	Met [ ] Not Met [ ]
PSYX-K9.	Identify and describe abnormal behavior in relation to group psychotherapy.	Met [ ] Not Met [ ]
PSYX-K10.	Describe psychopathology as related to group psychotherapy.	Met [ ] Not Met [ ]
PSYX-K11.	Describe personality theory as related to group psychotherapy.	Met [ ] Not Met [ ]
PSYX-K12.	Detail crisis intervention approaches suitable for group psychotherapy.	Met [ ] Not Met [ ]
PSYX-K13.	Specify diagnostic and assessment methods appropriate for group psychotherapy.	Met [ ] Not Met [ ]
	Skill Competency	Is this objective met?
PSYX-S1.	Recruit and screen prospective psychotherapy group members.	Met [ ] Not Met [ ]
PSYX-S2.	Recognize self-defeating behaviors of psychotherapy group members.	Met [ ] Not Met [ ]
PSYX-S3.	Describe and conduct a personally selected group psychotherapy model appropriate to the age and clientele of the group leader's specialty area (e.g., mental health counseling).	Met [ ] Not Met [ ]
PSYX-S4.	Identify and develop reasonable hypotheses about nonverbal behavior among psychotherapy group members.	Met [ ] Not Met [ ]
PSYX-S5.	Exhibit appropriate pacing skills involved in stages of a psychotherapy group's development.	Met [ ] Not Met [ ]
PSYX-S6.	Identify and intervene effectively at critical incidents in the psychotherapy group process.	Met [ ] Not Met [ ]
PSYX-S7.	Work appropriately with disruptive psychotherapy group members.	Met [ ] Not Met [ ]
PSYX-S8.	Make use of the major strategies, techniques, and procedures of group psychotherapy.	Met [ ] Not Met [ ]
PSYX-S9.	Provide and use procedures to assist transfer and support of changes by group psychotherapy members in the natural environment.	Met [ ] Not Met [ ]

	Met [ ] Not Met [ ]
PSYX-S10. Use adjunct group psychotherapy structures such as psychological homework (e.g., self-monitoring, contracting).	
PSYX-S11. Work cooperatively and effectively with a psychotherapy group co-leader.	Met [ ] Not Met [ ]
PSYX-S12. Use assessment procedures in evaluating effects and contributions of group psychotherapy.	Met [ ] Not Met [ ]
PSYX-S13. Assist individual change along the full range of development, from "normal" to "abnormal" in the psychotherapy group.	Met [ ] Not Met [ ]
PSYX-S14. Handle psychological emergencies in the psychotherapy group.	Met [ ] Not Met [ ]
PSYX-S15. Institute hospitalization procedures when appropriate and necessary in the psychotherapy group.	Met [ ] Not Met [ ]
PSYX-S16. Assess and diagnose mental and emotional disorders of psychotherapy group members.	Met [ ] Not Met [ ]

NOMINATION QUESTIONNAIRE

University: _____

Department: _____

Program: _____

Key Informant: _____

Nomination

During your completion of the *General Questionnaire* you were led through an evaluation of the fit between the programs of study at your institution and the curricular elements embodied in the ASGW Training Standards for group work.

Please now indicate whether, in your judgment, one or more of your programs of study could serve as an exemplar for Core Training or one of the Specializations in group work. Enclosed with this packet of materials are copies of the ASGW Training Standards for Core Training and for the four Specializations: Work Groups, Psychoeducational Groups, Counseling Groups, and Psychotherapy Groups. As you evaluate the training offered at your institution, please refer to the Standards to guide your nomination decisions.

NOTE: You may nominate your counselor training program as an exemplar in more than one category.

Level	Practice Area	Nomination
Core	**Core Training:** The program at my institution provides comprehensive coverage of the training elements described in the ASGW Training Standards for core training in group work skills.	[ ]
Specialization	**Task/Work Group Work:** At my institution we have a program of study for counselor specialists in working with task and work groups which provides comprehensive coverage of the training elements specified in the ASGW Training Standards for this specialization.	[ ]
	Psychoeducational Group Work: At my institution we have a program of study for counselor specialists in psychoeducational group work which provides comprehensive coverage of the training elements specified in the ASGW Training Standards for this specialization.	[ ]
	Counseling Group Work: At my institution we have a program of study in leading counseling groups which provides comprehensive coverage of the training elements specified in the ASGW Training Standards for this specialization.	[ ]
	Psychotherapeutic Group Work: At my institution we have a program of study for counselor specialists in leading psychotherapy groups which provides comprehensive coverage of the training elements specified in the ASGW Training Standards for this specialization.	[ ]
No Nomination Given	I do not wish to nominate any of our group work offerings as an exemplar program for either core or specialist training categories at this time.	]

Selected Instructional and Resource Examples

EXAMPLE 1

Instructions for Critiquing an Article on Group Work

GROUP ARTICLE CRITIQUE
(Montana State University)

Group Counseling Article Critique*

Please *briefly* answer the following questions about the study. For each question, please indicate if information for answering the question was provided in the article explicitly, implicitly, or you had to guess.

1. What were the questions or hypotheses being examined?
2. What theories were used to explain and guide the procedures and questions?
3. What previous studies does this study build upon and expand?
4. What are the characteristics of the group participants' population and how were they selected?
5. What are the characteristics of the group which affect group process (composition, leadership, format, location, schedule, length, potency, etc.)?
6. What measurement techniques are employed, and how do they meet criteria in the following areas: reliability, validity, norms, prior use, population appropriate, closely related to the purpose of the group, conceptually meaningful, cognitive, affective, behavioral, unobtrusive/nonreactive, outcome *and* process?
7. Was the study experimental (researcher initiated) or correlational (researcher studied and event that would occur without the researcher)?
8. Was the study carried out in a laboratory (setting established for research purposes) or in the field (the natural place where this group would occur)?
9. How many experimental, control, and placebo groups were there, and how were subjects assigned to groups?
10. Was a time series design employed (pre-pre, pre-testing, post-testing, and follow-up testing) which allows subjects to serve as their own controls?
11. What statistics were employed? Did they account for the relationships between multiple dependent and independent variables? Were individual members or whole groups (usually small *n* nonparametric statistics) used as units as analysis?
12. What indications are there that this study contributes to programmatic research by building on previous studies and serving as a base for future studies? To what extent is the information reported above offered in a clear and standardized format to allow for comparison and replication?
13. How are ethical issues such as informed consent, confidentiality, right of exit and follow-up dealt with?

---

*These questions are abstracted from Gazda, G. (1984), *Group counseling: A developmental approach*, pages 256–257.

EXAMPLE 2

Instructions for Journals and Logs

JOURNAL/LOG EXAMPLE
(University of North Texas)

Daybook: Specifications and Cover

Each student should purchase or provide a paper folder, 8½" × 11" in size with 3-ring paper holders for use in the *Daybook* assignment this semester. This will permit the addition of paper to the book as necessary. The cover of the *Daybook* should be well marked and use a format similar to the example provided below.

UNIVERSITY OF NORTH TEXAS

GROUP COUNSELING DAYBOOK

Instructor: _____

Property of:

Name: _____   Lab. Grp. Leader _____

Address: _____   Academic Term _____

Phone: _____

(If found, please return to owner or to Room 155H Stovall Hall, UNT, Denton, TX.)

Guide to Writing in the Daybook

The Daybook is like a diary but different in that it is not a simple chronicle of events and situations that occur in the laboratory group. Rather than summarizing what happened, your focus in writing should be upon your own feelings as you experienced them in the group. You may have feelings regarding other people in the group, the leader, yourself or the group in general.

Following are some guidelines:

1. Write in the Daybook as soon as you can following each group experience. This will make your recollection as current as possible.
2. Focus on your own affect, rather than upon other people or group process.
3. Be specific and concrete.
4. Try to make the Daybook an extension of the group experience rather than a summary. It should be an exercise in depth self-exploration.
5. The logical extension of "getting in touch" with your current feelings is to inspect them for motivation.

6. Treat the Daybook as you would any professional material that is highly confidential in nature. The Daybook will be read by the course instructor and your group facilitator.

Following are some excerpts from Daybooks that illustrate the kind of material that is most helpful to the writer:

Excerpt #1—. . . perhaps that's why I'm so interested in _____ as an individual. I'm also wondering if significant people for me develop because of their approval, trust, and liking—it has a big part to do with it. I have enjoyed very few people who gave me negative feedback. Criticism is difficult for me to accept—but I find a deeper respect and eventual high regard for those who give me criticism in a building way.

Excerpt #2—When Marilyn said we weren't totally strangers, it really hit me that that's exactly what I felt—a stranger, separate, and alone. While I was talking about myself the first time, I was glad because I wanted almost to be forced to be open, to reveal myself although it scared the hell out of me to do it. I wanted the group to focus on me because I wanted to be reassured that they wouldn't let me get by with being phony, that they wouldn't just leave me as I was.

Excerpt #3—So a woman is good, kind, open, and honest, and really has some basic strong points. But these are not selling points in today's market. Is what I am asking too much? I really can't believe that it is. But I find myself doubting me and even the strong points when I face the everyday world I live in. I almost want to shout, "I have played the game fair and done everything I was taught to do and still it isn't enough. Why? Why? Why?"

Excerpt #4—I winced a little as Frank suggested that Jim was not being open. It was obvious that Jim felt great pain at such a charge. I too felt the pain because even though I would like very much to be open, I don't seem to know how.

UNIVERSITY OF NORTH TEXAS

Structure for *Daybook* entries.

Session No._____ Date_____

1) *Group goals.* Were the group goals defined? Do they change from session to session?

2) *Personal goals.* Are your own goals well-defined, unclear or in the process of development? Do they change from session to session? Are they specific or general?

3) *Group process.* What was the level of interaction, intellectual, feeling oriented, additive? Is the group stuck or moving? Are there sub-groups? What is the emotional climate of the group in general?

4) *Personal/individual*. (Names are O.K., but not necessary). (a) What are the attitudes, feelings, beliefs and reactions/behaviors of individual group members? *Myself: How did I feel, respond and behave? Did anything get triggered in me? What avenue of self-exploration can I pursue to learn more about myself?

> *This should be the area where you devote most of your attention.

5) *Session*. What did this session accomplish: (a) for the group, and (b) for me?

EXAMPLE 3

Orientation Materials for a Laboratory Group

THE LABORATORY EXPERIENCE IN A SMALL GROUP*
(Rollins College)

Confidentiality

Virtually all conversation in the small group is confidential information to be exchanged only among members of that group.

General observations and learnings about group process may be discussed outside the group, but not as an alternative to discussing such matters within the group as well.

In journal entries or in class discussion take great care to protect the identity of your group's members. Remember that a person's identity could be deduced by your comments, even though you do not mention a name. For example, "Someone in our group was discussing the birth of his child," can be attributed to the *only* male in your group!

Journals are seen only by the course instructor and coleaders, nobody else. The function of the journal is to present *your* thoughts, feelings, perceptions, motives, not the description of others' behavior. If you have a question about what to write and whether it might violate someone's confidence, consult with the instructor.

Coleaders meet weekly with the professor for supervision. These conversations will focus on the group's structure, patterns, and processes rather than on content or the life circumstances of members. Even so, there may be occasions when a member's identity is known to the instructor or when a particular fact or event is mentioned during the supervision session. If a member wishes to keep certain information confidential within the group and exclude that information from the instructor's awareness (assuming that no College policy violation or illegal activity is involved), the coleaders should be advised.

Discussion of Small Group Processes

Member observations of such process issues as avoidance of intimacy, underlying conflict, excessive silence, and the like should be discussed *within the member's group*, not in the large class. Example (not specific to any member) may be cited in class to illustrate a concept, such as developing trust, so long as the example is stated in general terms that neither identify a member nor violate a confidence.

Students may ask questions or seek clarification about group process in relation to class material so long as such a discussion does not replace or detract from within-group attention to the topic or event.

---

*Adapted from a similar handout by Dr. Judith Provost.

EXAMPLE 4

Instructions for Preparing a Group Plan

GROUP PROPOSAL
(Montana State University)

Listed below are topic areas which can be addressed when proposing a counseling group. Where there is overlap, a specific point needs to be made only once. Try to limit your actual proposal to between five and ten pages (typed, double-spaced). Please use references and provide a reference list according to APA style. Feel free to attach appendices.

Introduction: Explain why the group proposed here is important and worthwhile. Social trends, neglected issues, personal experience and/or research evidence may be included in the explanation.

Population and Concerns: Which population will be helped by this group?* What kinds of problems will it help with?* Describe the populations in some depth addressing relevant culture, gender, and developmental issues. Use a theory (or theories) to explain the population's concerns and to identify goals for improvement.

Group Counseling Theories: What group counseling theory or theories will be used to guide the group?* What are the theories' basic assumptions, what goals do they provide, and how do they explain client change?* How do these theories match the population and concerns described above? If you are using more than one theory, how will they be integrated so they are complementary rather than contradictory?

Leadership: What personal characteristics will be important for leaders working with the population and concerns described above according to the theories also described above? What training and/or supervision should the leaders have?* What functions will the leaders fulfill and what leadership techniques will they employ to fulfill them? What possible effects would individual leadership have compared to coleadership? How will the leaders fulfill their responsibilities to protect the rights and promote the welfare of members?*

Membership: How will group members be recruited and what effects might this recruitment process have?* What are the optimal and acceptable number of group members? What criteria and methods will be used for screening out and selecting in group members?* What information will be gathered on members prior to entering the group? How will this information be used? What dimensions of development will be important to consider when determining group composition? In what ways will the group be homogeneous and/or heterogeneous? What would be an ideal group composition? How will group members be prepared for the group experience? What are members' rights and responsibilities?* What roles and behaviors will be expected of members in the group?* What risks are there in participating in the group?*

Group Development: In what ways would you characterize the development of the group over time? Include in your discussion changes in membership, changes in members' concerns, stages the group may pass through, group dynamics, and changes in members' roles. How will use of theories, leadership functions and techniques change in response to the group's development?

Research and Evaluation: How will termination and follow-up appraisals be performed to evaluate the effectiveness of the group?* What provisions will be made for persons who do not progress or who are harmed as a result of the group experience?* What kinds of research questions might be asked about the process and outcome of the group? Describe potential research designs for answering questions about the group. How will members' involvement in research be managed? What measurement techniques will be involved in evaluating and doing research on the group? Address the following characteristics of measures used to evaluate and/or do research on the group: relevance to questions about the group; appropriateness to the population being studied; assessment of cognitive, emotional and behavioral domains; unobtrusiveness; reliability; validity; and availability of appropriate norms. What statistical analysis will be used to process data? How does the analysis manage multiple independent and dependent variables and the interdependence of group members' scores?

Ethics: Review the "Ethical Guidelines for Group Counseling" (ASGW, 1989). The questions marked with an * above are closely related to these guidelines. Evaluate the extent to which your proposal has addressed the guidelines. Address here any guidelines which were not covered in other sections.

EXAMPLE 5

Guidelines for Portfolio Construction

PORTFOLIO GUIDELINES
(Southern Illinois University at Carbondale)

A portfolio is required for all participants. You will need to acquire a three-ring looseleaf binder for this project. Tabbed dividers are optional, but are highly recommended.

The portfolio itself consists of several components including:

1. notes from the observation group
2. notes from the class and book chapter summaries
3. session outlines for each of your group sessions
4. critiques or conceptualizations for each of your group sessions
5. a personal profile on each of your group members
6. supervision notes and individual session summaries
7. a personal log or journal
8. an appendix.

What the Components Mean
Following is a breakdown of each of the eight major components and the structural format for the organization of your portfolio.

1. Notes from the observation group consist of:
   A. Your process observations (what did you see happening)
   B. Objectives and behavioral outcomes (what was expected to happen and how do you know if it did)
   C. What worked or didn't work, what can you incorporate

2. Notes from the class include:
   A. What was covered in class (key points and concepts)
   B. What was most important for you
   C. What is happening within the class itself (as group development)
   D. Chapter summaries/critiques from the text book

3. Session outlines for each of your group sessions should include:
   A. Objectives for the session
   B. Topics to be covered
   C. Activities to be used (include your rationale & how it reflects your objectives)
   D. Process questions for each activity and session processing
   E. Behavioral outcomes (how will you know you have achieved your purposes or objectives)

4. Conceptualizations/critiques of each session (to be completed after each of your sessions) will consist of information such as:

A. What did or did not work in the session
B. What process occurred in the session (microprocess)
C. Where is your group in the process (mass-group/macroprocess)
D. Problems encountered in the session
E. Number of members present

    A standardized 1-page form will be given to you for addressing "A" through "E" along with some additional factors.

5. Personal profiles on each of your group members should include:
A. Name, age, sex, social security number, phone, etc.
B. Any special considerations (e.g., hearing impaired, learning disabilities, etc.)
C. Accumulated information (values, interests, decision making style, lifestyle, aspirations, self-concept, etc.)
D. Instrument information (from SDS and CDI reports)
E. Your personal observations and impressions.

    This is a "living" component which will change and evolve over time as you learn more about your group members.

6. Supervision notes component has 2 elements:
A. Questions and issues you wish to address in supervision
B. A synopsis of the feedback and content of each supervision session (We *strongly* advise you to tape your supervision sessions for later review.)

7. Personal log consists of:
A. Thoughts, feelings, or observations about yourself in the contexts of group facilitator, class student/group member or supervisee. You may wish to address your performance in regard to strengths, areas to concentrate on, concerns and/or questions you may have. This is an opportunity to communicate in another way with your supervisor.
B. You may write as often as you wish, as much as you like, but at least one page weekly.

8. Appendix should include:
A. Any handouts, activities, or other materials that don't fit logically in other categories, or that are not being used by you in your group.
B. The appendix should be utilized as a cache of alternatives and additional information for your use.

How to Put It Together

You will observe 16 sessions of the model group, and attend 16 sessions of the class. Initially, you will only have observation notes, class notes, the personal log, and appendix to deal with. The personal profiles will develop later.

You should divide your portfolio into 19 sections: one section for each of the 16 class/observation sessions, one for your personal log, one for the appendix, and one for the profiles. As you attend each session the class notes and observation notes should be included in the appropriate section (1–16). Of course, your personal log and appendix should be added to as needed.

As your own groups and supervision begin, your session outlines, session critiques, and supervision notes should be placed with the observation and class notes of the corresponding session. In other words, the notes, outlines, etc., from your first group session should go with session 1 of the observation group, your session 2, with observation/class session 2 and so on. The personal log, appendix, and personal profiles (as they are developed) should continue to be added to and revised, and remain separate sections of the portfolio. Most groups will have 18 sessions and the final. The extra sessions materials would logically fit into the 16 sessions sections of the portfolio. Check with your supervisor if this becomes a problem.

Final Words (as if you didn't have enough)
All entries should be typed double spaced, or *legibly* handwritten. Supervisors will be checking your portfolios periodically throughout the semester as an added tool for both communication and evaluation.

EXAMPLE 6

Processing Group Activities

SESSION OUTLINE
(Southern Illinois University at Carbondale)
Session # _____

Objectives *(enumerate)*:

Behavioral Outcomes *(enumerate)*:

Activities, Rationale, and Processing Questions for Each Activity:

TIME	ACTIVITY
_____	_____
_____	_____
_____	_____
_____	_____

SESSION PROCESSING QUESTIONS

_____

_____

_____

_____

_____

_____

_____

_____

SAMPLE OUTLINE
Written Conceptualization of Session # _____

1. How was introduction handled?
   Linkages to previous sessions/assignments?

2. Number in attendance?

3. What group development/therapeutic factors were you working on during this session?

4. How did activities contribute to group and/or individual development?

5. What were the critical incidents during the session?

6. Other positive and negative issues which came up during the session?

7. Linkages made between ideas.
   Linkages made between people.

8. How were processing and closure handled?

9. Issues to focus on for next session.

10. Other problems/issues.

EXAMPLE 7

Bibliography

ASSIGNED READINGS
Preparing Group Work Specialists (EDU 580)
University of Maine
Spring, 1993

Required Readings

Conyne, R. K. (1989). *How personal growth and task groups work*. Newberry Park, CA: Sage Publications.

Conyne, R.K., Dy, H.A., Kline, W.B., Morran, D.K., Ward, D.E., & Wilson, F.R. (1992). ASGW standards for training group workers: Context for revising the Association for Specialists in Group Work training standards. *Journal for Specialists in Group Work, 17*(1), 10–19.

Napier, R.W., & Gershenfeld, M.K. (1983). *Making groups work: A guide for group leaders*. Boston, MA: Houghton Mifflin.

Yalom, I.D. (1985). The theory and practice of group psychotherapy. New York: Basic Books. (Selected excerpts will be assigned in class).

Module I: Task/Work Groups

Astin, A. (1987). Competition or cooperation? Teaching teamwork as a basic skill. *Change, 19*, 12–19.

Banning, J.H. (1988). Building community: A macro and micro approach. *The Campus Ecologist, 6*(3), 1–2.

Baxter, L.A. (1982). Conflict management: An episodic approach. *Small Group Behavior, 13*(1), 23–42.

Brandler, S.M. (1988). The jigsaw puzzle: An experiment in understanding group process. *Social Work with Groups, 11*(2), 99–109.

Conyne, R.K. (1985). Organization change: The social climate group. In Conyne, R.K. (Ed.), *The group workers' handbook* (pp. 196–210). Springfield, IL: Charles C Thomas.

Falk, G. (1981). Unanimity versus majority rule in problem-solving groups: A challenge to the superiority of unanimity. *Small Group Behavior, 12*(4), 379–399.

Futoran, G.C., Kelly, J.R., & McGrath, J.E. (1989). TEMPO: A time-based system for analysis of group interaction process. *Basic and Applied Social Psychology, 10*(3), 211–232.

Glassman, U., & Kates, L. (1988). Strategies for group work field instruction. *Social Work with Groups, 11*(1/2), 111–121.

Graybeal, S.S., & Stodlosky, S.S. (1985). Peer work groups in elementary schools. *American Journal of Education, 93*(3), 409–428.

Hulse-Killacky, D. (1986). Leadership strategies for managing conflict. *Journal for Specialists in Group Work, 7*, 112–118.

Kormanski, C. (1982). Leadership strategies for managing conflict. *Journal for Specialists in Group Work, 7*, 112–118.

Palmer, P. (1987). Community, conflict and ways of knowing: Ways to deepen our educational agenda. *Change, 19*, 20–25.

Pugh, M.D., & Wahrman, R. (1983). Neutralizing sexism in mixed sex groups: Do women have to be better than men? *American Journal of Sociology, 88*(4), 746–762.

Ramsey, M. (1982). Organization planning and the nominal group technique. *Journal for Specialists in Group Work, 7*(1), 21–29.

Reed, B.G. (1981). Gender issues in training group leaders. *Journal for Specialists in Group Work, 6*(3), 161–170.

Ridgeway, C., & Johnson, C. (1990). What is the relationship between socioemotional behavior and status in task groups? *American Journal of Sociology, 95*(5), 1189–1212.

Rogers, J.L. (1988). New paradigm leadership: Integrating the female ethos. *Initiatives, 51*, 1–8.

Ruch, C.P., & Hall, G.E. (1982). The effect of OD interventions on stages of concern (SoC). *Journal for Specialists in Group Work, 7*(1), 39–47.

Schlinder-Rainman, E. (1981). Training task group leaders. *Journal for Specialists in Group Work, 6*, 171–174.

Toseland, R.W., Rivas, R.F., & Chapman, D. (1984). An evaluation of decision-making methods in task groups. *Social Work, 29*(4), 339–349.

Wall, V.D., & Nolan, L.L. (1987). Small group conflict: A look at equity, satisfaction, and styles of conflict management. *Small Group Behavior, 18*(2), 188–211.

Whipple, W.R. (1987, October). Collaborative learning: Recognizing it when we see it. *Bulletin of the American Association of Higher Education*, 3–7.

Wood, J.T. (1982). Sex differences in group communication: Directions for research in speech communications and sociometry. *Journal of Group Psychotherapy, Psychodrama, and Sociometry, 34*, 24–31.

Module II: Guidance/Psychoeducation Groups

Allen, J., & Anderson E. (1986). Children and crisis: A classroom guidance approach. *Elementary Guidance and Counseling, 21*(2), 143–149.

Apgar, K., & Coplon, J.K. (1985). New perspectives on structured life education groups. *Social Work, 30*(2), 138–143.

Bowman, R.P. (1987). Small-group guidance and counseling in schools: A national survey of school counselors. *The School Counselor, 34*(4), 256–262.

Bruckner, S.T., & Thompson, C.L. (1987). Guidance program evaluation: An example. *Elementary School Guidance and Counseling, 21*(3), 193–196.

Bundy, M.L., & Boser, J. (1987). Helping latchkey children: A group guidance approach. *The School Counselor, 35*(1), 58–65.

Cohen, E.G., & Benton, J. (1988). Making group work. *American Educator*, 12(3), 10, 12–17, 45–46.

Coleman, M., & Webber, J. (1988). Behavior problems? Try groups! *Academic Therapy*, 23(3), 265–274.

Cooper-Haber, K., & Bowman, R.P. (1985). The Keenan project: Comprehensive group guidance in high school. *The School Counselor*, 33(1), 50–56.

Crosbie-Burnett, M., & Pulvino, C.J. (1990). Children in nontraditional families: A classroom guidance program. *The School Counselor*, 37, 286–293.

Deck, M.D., & Saddler, D.L. (1983). Freshman awareness groups: A viable option for high school counselors. *The School Counselor*, 30(5), 392–397.

Delaney, J.D. (1986). Developing a middle school homeroom guidance program. *N.A.S.S.P. Bulletin*, 70(487), 96–98.

Deutsch, R., & Wolleat, P.L. (1981). Dispelling the forced choice myth. *Elementary School Guidance and Counseling*, 16(2), 112–120.

Egge, D.L., Marks, L.G., & McEvers, D.M. (1987). Puppets and adolescents: A group guidance workshop approach. *Elementary School Guidance and Counseling*, 21(3), 191–193.

Gumar, J. (1986). Working in groups with middle graders. *The School Counselor*, 33(3), 230–238.

Gumar, J. & Scott, L. (1985). Training group leaders in ethical decision making. *Journal for Specialists in Group Work*, 10(4), 198–204.

Jacobson, T.J. (1984). Self-directed job search training in occupational classes. *Journal for Specialists in Group Work*, 10(4), 198–204.

Myrick, R.D., Merhill, H., & Swanson, L. (1986). Changing student attitudes through classroom guidance. *The School Counselor*, 33(4), 244–252.

Nufrio, R.M. (1988). *Elementary counseling: A program model*. (ERIC Document Reproduction Service ED 294 124).

Pinsker, M., Porter, S., Seaton, C., Beasely, R., Legg, P., & Tester, C. Project success—a group contingency model for ninth grade. *N.A.S.S.P. Bulletin*, 69 (1182), 127–128.

Ritchie, M.H. (1989, October). *Research on the roles preparation and effectiveness of school counselors*. Paper presented at the Annual Meeting of the North Central Association for Counselor Education and Supervision, Milwaukee, WI.

Sattes, B., & Miller, M. (1989). Survey of effective elementary guidance programs: Results of a joint survey. (Contract No. 400–86–0001). Charleston, WV: Appalachia Educational Laboratory.

Simmons, C.H., & Parsons, R.J. (1983). Empowerment for role alternatives in adolescence. *Adolescence*, 18(69), 193–200.

Trimmer, H.W. (1984). Group job search workshops: A concept whose time is here. *Journal of Employment and Counseling*, 21(3), 103–116.

Module III: Counseling/Interpersonal Problem-Solving Groups

Anderson, W. (1981). Developing appropriate exercises for microlabs. *Journal for Specialists in Group Work*, 6(4), 211–216.

Association for Specialists in Group Work. (1989). *Ethical guidelines for group counselors.*

Barnette, E.L. (1989). Effects of a growth group on counseling students' self actualization. *Journal for Specialists in Group Work, 14*(4), 202–210.

Borgers, S.B., & Tyndall, L.W. (1982). Setting expectations for groups. *Journal for Specialists in Group Work, 7,* 109–111.

Capuzzi, D., & Gross, D.R. (1992). *Introduction to group counseling.* Denver, CO: Love Publishing Company.

Carroll, M.R., & Wiggins, J. (1990). *Elements of group counseling: Back to basics.* Denver, CO: Love Publishing Company.

Childers, J.H., & Couch, R.D. (1989). Myths about group counseling: Identifying and challenging misconceptions. *Journal for Specialists in Group Work, 14*(2), 105–111.

Cohen, A.M., & Smith, R.D. (1976). The critical incident in growth groups: Theory and technique. La Jolla, CA: University Associates, Inc.

Corey, G., Corey, M.S., Callanan, P.J., & Russell, J.M. (1988). *Group Techniques.* Monterey, CA: Brooks/Cole Publishing Company.

Day, R.W. (1981). WELCOME/BEWARE: A structured activity for use in the initial stages of counseling and therapy groups. *Journal for Specialists in Group Work, 6,* 235–239.

Dobson, J.E., & Campbell, N.J. (1986). Laboratory outcomes of personal growth groups. *Journal for Specialists in Group Work, 11*(1), 9–15.

Donigian, J., & Malnati, R. (1987). *Critical incidents in group therapy.* Monterey, CA: Brooks/Cole Publishing Company.

Frew, J.E. (1986). Leadership approaches to achieve maximum therapeutic potential in mutual groups. *Journal for Specialists in Group Work, 11*(2), 93–99.

Hawes, E.C. (1985). Personal growth groups for women: An Adlerian approach. *Journal for Specialists in Group Work, 10*(1), 19–27.

Jacobs, E.E., Harvill, R.L., & Masson, R.L. (1988). *Group counseling: Strategies and Skills,* Pacific Grove, CA: Brooks/Cole Publishing Company.

Jordan, J.V. (1990). Courage in connection: Conflict, compassion and creativity. *Work in Progress,* No. 45. Wellesley, MA: Stone Center Working Paper Series.

Pearson, R.E. (1983). Support groups: A conceptualization. *The Personnel and Guidance Journal, 61*(6), 361–364.

Roark, A.E., & Sharah, H.S. (1989). Factors related to group cohesiveness. *Small Group Behavior, 20*(1), 62–69.

Sklare, G., Keener, R., & Mas, C. (1990). Preparing members for "Here-and-Now" group counseling. *Journal for Specialists in Group Work, 15*(3), 141–148.

Stockton, R., & Morran, D.K. (1981). Feedback exchange in personal growth groups: Receiver acceptance as a function of valence, session, and order of delivery. *Journal of Counseling Psychology, 28*(6), 490–497.

Wilson, F.R., Conyne, R.K., Bardgett, D.A., & Smith-Hartle, A. (1987). Marketing of group counseling services. *Journal for Specialists in Group Work*, *12*, 10–17.

Winter, S.K. (1976). Developmental stages in the roles and concerns of group co-leaders. *Small Group Behavior*, *7*(3), 349–368.

Module IV: Psychotherapy/Personality Reconstruction Groups

Brower, A.M. (1986). Behavior changes in psychotherapy groups: A study using an empirically based statistical method. *Small Group Behavior*, *17*(2), 164–185.

Corder, B.F., & Whiteside, R. (1990). Structured role assignment and other techniques for facilitating process in adolescent psychotherapy groups. *Adolescence*, *25*(98), 343–351.

Friedlander, M.L., Thibodeau, J.R., Nichols, M.P., Tucker, C., & Snyder, J. (1985). Introducing semantic cohesion analysis: A study of group talk. *Small Group Behavior*, *16*(3), 285–302.

Kottman, T.T., Strother, J., & Deninger, M.M. (1987). Activity therapy: An alternative therapy for adolescents. *Journal of Humanistic Education and Development*, *25*(4), 180–186.

Stein, R.T. (1982). High-status group members as exemplars: A summary of field research on the relationship of status to congruence conformity. *Small Group Behavior*, *13*(1), 3–21.

Thune, E.S., Mandersheild, R.W., & Silbergeld, S. (1981). Sex, status, and co-therapy. *Small Group Behavior*, *12*(4), 415–442.

Toro, P.A., & Rappaport, J. (1985). *Social climate comparison of mutual help and psychotherapy groups.* (Report No. CG–081–643). Rockville, MD: National Institution of Mental Health. (ERIC document Reproduction Service No. ED 263 486).

Tschuschke, V., & MacKenzie, K.R. (1989). Empirical analysis of group development: A methodological report. *Small Group Behavior*, *20*(4), 419–427.

Unger, R. (1989). Selection and composition criteria in group psychotherapy. *The Journal for Specialists in Group Work*, *14*(3), 151–157.

Yalom, I. (1983). *Inpatient group psychotherapy.* New York: Basic Books.

List of Institutions Providing Exemplary Curricular Experiences

Institutions Providing Exemplary Curricular Experience
(In order of textual presentation)

CHAPTER	CONTRIBUTING PROGRAMS
1	**Comprehensive Program** University of Georgia
3	**Cluster 1: Definition** Rollins College University of Cincinnati Indiana University–Purdue University at Fort Wayne University of Maine
	Cluster 2: Preparation University of Cincinnati Southern Illinois University at Carbondale Indiana University–Purdue University at Fort Wayne Indiana University University of Maine
	Cluster 3: Therapeutic Dynamics and Leader Skills Rollins College Montana State University Southern Illinois University—Carbondale University of Cincinnati Indiana University Indiana University–Purdue University at Fort Wayne Wright State University

CHAPTER	CONTRIBUTING PROGRAMS

Cluster 4: Research and Evaluation
Rollins College
Montana State University
Southern Illinois University—Carbondale

4 **Cluster 1: Definition**
University of Nebraska—Kearney
Montana State University
Rollins College

Cluster 2: Preparation
East Tennessee State University
University of Cincinnati
Indiana University
Indiana University–Purdue University at Fort Wayne
Montana State University

Cluster 3: Therapeutic Dynamics and Leader Skills
Rollins College
University of Louisville
University of Cincinnati
Idaho State University
California State University—Fullerton
. Governors State University
Indiana University–Purdue University at Fort Wayne
Montana State University
Indiana University
University of North Texas

Cluster 4: Research and Evaluation
Montana State University
Indiana University
University of Louisville
Governors State University
East Tennessee State University
University of Cincinnati
Idaho State University
Indiana University–Purdue University at Fort Wayne
University of North Texas

Cluster 5: Ethics
East Tennessee State University
University of Cincinnati
Rollins College
Montana State University
Indiana University

CHAPTER	CONTRIBUTING PROGRAMS

5   **Task Group Exemplars**
University of Cincinnati
University of Maine
Eastern Michigan University

Psychoeducation Group Exemplars
University of Cincinnati
Southern Illinois University—Carbondale

6   **Cluster 1: Definition**
University of Georgia
University of Nebraska at Kearney
Montana State University
Eastern Washington University

Cluster 2: Preparation
Rollins College
East Tennessee State
University of Cincinnati
Indiana University
Indiana University–Purdue University at Fort Wayne
Montana State University

Cluster 3: Therapeutic Dynamics and Leader Skills
Rollins College
University of Louisville
University of Georgia
University of Missouri—Columbia

Cluster 4: Research and Evaluation
Montana State University
University of Georgia
Indiana University
University of Louisville
University of Missouri
East Tennessee State University
University of Cincinnati
Idaho State University

Cluster 5: Ethics
Rollins College
University of Cincinnati
University of Georgia
Montana State University

Index

4032